D0993932

Issues in Voluntary and Non-profit Management

This reader is one part of an integrated Open University course, so the selection is related to other material which is available to students. It is designed to stimulate a critical understanding on the part of students. The opinions expressed in this reader are not necessarily those of the Course Team or of the University.

Issues in Voluntary and Non-profit Management

A Reader edited by
Julian Batsleer, Chris Cornforth and Rob Paton
at the Open University

Addison-Wesley Publishing Company

Wokingham, England • Reading, Massachusetts • Menlo Park, California
New York • Don Mills, Ontario • Amsterdam • Bonn • Sydney • Singapore
Tokyo • Madrid • San Juan • Milan • Paris • Mexico City • Seoul • Taipei

in association with

The Open
University

Selection and editorial material copyright © The Open University 1992

This book is a component of the Open University course B789 *Managing Voluntary and Non-profit Enterprises*. Details of this and other Open University courses are available from the Central Enquiry Service, The Open University, PO Box 71, Milton Keynes MK7 6AG. Tel. 0908 653078.

All rights reserved. No part of this publication may be reproduced, stored in a retrieval system, or transmitted in any form or by any means, electronic, mechanical, photocopying, recording or otherwise, without prior written permission of the publisher.

Many of the designations used by manufacturers and sellers to distinguish their products are claimed as trademarks. Addison-Wesley has made every attempt to supply trademark information about manufacturers and their products mentioned in this book.

Cover designed by Designers & Partners of Oxford and printed by The Riverside Printing Co. (Reading) Ltd.
Typeset by Colset Private Limited, Singapore.
Printed in Malta.

First printed 1991.

British Library Cataloguing in Publication Data

Issues in voluntary and non-profit management.
  I. Batsleer, Julian II. Cornforth, Chris
  III. Paton, Rob
  658.048

ISBN 0-201-56547-1

Preface

This book was prepared as the Course Reader for *Managing Voluntary and Non-profit Enterprises* (B789), a distance-taught Open University course which counts towards nationally recognized, competence-orientated qualifications in both management and health and social welfare. The course includes 12 specially written teaching texts; video tapes and audio cassettes; tutorials and a residential school; a personal organizer containing reminder sheets and check-lists to help carry the course into the work place; and assignments and end of course assessment. This Course Reader contains much of the more general, conceptual material of the course – the other components concentrate more on the practical application of ideas on a day-to-day basis.

When we first started planning the course we soon realized just how little serious writing there has been in this field. The literature on management in voluntary and non-profit organizations in the UK has not kept up with their growing importance in society. Some useful 'how to do it' books do exist, but relevant, reflective and accessible writing for those seeking a more sustained treatment is practically unavailable. The US literature by contrast is considerable – although it addresses a very different context. We hope this volume goes some way towards filling the gap and that it will interest and assist practitioners, trainers, teachers and students in many different contexts.

Acknowledgements

We are immensely grateful to the contributors who wrote pieces specially for this book. They have tolerated our presumptuous specifications, critical comments and intrusive editing with co-operation, good humour and patience. Many had to work very hard, often to harsh deadlines. We hope they are as satisfied with the result as we are.

Three other people made essential contributions: Jean Attenborough provided characteristically reliable and tireless administrative support; Sharon Rich provided intelligent, rapid and accurate word processing; Amanda Smith, our editor, accepted late hand-overs cheerfully, and still found time to clarify and improve every page of the text. It is a privilege to have this kind of assistance.

Julian Batsleer, Chris Cornforth, Rob Paton   April 1991

Acknowledgements

Grateful acknowledgement is made to the following sources for permission to reproduce material in this reader:

Text

Paton, R. (1989) 'The social economy: value-based organizations in the wider society', *Management Issues*, Issue No. 2, pp. 6–7, Autumn 1989 and Issue No. 3, pp. 3–7, Winter 1989; Handy, C. (1988) *Understanding Voluntary Organizations*, Penguin Books, © Charles Handy 1988. Reproduced by permission of Penguin Books Ltd; Landry, C., Morley, D., Southwood, R. and Wright, P. (1985) *What a Way to Run a Railroad: An Analysis of Radical Failure*, Comedia Consultancy Group; Kramer, R.M. (1989) 'Voluntary organizations in the welfare state', *Working Paper 8*, Centre for Voluntary Organizations; Stanton, A. (1989) 'Citizens of workplace democracies', *Critical Social Policy*, Issue 26, Vol. 9, No. 2, Autumn 1989.

Figures

Figures 2.1 and 2.2: Handy, C. (1988) *Understanding Voluntary Organizations*, Penguin Books, © Charles Handy 1988. Reproduced by permission of Penguin Books Ltd; Figures 7.1 and 7.2: (1990) *Voluntary Sector Salary Survey*, Manufacturing Science and Finance Union; Figure 8.1: Beugen, P. (1985) 'Supporting the volunteer life cycle', *Voluntary Action Leadership*, Volunteer – The National Centre; Figures 13.1, 13.2, and 13.3 : Butler, R.J. and Wilson, D.C. (1990) *Managing Voluntary and Non-Profit Organizations: Strategy and Structure*, Routledge; Figure 13.6: (1984) *Centralization and Autonomy: A Study in Organizational Behaviour*, Holt Rinehart and Winston. Reproduced by permission of Cassell; Figure 16.2: 'Community Care Projects' (1989) *Joint Projects: Patterns of Management*, National Council for Voluntary Organizations; Figure 16.3: Taylor, M. and Lansley, J. (1990) 'Idealogical Ambiguities of Welfare', *Proceedings of the 1990 Conference of the Association of Voluntary Action Scholars*, Centre for Voluntary Organizations.

Tables

Table 9.1: Stanton, A. (1989) 'Citizens of workplace democracies', *Critical Social Policy*, Issue 26, Vol. 9, No. 2, Autumn 1989; Table 14.1: Butler, R.J. and Wilson, D. (1990) *Managing Voluntary and Non-Profit Organizations: Strategy and Structure*, Routledge; Table 16.1: Dluhy, S. (1990) *Building Coalitions in the Human Services*, Sage Publications Inc.

Notes on Contributors

Rob Paton has social science degrees from Oxford and the University of Pennsylvania. After a period of community work he joined the Open University initially to research worker co-operatives but later as a lecturer in Systems. His recent publications include *Reluctant Entrepreneurs* (Open University Press) and *Management Development in Voluntary Organizations: a handbook* (with Carolyn Hooker, published by the Training Agency). He is currently Director of the Voluntary Sector Management Programme in the Open University School of Management and Chair of the Course Team for *Managing Voluntary and Nonprofit Enterprises*.

Professor Charles Handy, writer, teacher and broadcaster, is Visiting Professor at the London Business School and consultant to a wide variety of organizations in business, government, the voluntary sector, education and health. He has written many books including *Understanding Organizations* and an influential study of management education and development for the government, *The Making of Managers*, which compared management education in Britain with Germany, France, the USA and Japan. He was a member of the course team for the Open Business School course *The Effective Manager*. Professor Handy is currently vice-chairman of the Royal Society of Arts and is also a regular guest speaker on Radio 4's *Thought for the Day*.

Charles Landry runs Comedia Consultancy, an organization specializing in cultural planning for cities including Liverpool, Birmingham and Glasgow. Comedia also produces arts plans and organizational reviews for enterprises in the non-profit sector.

David Morley is a Senior Lecturer at Goldsmith College, London. He specializes in audience research work particularly in relation to television and new communications.

Russell Southwood is involved in a consultancy company called Boyden Southwood which specializes in work in the arts, media and leisure industries.

Patrick Wright spent five years (1982–1987) as the Head of the Management Development Unit of the National Council for Voluntary Organizations. He is now working as an independent consultant to voluntary organizations. He has published *On Living in an Old Country* (1985). *A Journey through Ruins* will be available in Spring 1991.

What a Way to Run a Railroad, from which Article 3 is taken, is the culmination of long-standing discussions over several years between the four authors mentioned above.

Tim Dartington is Head of Management Development at the National Council for Voluntary Organizations. He has contributed regularly on management issues in NCVO News. He wrote *The Limits of Altruism, elderly mentally infirm people as a test case for collaboration* (King Edward's Hospital Fund for London, 1986) and co-authored *A Life Together: the distribution of attitudes around the disabled* (London, Tavistock Publications, 1981).

Chris Cornforth is Allied Dunbar Lecturer in Voluntary Sector Management at the Open University. He was a member of the Course Team for *Managing Voluntary and Non-profit Enterprises* and is currently Course Team Chair of *Winning Resources and Support*, a course which focuses on fund-raising, public relations and campaigning. He has a particular research interest in the viability of democratic forms of organization and management. He co-authored the book *Developing Successful Worker Co-operatives* (1988) and co-edited *The State, Trade Unions and Self-Management* (1989).

Jeane L. Nadeau BA, CQSW, Cert. in Group Work SW, has been a management consultant/trainer in the non-profit sector since 1982. She is committed to assisting organizations and managers to respond to the challenge of managing within the new and radical ethos created by Equal Opportunities Policies. Her background is in social work (12 years) as a lecturer, day centre manager, officer/member of voluntary management committees and psychiatric social worker, and before that in the computer system industry (8 years) as a senior systems consultant and team manager.

Sue A. L. Sanders, LUD, Cert. of Ed., is a published writer, her most recent work being as contributor to *Learning Our Lines, Sexuality and Social Control in Education* (Women's Press). Previously her articles on women's issues, fiction and poetry have appeared in various publications. She works in the non-profit sector as a management consultant and trainer, having been both a director and an administrator of fringe theatre companies for ten years. She is a teacher in adult education and has taught in colleges and schools in London and in Sydney, Australia.

Chris Ball is a Regional Officer of the Manufacturing Science and Finance Union and Secretary to the Union's voluntary sector National Advisory Committee. He completed an Open University degree in the Faculty of Social Sciences before going on to gain a Masters and then a PhD in Industrial Relations at the London School of Economics. He has combined research and practice in several articles and pamphlets, including *Trade Unions and Equal Opportunities Employers* (1990).

Elaine Willis has been Deputy Director of The Volunteer Centre UK since 1987. The Centre provides information, training and support to those who work with volunteers. It also seeks to persuade those who make policy and planning decisions about volunteer involvement to do so more effectively. Elaine has contributed to several written publications including *Measuring Up – guidelines on the self-evaluation of volunteer projects* (1986), *The Promotion of Volunteering* (1989) and *Advocacy: some perspectives for the 1990s* (1990). She has also worked as a Project Manager of a youth unemployment project and as a National Development Officer on a government-funded unemployment and volunteering scheme.

Alan Stanton qualified and practised as a solicitor and later as a social worker and now works as a researcher. His PhD in 1988 was for research on collective and collaborative teams in 'human service' agencies. His wide involvement in the voluntary sector includes volunteering, and serving on management committees such as Citizens' Advice Bureaux, a community accountancy project, a trust for Indian tribal women, and a local video project.

Elliot Stern works at the Tavistock Institute of Human Relations where he is head of the Evaluation Development and Review Unit. He has undertaken research and consultancy assignments in the voluntary sector, most recently with the Self Help Alliance and the British Association of Settlements and Social Action Centres. He has also undertaken research and evaluation in the fields of education, local economic development and vocational training.

Vanja Orlans is Associate Research Fellow at the Stress Research and Control Centre at Birkbeck College, University of London, and a Chartered Psychologist of the British Psychological Society. She has over ten years' experience working with individuals, groups and organizations on the problems of stress, and is the author of many articles concerned with such issues. She has recently worked with several trades union organizations on the diagnosis and management of organizational stress.

Margaret Harris is Assistant Director of the Centre for Voluntary Organisation and Lecturer in Social Administration at the London School of Economics. She has worked in local government and as a volunteer advice worker and trainer with the Citizens' Advice Bureaux. She has published several articles on voluntary management committees and other aspects of voluntary sector organization and management. Her current work includes teaching on the LSE's Masters degree in Voluntary Sector Organization and research on the management of religious organizations.

David Wilson is a Senior Lecturer in organizational behaviour at the University of Warwick. His latest research-based book in the voluntary sector deals with issues of strategy, change and organizational culture. He has written widely on the subject and actively consults for and researches the non-profit sector. He has three other books in the areas of strategic decision making and organizational behaviour.

Ralph M. Kramer is a professor in the School of Social Welfare at the University of California, Berkeley. Before joining the Berkeley faculty in 1964, where he also received his BA and MSW degrees, Professor Kramer was employed for 17 years as a psychiatric social worker, family service agency executive and executive director of a social planning council. He is the author of numerous articles on citizen participation, social planning and the voluntary sector. His books include *Voluntary Agencies in the Welfare State, Participation of the Poor*, and *Community Development in Israel and the Netherlands*. As part of a Fulbright Research award, Professor Kramer has recently directed a study of the role of voluntary agencies in England, the Netherlands, Norway and Italy.

Julian Batsleer has spent his working life in adult and higher education. In the early 1970s he undertook research into the policy and management of charitable organizations – long before it was fashionable elsewhere. As well as social policy and administration, his teaching has included trade union studies and industrial relations. In the mid-1980s he was responsible for the establishment of a voluntary sector management training service in Greater Manchester. Since 1987 he has worked for The Open University and is a member of the Open Business School's Course Team for the *Managing Voluntary and Non-profit Enterprises* course.

Stephen Randall is Team Leader of the Trade Union and Basic Education Project which is based in Manchester and is a unit within the North West District Workers' Educational Association. TUBE has been in existence for nine years and has a brief to work with black and other community groups in the inner-city areas. The team comprises community education workers, operating alongside user-groups, helping them devise and design learning programmes appropriate to their perceived needs. As well as offering educational provision TUBE plays a role as a community forum and, in this capacity, stages day schools and conferences on issues of concern to the community. Thus the project has organized seminars on the numerous immigration bills; black workers and the labour movement; and black pupils and educational underachievement. Born and brought up in Liverpool 8 (Toxteth to the media), Stephen Randall attended Lancaster University as a mature student where he graduated in History and Philosophy.

Introduction

The last decade has seen growing interest in the management of voluntary and non-profit organizations. The signs include the rapid growth in management training courses and management consultancies aimed primarily at voluntary and non-profit organizations; the increasing recruitment of professional managers from both the private and the public sectors; the emergence of professional bodies such as the Institute of Charity Fundraising Managers; and a rush of new journals for both academics and practitioners.

Two sets of influences have stimulated these developments. The first and more obvious one is the sweeping political changes of the 1980s. The Conservative government's radical social and economic policies have affected both the funding available to voluntary organizations and the ideological climate in which they exist. Increasingly voluntary organizations have been seen as one vehicle for implementing government programmes. As a result large sums of money have been channelled into areas such as employment creation and training schemes, which were seen as political priorities, while other areas have been cut back. Government has also stimulated private giving to the voluntary sector through tax incentives and by encouraging the private sector to recognize its responsibilities to the community. At the same time tight control of local government expenditure and the abolition of the metropolitan councils has constrained or removed other sources of finance.

Increasing dependence on finance from central government has meant that many voluntary organizations have had to face new challenges and pressures. Such organizations may have experienced rapid growth as they responded to new government initiatives and then faced changes in requirements and funding at short notice as the emphasis of government programmes shifted to meet new political priorities. As in the public sector, voluntary organizations have also been subject to increasing public scrutiny and pressure to see that public money is used in an efficient and effective manner. In addition there are clear signs that more recent changes such as the introduction of contracting for service delivery and community care are likely to have equally profound effects in the long term.

Undoubtedly the voluntary sector has also been affected by broader ideological changes in society towards what has loosely been called an enterprise culture. There appears to have been a growing recognition of the importance of enterprise and initiative, and the dangers of an over-reliance on funding from the state. However, at the same time there have been mixed reactions to the attempt to portray private sector models of management as the solution to problems in the public and voluntary sectors.[1]

Although these changes have placed heavy new demands on management within the voluntary sector they are certainly not the only reason why management is being discussed and re-examined. A second set of influences emanates more from within the sector itself, where there have been persistent attempts not just to ensure effective forms of organization but also to reconcile management practice with the values of voluntary organizations and the pursuit of various progressive aims, such as greater equality and participation. An important early step in this process was the formation of a working party under the chairmanship of Charles Handy which looked at effectiveness in the voluntary sector. The report of the working party entitled *Improving Effectiveness in Voluntary Organizations* was published in 1981. A key recommendation was the establishment of a Management Development Unit (MDU) at the National Council for Voluntary Organizations. While the MDU did much to encourage the growth of management training within the sector it also played an important role in stimulating a critical debate about what sorts of management theories and practices are appropriate to voluntary organizations.

An important contribution to this debate has come from attempts to reappraise and learn from the experiences of a variety of radical projects, started during the 1970s and early 1980s, which attempted to do away with managerial hierarchies and to introduce democratic and collective ways of working.

Throughout the 1980s voluntary organizations were grappling with the imperative of equal opportunities too. This has had, and is likely to continue to have, both diffuse and far-reaching effects on management thinking and practice within the sector. While challenging many taken-for-granted assumptions about management it has also sought to formalize new codes of good practice and professional conduct. For example, equal opportunities training involves and extends much basic management training in areas such as recruitment, supervision and staff development. In addition it has challenged management to address new questions about the nature and delivery of services provided by voluntary organizations and whether they do in fact reach all parts of the community.

More recently and increasingly, concern with what is sometimes called 'empowerment' has been capturing a place on progressive management agenda. Like statutory welfare agencies, many voluntary organizations have been criticized for fostering the dependence of 'clients' rather than enhancing the choices, independence and identities of those they serve. This has led some voluntary organizations to seek new ways of involving users in their management and the provision of services or to develop forms of user management.

Perhaps because of these competing pressures and influences, management thinking and practice in the voluntary sector are in a state of flux. While it is recognized that many traditional management concepts and techniques are relevant and valuable, there is also widespread scepticism that the wholesale adoption of practices and techniques developed primarily in the private sector will be either appropriate or effective. The concern, and the task for those in a position to reflect or research and then to write about these issues, has been, first, to identify the distinctive characteristics of voluntary and non-profit organizations; second, to adapt existing theories and practices to suit these different circumstances; and, third, to articulate the principles implicit in the practical wisdom and hard-won experience of the sector's many unsung heroes – the individuals and groups who not only hold together diverse coalitions of backers for precariously resourced projects but also inspire high levels of commitment from co-workers and volunteers under the most trying and uncertain conditions. This book is one contribution to that task.

In this book we examine a variety of important and topical issues in the management of voluntary and non-profit enterprises, by drawing together the work of researchers and practitioners. There are three main aims for people working in, or involved with, the voluntary sector.

(1) To inform them about recent and ongoing debates concerning the distinctiveness of management in voluntary and non-profit organizations and the challenges that these debates present.

(2) To introduce some useful concepts and approaches which could help to shape and improve their own practice.

(3) To alert them to new trends and developments that are likely to affect management in the voluntary sector in the future.

The book is divided into five parts. Part One begins by focusing on the distinctive characteristics of voluntary and non-profit enterprises. The article by Rob Paton does this by locating the position of voluntary and non-profit enterprises within a framework which divides the economy into six different sectors. It explores both the similarities and the differences between voluntary and non-profit enterprises and other parts of the economy, for example the public sector and small businesses. The article by Charles Handy looks in more detail at the variety of organizations within the voluntary sector and develops a typology based on the functions they perform. Both authors, in different ways, highlight the essential ambiguity concerning the character and purpose of many voluntary and non-profit enterprises.

Part Two takes up the debate about what are appropriate forms of management in the voluntary sector. The article by Charles Landry and his colleagues presents an analysis of the failure of many radical enterprises and projects set up in the 1970s, which tried to develop new alternative or collective ways of working. Drawing on their own experience the authors argue forcefully that in rejecting hierarchy they also threw out important management functions and that, again and again, this led to the failure of the enterprises.

The article by Tim Dartington welcomes the new interest in management but warns that 'over-professionalizing' the voluntary sector and importing inappropriate management techniques from other sectors has its own dangers. Rob Paton and Chris Cornforth in their article attempt to take the debate a stage further by analysing some of the main distinctive features of the voluntary sector and drawing out their implications for management.

Part Three addresses issues concerning the management of people in voluntary and non-profit enterprises. Many voluntary organizations can rightly claim to have been in the vanguard of organizations trying to develop and implement effective equal opportunities policies in the UK. The article by Jeane Nadeau and Sue Sanders draws on their experiences as managers and consultants in this field. They highlight some of the common problems and difficulties that occur in implementing equal opportunities policies and suggest ways of addressing them.

The article by Chris Ball discusses some of the issues and dilemmas that voluntary organizations face in deciding what are appropriate remuneration policies and employment practices. In particular, he examines the advantages and disadvantages of the common practice within the voluntary sector of determining rates of pay by linking it to scales in the public sector.

Elaine Willis's article presents a guide to good practice in the management of volunteers. She argues that all too often organizations focus exclusively on the face-to-face management of volunteers and fail to consider adequately the wider implications of having volunteers, for example as regards organization policy or information systems.

A widespread concern in many voluntary and non-profit organizations has been to try to find ways of reducing hierarchy and of working more 'collectively'. The article by Alan Stanton analyses the development of teams committed to work collectively, based on his research in social services agencies. This can also be read as a rejoinder to Charles Landry *et al.*'s analysis of radical failure: by no means all radical projects ended in failure and some important lessons about collaborative working were learned.

The theme of Part Four is organization and effectiveness. The article by Elliot Stern contributes to the lively debate about evaluation in voluntary and non-profit organizations. He examines some of the dilemmas and pitfalls of evaluation and highlights several weaknesses in current practice based on his extensive experience as an external evaluator of innovatory projects.

Too much pressure and stress can impede individual performance and consequently reduce organization effectiveness. The article by Vanja Orlans analyses some of the common and often distinctive sources of stress in voluntary and non-profit enterprises. She argues that many of these are organizational in nature and demand organizational solutions.

It is widely acknowledged that the composition and functioning of a voluntary organization's management committee or board has an important influence on the organization's effectiveness. Margaret Harris draws on her own research to examine some of the common problems and difficulties concerning the role and functioning of management committees of small local organizations, the reasons why they arise and what lessons can be learned from this experience.

The article by David Wilson draws on organization theory to outline the four main structural forms adopted by the majority of large voluntary organizations, and the factors that are relevant to the choice of structure. In doing so he uses material from one of the few research studies on the structure of voluntary organizations in the UK.

The fifth and final part of the book focuses on some of the important changes occurring in the environment of voluntary and non-profit organizations and examines some of their managerial and strategic implications.

Another contribution by David Wilson reviews the development of competitive strategies by voluntary organizations over the last decade. He asks, on both theoretical and quite pragmatic grounds, whether it is not time to pause and consider whether a scramble to define 'market niches' is really the way forward.

Ralph Kramer reviews the experience of contracting out public services, drawing in particular on research in North America, and highlights some important lessons for voluntary and non-profit enterprises.

The final chapter by Julian Batsleer and Steve Randall examines how wider political and social changes in the UK have influenced, and will continue to influence, the role of voluntary organizations. They suggest that there are several different interpretations of the relationship between the voluntary sector and the state over the provision of social services. They argue that each interpretation has different strategic implications for voluntary organizations, particularly affecting the degree to which they compete or collaborate with each other.

One issue runs throughout all these articles, whether written by academics or practitioners: the question of the relevance of 'mainstream' management and organization ideas and practices for voluntary and non-profit enterprises. All the authors, either in whole or in part, are grappling with whether, how far and under what circumstances concepts from other contexts can illuminate the predicaments or successful approaches they have observed in voluntary and non-profit organizations. Readers will have to decide for themselves how successful their efforts have been.

Note

(1) Similar developments and debates have also been taking place in the management of public services. See, for example, Stewart, J. (1988) *Management in the Public Domain*, Local Government Training Board, Luton.

Some of the articles reprinted in this book have been edited. The use of square brackets and ellipses in these articles indicates that material has been added or deleted by the editors.

Contents

PART ONE

Voluntary and Non-profit Enterprises in Context: Their Distinctive Characteristics

1

The Social Economy:
Value-based Organizations in the Wider Society

Rob Paton

What do we mean by 'voluntary and non-profit organizations'? What do they have in common? Is it helpful to think of them as a distinct 'sector'? Elsewhere in Europe these questions would be answered in terms of the social economy. France and Spain have government institutes concerned with its promotion, and the European Commission's latest division or 'D.G.' (Directorate Générale) has support for the social economy as its main purpose. But what does 'the social economy' refer to? The usual answer is a legal one in terms of co-operatives, mutual societies and non-profit associations. This approach has obvious problems resulting from the differences in legal systems: for example, some non-profit organizations use the form of a limited company; charities are a legal form unique to the UK; what about trusts and foundations? – and so on. Indeed, the use of the term social economy by our continental neighbours has about as much clarity and precision as the British use of 'voluntary sector'. This article adopts the term social economy but offers a new approach to its definition, one based on organizational considerations that address the experience and concerns of managers more directly.

■ Introduction

For years people have complained that the term 'voluntary sector' is vague and confusing. Originally, the 'voluntary' in voluntary sector and voluntary organization meant 'independent of government' – as in the 'voluntary hospital movement'. This usage survives for church schools, which are, technically, 'voluntary aided schools'. The trouble with this approach is that it begs an awfully big question – are voluntary organizations independent of government? This has been questionable for many voluntary organizations for some years, but with 'purchase of service' contracting and other changes in government policy, it becomes even more contentious.

Moreover, this usage is archaic. The meaning that many people now give to 'voluntary' derives from the idea of volunteering. For example, one person who knows the sector well writes:

> 'Even when the work is done by paid staff, these groups are still called "voluntary", partly because of their connection to volunteer groups and partly because they are managed by voluntary (unpaid) management committees.' *(Adirondack, 1989)*

On this basis voluntary organization = volunteer-dependent organization and/or voluntarily managed organization. The trouble is that this sort of definition includes many organizations that are not at all what (some? many?) people have in mind – think of trade unions, or schools with elected governors and parent volunteers, or the police force with its many voluntary 'special constables' and its formal accountability to a committee with many elected unpaid councillors.

A further problem is that 'voluntary' (in whatever sense or senses) is applied both to a particular sort of organization and to a whole sector. A coherent definition of a particular sort of organization is not too difficult – but then for many purposes the sector becomes too narrowly defined, excluding many non-statutory agencies and non-profit organizations. Alternatively, one can define the sector in a fairly coherent way – but then it contains many organizations that would not normally be considered voluntary organizations (trade unions, churches, alternative trading organizations).

The term 'charity' is no better. The idiosyncratic development of English case law means that defining the sector in terms of charities would include some major public schools, as well as quangos like the Medical Research Council, and a host of small parochial charities that are not organizations in the usual sense.

These difficulties are well known and have resulted in a rash of alternative labels – non-profit, third sector, non-statutory sector – which, if they have a clear basis, seem to derive from a *residual* conception of the sector: it is what is left if you exclude business and government. This simply begs more questions: for example, do the organizations that comprise it have enough in common to warrant being considered as a sector; do we really include the Mafia or Oxford University or families...?

Clearly, a new understanding of the voluntary sector is needed – one that will convey both its distinctiveness and its variety, without the misleading associations. It is a matter of the sector knowing itself better, of having a clearer, positive identity.

■ Locating the social economy

The usual distinction between the public and the private sectors is no longer an adequate starting point in considering the different ways goods and services are produced and delivered in modern societies. For one thing it has become politically contentious. More importantly, several writers (of whom John Kenneth Galbraith is an eloquent example) have argued that it is increasingly irrelevant. A valid image of the modern economy would distinguish between, on the one hand, the corporate sector of very large economic groupings exercising a substantial degree of control over their markets, planning their operations over an extended time horizon and able to call on extensive government support in a wide variety of ways and, on the other hand, the 'dispersed' sector – the many small and medium-sized businesses whose ability, individually, to ride the waves of change is usually much more limited. According to this argument, the classical picture of the way economies are supposed to work applies reasonably well to small and medium-sized enterprises and very inadequately to the corporate sector.

In fact, economists, organizational theorists, banks, government policy makers and management trainers all recognize that small and medium-sized firms are different. But, if a distinction between large/institutionalized and smaller/entrepreneurial is useful for profit-making organizations, why not apply it to non-profit organizations as well? The result is a four sector economy in which three sectors (the public, the corporate and the small firm) are all familiar. The fourth – small and medium-sized organizations orientated towards the provision of some kind of common benefit or public good – is, of course, that ill-defined and disputed sector for which the continental term *social economy* is proposed.[1]

This picture is still incomplete, however, because it does not include two large areas of economic and social activity. One is the 'Can I have it in cash?' economy of goods and services that are traded but never appear in the national income statistics (or Inland Revenue or VAT records). The other is the provision of social, recreational, cultural, regulatory, health, childcare and other services through the spontaneous mutuality of family, friendship and community networks. Adding these two informal sectors – which can be called the *hidden economy* and, for want of a better term, the *natural economy*[2] – to the picture gives a six sector model of the provision of goods and services (see Figure 1.1).

The corporate sector	The public sector
Small businesses	The social economy
The hidden economy	The natural economy

Figure 1.1 The social economy in context.

But are these sectors distinct? Surely the boundaries between them will be rather blurred? Yes, indeed – but does this matter? If one abandons the search for clear-cut *categories* of organization (unless one is a lawyer or a tax inspector, such a search is quite unnecessary) and thinks instead of *dimensions*, then the 'problem' of overlapping boundaries, fuzziness, etc. disappears. In fact, the arrangement of the sectors in Figure 1.1 is given by placing them in terms of two underlying dimensions. First, horizontally, what sort of purposes do the organizations serve? The range is from those concerned with private profit, through mutual benefit organizations, to those that exist for the benefit of others. Second, vertically, how *institutionalized* are the groupings involved? The range is from the thoroughly informal (family or friendship networks; small scale, opportunistic trading relationships) to small or medium-sized organizations and on to the large, more or less permanent bureaucracy.

Since these are dimensions (rather than categories) the sectors in Figure 1.1 have broad boundaries. But if it is actually the case that many organizations are neither one type nor the other, then this is hardly a disadvantage. The real tests of this approach are, first, whether it highlights the common features of organizations *within* a given sector and, second, whether it illuminates the character of organizations that fall between the sectors. To see whether this is so for organizations in and around the social economy requires a closer examination of the suggested boundaries.

The horizontal dimension concerns the underlying purposes of organizations. The main problem here is that organizations, like people, sometimes claim they are dedicated to one purpose while it appears to observers that they give more attention to rather different purposes. In general, of course, people have a mixture of motives in their organizational activity. Staff in social economy organizations may look for and find vocations, but they also pursue careers. At one extreme the maintenance of the organization or the rewards it offers (status, social relationships, personal advancement, etc.) have become the main concern of staff. At the other extreme are organizations whose members share a strong commitment to a common cause – be it organic gardening, scouting, assisting those with AIDS, or feminism. These latter organizations are the heartland of the social economy. Since they are marked by a distinctive value system and a more intense involvement by members, they will be referred to as value-based organizations.

Hence although one cannot always assume that an organization set up to pursue a common or public benefit is really still doing so, the idea of a common benefit orientation, which can vary in strength, is still useful.[3]

The vertical dimension concerns how institutionalized organizations are – which depends on size and the uncertainty of the organization's environment. At one end of the range are the large, well-established agencies or institutions, employing hundreds or thousands of people and having a recognized role, a comparatively secure resource-base and the capacity to adapt to change by introducing new activities and services. In contrast, smaller organizations may have few paid staff and face a continual struggle either to define, articulate and address a particular social need or to promote the value of particular activities or services in a way that attracts human and financial resources and sustains a common commitment.

The two dimensions are related: size has an important connection with the strength of the common benefit orientation. Small and medium sizes (in terms of the number of paid staff and/or active supporters in a given unit) provide the best conditions for maintaining an organization's distinctive values. In too large an organization, the tendency is for bureaucratization and a dilution of commitment to the common cause. Hence the two dimensions do generate a coherent pattern – *the small or medium-sized value-based organization founded on commitment (arising from devotion, compassion, enthusiasm, solidarity, defiance, etc.) and working for a common or public benefit*. Such organizations may or may not be voluntary. These attributes also occur in alternative trading organizations (for example Traidcraft), in many worker co-operatives, in religious, artistic and political organizations, and in intentional communities (for example communes).

With these points in mind, Figure 1.2 overleaf presents an application of this view of the social economy annotated with examples of organizations falling in the various boundary zones.

■ Shifting boundaries

So what does this view have to recommend it? What does it clarify? First, the sectors are distinguished in terms of fundamental organizational characteristics that have been shown by innumerable studies to have a pervasive impact on the way organizations run. Hence, for anyone interested in organizations and management this is a coherent, theoretically grounded approach.[4]

Second, this view locates the sector in relation to the rest of the economy and society. Hence it provides a convenient way of charting movements between the sectors and of examining the relationships, tensions and influences that arise between them.[5]

For example, historically, many organizations have originated as small societies or mutual aid networks and (for better or worse) progressed *through* the social economy to become established companies or institutions (for example the Abbey National, the Co-op movement, the Consumers Association). As another example, government policies aimed at reducing the size of the public sector have had the effect of shifting activities into other sectors. Some have moved into the corporate sector (major privatizations), some into the small firm sector (the contracting-out of ancillary services) and some into the social economy. This last movement, which promises (or threatens) to transform the sector, includes the shift from public housing to provision by housing associations, the adoption by local authorities of the role of purchaser of welfare and other services and the provision for schools and health facilities to opt for much greater financial autonomy under independent trusts.

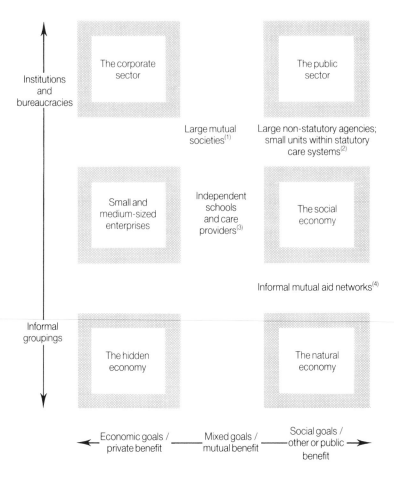

Notes

(1) for example, building societies, retail co-ops, the Automobile Association
(2) for example, large housing associations, Barnardos; local authority family centres, cottage hospitals
(3) for example, charitable public schools, nursing homes (private but professionally run)
(4) for example, baby-sitting circles, mother and toddler clubs

Figure 1.2 Types of organization in and around the social economy.

■ The diversity of organizations in the social economy

Organizations in the social economy exist for many purposes and play many different roles in the wider society. By considering those roles in relation to the other sectors some of the differences between them (and between the sectors themselves) can be sketched out. One role, clearly, is to attempt to redress the shortcomings and failures of governments. The level of public services is always a compromise between high and low spenders and is bound to leave many people dissatisfied with what they see as inadequacies in provision. These people organize, support or campaign for additional services – hence the emergence of Oxfam, community self-help initiatives, and so on. But equally, government departments have long realized that the creation or support of (more or less) independent bodies provides an alternative vehicle for delivering public services – and a useful contribution to policy-making – especially when they utilize volunteer effort (as, for example, in the Citizens' Advice Bureaux) where they will have enormous cost advantages in comparison to other modes of provision.[6]

Similar contradictory tendencies are clear when the social economy's relationship with the business sector is examined. One role that value-based organizations play is, in effect, to be businesses, to *invade* the market and capture parts of it for common benefit ends. They can do this because they often have advantages when competing with private companies. The value basis of organizations in the social economy generates a different relationship with potential customers and ready access to them through, for example, membership lists. Hence the increasing importance of charitable trading in all its many forms. Moreover, common benefit organizations can obtain substantial cost advantages, often because the value-based organization can offer as a *benefit* what in other organizations is experienced as a *cost* – namely, the chance to contribute. Similarly, religious or alternative communities can be competitive through low labour costs compensated for by non-material rewards. Cost advantages may also arise in many other ways.

However, charitable or non-profit organizations are also formed as a way of extending the market into areas where normal private companies and market relationships are problematic. For example, Community Businesses may be set up where an activity is insufficiently profitable for a private company (for example, remote island shops). There again, with many health, welfare and educational services it is often not clear quite what is being bought. So the child/patient/old person will be 'looked after' – but what does this mean in practice, and wouldn't it be in a proprietor's interest to cut corners? The use of a non-profit legal form is a signal to potential customers that private interest will not undermine service standards. Hence the emphasis British United Patients Association (BUPA) gives to its non-profit status in brochures and promotions.

In the same way, some organizations in the social economy can be seen as responses to failures in the natural economy – Age Concern and the NSPCC are obvious examples – but, at the same time, the role of other organizations is in extending the natural economy. This is most obvious in mutual aid organizations associated with disabilities, illnesses or trauma (victim support schemes, Women's Aid, etc.). Devotees of state provision sometimes claim that such organizations are really compensating for the inadequacies of the publicly provided services; but this reflects a serious misunderstanding of the nature of the relationships involved and the support provided. The detached concern of the professional is not the same as the understanding and relationship between 'fellow sufferers'.

In summary, organizations in the social economy do not just campaign against and compensate for the shortcomings of governments; they are also deliberately used and created as vehicles for government policies. They have a role in securing and using particular segments of the market for common benefit ends; but they are also a means of expanding the market into the provision of services for which profit-orientated organizations are unsuitable. They are a response to failures of the natural economy but also a means of extending and recreating it. With organizations playing such very different roles – *quite often simultaneously* – it is not surprising that there has been confusion and disagreement over what the term voluntary sector refers to and the place of voluntary organizations in, for example, social policy and welfare.

■ What sort of organization are we anyway?

Commercial organizations can draw on a well-developed body of principles and practices based on the logic of profit and which incorporate such concepts as competitive positioning, measurable targets, the division of labour, optimization, performance-related remuneration, and so on. Likewise the public sector (based on a logic of accountability) can turn to an honourable tradition of public administration founded on concepts of service, impartiality, strict hierarchical control, universality and the like. By comparison, the organizational principles and practices of the social economy are far more limited or, at least, less clearly articulated.

Because they are founded on a logic of *commitment*, value-based organizations tend to generate a style of organization in which people 'do what needs to be done' and effort is highly valued. This is important but in itself a limited and even problematic prescription for getting things done. Not surprisingly, then, organizations in the social economy sometimes look to other sectors for practices and principles. This may also be a necessary result of their attempts to secure resources in or from those sectors. There is more to this than importing approaches (and staff) from private and public sectors. The social economy is also strongly influenced by the principles and practices of the natural economy – which is based on a logic of *affinity* expressed through informality, mutuality and voluntarism.

As a result, those involved may have very different ideas about the sort of organization they are trying to run. For example, the National Tramways Museum must simultaneously be:

- the provider of a well-marketed, regionally competitive, 'leisure experience', including a profitable gift shop and cafeteria
- a public service organization operating to professional standards in its roles both as a cultural resource (providing interpretative materials, keeping a

film archive, encouraging school visits, etc.) and as a training organization for young unemployed people
- a club for enthusiasts, providing recreation, a chance to acquire, develop and exercise skills and a congenial social milieu.

All these aspects of the museum are essential for its continuing viability: the economic equation depends on a substantial trading income, grant aid to develop and extend the exhibitions and environment and, crucially, a substantial amount of free (often skilled) labour in the painstaking restoration of trams, in selling tickets and supervising the site, and in planning and managing the organization.[7]

The co-existence of such very different conceptions of what sort of organization one is trying to be produces many of the tensions that commonly arise in organizations in the social economy. Do paid workers have the status of professional staff, or are they basically volunteers who can work full-time? Are we a not-for-profit business that must earn its income – or are we an organization that exists to respond to particular needs among the poor as well as the well-off? Is it, or is it not, an option for a small housing association that has adopted a local authority pay scale to say it cannot afford to pay increments this year? Should (say) an AIDS or a children's charity be trying to cultivate a distinctive competence and a competitive advantage in relation to rival agencies – or should it be collaborating with them and sharing its expertise and experience? What does an equal opportunities policy mean for the enthusiastic, self-selected friendship group that is turning into an organization with the help of public money?

The 'pull' exerted by these other sectors results in a pervasive ambiguity and uncertainty concerning the nature and role of many organizations in the social economy. This complicates the management process enormously.

■ Conclusions

Thinking in terms of value-based organizations and of the social economy defines the problematic 'independent' sector more clearly and sets it in context. It captures better not only what organizations in this sector do have in common but also their diversity and the range of conflicting pressures and expectations to which they are subjected. This approach will not, of course, be sufficient for all purposes: often it will be important to distinguish particular categories of organization within the social economy (for example, large agencies, community-based organizations, membership associations). Nevertheless, it provides a simple and coherent framework for understanding a family of organizational forms whose name and nature has been a chronic source of confusion and controversy.

Notes

(1) The continental usage of the term social economy is somewhat different from, but not incompatible with, the framework presented here. A full treatment is beyond the scope of this paper but see Van Til (1988).

(2) Natural, in the sense that kinship can be considered the original form of social organization from which all other organizational forms have become differentiated.

(3) Difficult questions about the real goals of organizations arise in relation to the private and public sectors, too, of course. Sophisticated studies of takeovers and mergers have repeatedly failed to show that they generate, directly or indirectly, a sustained improvement in earnings for shareholders. Many economists have been forced to conclude that takeovers commonly have more to do with the aggrandisement of senior executives than any economic logic. On the other hand, human beings do tend to attribute great value to activities that they undertake initially for economic motives. Hence the enormous commitment often shown by those who might otherwise be considered as simply doing a job.

(4) By implication, it will probably not serve the purposes of those with, for example, a primarily social policy concern, or perhaps a political science or economics orientation. For the importance of organizational goals on the character of an organization see, for example, the classic work of Etzioni (1961). For the impact of institutionalization (that is, size and environmental stability) see Pugh and Hickson (1976).

(5) The social economy is certainly not alone in needing to be understood in context. For example, the behaviour of many small firms can only be understood in relation to the large firms they depend on or from which they have emerged (for example, the wave of management buy-outs in the 1980s) and the tax evasion and avoidance possibilities of moonlighting and cash payments.

(6) The relationship between government bodies and organizations in the social economy often displays the same kind of uneasy symbiosis that exists between large firms and small firms in the private sector: each needs the other, yet fears it is being taken advantage of.

(7) Many thanks to Cliff Pelham, an Open Business School Diploma student in the mid-1980s, for this example.

References

Adirondack, S. (1989) *Just about Managing*. London: Voluntary Service Council.

Etzioni, A. (1961) *A Comparative Analysis of Complex Organizations*. New York: The Free Press.

Pugh, D. S. and Hickson, D. J. (1976) *Organizational Structure in Its Context: the Aston Programme I*. Aldershot: Gower Publishing.

Van Til, J. (1988) *Managing the Third Sector: Voluntarism in a Changing Social Economy*. Washington: The Foundation Centre.

2

Types of Voluntary Organizations[1]

Charles Handy

The organizations that make up the voluntary sector are very diverse, often springing from quite different social and political traditions. The annual conference of the Charities Aid Foundation is worlds apart from the Annual General Meeting of, say, an inner-city Council of Voluntary Service. Any serious treatment of management issues in the sector must start, therefore, by distinguishing between different sorts of organization. The classic distinction is between mutual support groups, service delivery agencies, and campaigning bodies. The following article explains this distinction and its management implications with clarity and force.

[…]

There are three broad types of voluntary activity:

- *Mutual support* – those organizations which are created in order to put people with a particular problem or enthusiasm in touch with others like themselves who can give them understanding, advice, support and encouragement. Many voluntary organizations start this way, be they for sufferers from multiple sclerosis, parents of drug addicts, or alcoholics. The associations to do with hobbies and sports also fall into this category; model railway enthusiasts, Bugatti car owners and kite-flyers have their support networks too – indeed, the network is what it is all about.

- *Service delivery* – the biggest and most visible of the voluntary organizations are in the business of providing services to those in need: the RNIB, Mountain Rescue, the Royal National Lifeboat Institution, Save the Children, the Marriage Guidance Council [Relate], the Spastics Society and many more. Some of these organizations have so many paid staff (the Spastics Society has over 1200) that it is hard at first to tell them apart from their counterparts in the statutory sector.

- *Campaigning* – some organizations, of which CND is the best-known example, were created to campaign for a cause or to act as a pressure group in a particular interest, be it against racism in education or in favour of women's rights.

The categorization is crude, of course, and many voluntary organizations fit all three categories or slip unwittingly into a fourth. Is CND, for instance, only about campaigning or is it also a mutual-aid organization, a support network for enthusiasts for peace? There lies the rub, for in this unconscious blending of the categories lies much organizational confusion.

The fact is that each of the categories carries with it an unspoken and implicit assumption about the nature of organizations and how they ought to run.

A mutual-support group needs only the minimum amount of organization to service the members, to find reasons for meetings, to send out occasional circulars, to let its existence be known to people who might need it. The only qualification for membership is that you fit the description of the organization. Any single parent can join an association for single parents; any alcoholic can join Alcoholics Anonymous. No one is going to vet them for intelligence, analyse their job record or give them an aptitude test.

Mutual-aid groups do not want to be 'managed'; they detest the thought and are reluctant to divert any of their caring energies to the tasks of administration or of organization, which seem to them to be a distraction. At most they want to be 'serviced' by a secretary or a co-ordinator, with everyone joining in for any policy discussions that might be required. [See Figure 2.1.]

Service-delivery organizations, on the other hand, are all about organization. They exist to meet a need, to provide help to those who need it. They take pride in being professional, effective and low-cost. It follows that they need to be selective about their recruits, demanding in their review of standards, prepared to reprimand where necessary, even to dismiss someone whose work is inadequate.

You cannot join the delivery part of these organizations just because you agree with their work. They want and need professional qualifications and will pay proper, or nearly proper, salaries for them. You can help, by all means. You can raise money, mail literature, badger local authorities, be elected to their council; but you cannot, by your choice, join the core.

These are 'managed' organizations – they have to be. They will therefore have within them much of the paraphernalia of bureaucracy: jobs which carry formal definitions, with formal responsibilities and formal accountability to other bodies; the impersonal feel of an organization which can continue to operate in the same way even if the individuals in it change and move.

Campaigning organizations are led rather than managed. True, they need their administration to be done effectively, meetings well organized, literature well written and printed on time, but these are subordinate functions. The essence of the organization is that of adherence to a cause, focused on a leader, often a charismatic one whose personality infects the organization. The only qualification

The local single parents' group was in distress. The room which had been theirs for meetings, events and parties and had acted as their informal centre had been reclaimed by the landlord for his own use.

An informal meeting of some of the core group was arranged one evening in the home of one of the parents. As was the custom, all the children of the parents came too. They were, after all, the 'badges of belonging'; you could hardly be a single parent in need if you weren't obviously surrounded by your children. But it did make the meeting rather chaotic, since no one was prepared to be crèche minder for the evening – everyone wanted to be in on the discussion.

Ideas abounded for new ways of finding facilities. But who was to do the follow-up work after the meeting? Who was, as it were, the executive officer of the group? There were no volunteers. As single parents they were far too busy scraping together a living, looking after their children and tending the home to have time to do another job of sorts. Should they find someone, then, who wasn't a single parent to work for them? That would be to breach the most basic rule of their group: only single parents could be involved. Even ex-single parents were excluded.

The meeting took only one decision in the end: to meet next month at the home of one of the other members. So, one felt, it would go on, for no one wanted what was to them the 'chore' of organizing, and maybe meeting together was what it was all about anyway.

Figure 2.1 The group meeting.

for belonging is that you believe, and the more believers the better. It is, in fact, more a movement than an organization; or, at least, the organization is but the formal part which serves the movement, efficiently but preferably invisibly. Organization is, as with mutual-aid organizations, a necessary chore, to be done but not too obviously.

Each set of assumptions hangs together. And [...] there are different ways of organizing different structures and cultures for each set. The confusion and the problems start when the sets overlap.

That happens all too frequently because organizations do not usually stand still or stick to their last. They tend to grow and develop as they prosper. Members of a mutual-aid organization, for instance, will begin to think that in addition to supporting one another in distress they ought to do something practical about it, start a school, create a hospital, build a home. Some of the members will then want to do something about the lack of public appreciation of their predicament, may even want to get some laws changed or taxes eased. Quite sensibly and naturally the mutual-aid society has moved into service delivery and into campaigning. The logic is clear, but the clash of assumptions can be heard from miles away. [See Figure 2.2 overleaf].

It can work the other way. A campaigning organization finds it cannot rest content with words. It must put its actions where its mouth is and move into an appropriate service delivery, or at least offer a support network to those who suffer.

Over a century ago it had started – an association for the young and the lonely of our cities, provided only that they were female and Christian. What they needed were places to forgather to find fellowship, friendship and Christian ways. It had moved on since then, running projects for women as well as a string of cheap but decent hostels for women of any faith. It was involved in campaigning internationally for the cause of women generally, for peace and for better international relations.

As a result some of the meetings were interesting. Proposals for tighter budgeting, more realistic financing of building projects and better evaluation of standards of hostels, occupancy rates and returns on capital alternated, not always harmoniously, with pleas for the local members to be more involved, for space to be allocated for prayer meetings and social clubs at no charge. Should non-members be allowed to say? Should non-Christians be allowed?

What was the point of an association which let in everyone? some asked. What was the point of hostels half-empty? came back the rejoinder. Well, then, what about all this advocacy – so loud, so radical, so expensive? What had it to do with fellowship – wasn't it only a glamorous distraction from their real business, international junketing in place of caring?

The passion of their voices drowned out the logic. Personalities became more important than argument, as often happens when organizations use one mechanism for three very different tasks.

Figure 2.2 The threefold organization.

Des Wilson has said that a campaigning organization has a moral responsibility to put its expertise into practice, to inject it into the system and pass it on to the public.

'What I loved about Shelter', he said, 'was that combination of daily helping families and campaigning. It was a wonderful healthy balance.'

You can see his point, but the moral combination works only if there are in effect two separate organizations doing the two separate tasks under one umbrella. To the director on top of the umbrella, and to the world outside, it is one organization, but to the wise director it is two organizations underneath.

When voluntary organizations talk about the importance of values they are right. But values become the subject of an argument whenever the categories get combined and confused. A pure mutual-aid organization has no problems about values until it starts to try to provide a service. The assumptions and values conflict, because it becomes necessary to define what is meant by success, which you cannot do unless you are clear what it is you are trying to do and at what cost and to what standards.

'If we save one child from dying in the gutter, this society is justified,' cried a member at the AGM.

'What – even if it involved neglecting a hundred children not yet in the gutter?' replied the chairperson. It was a concealed debate between a campaign and a service-delivery outlook.

Organizations can, of course, keep it simple and therefore straightforward. Some of the most successful do just that. Alcoholics Anonymous sticks to what it does so well. It is not trying to become a campaigning organization, although the temptation must at times be great. The Samaritans do only what they do so well. They have not moved into the hospice movement, although there could be a logic in such a move.

Most organizations, however, have grown like Topsy and end up as some sort of amalgam of all three categories. There is nothing wrong with that. It may indeed, as Des Wilson says, be the only way to stay honest. It will, however, make life more complicated because the organizational assumptions will clash.

[...]

Note

(1) From Handy, C. (1988) *Understanding Voluntary Organizations*, pp. 12–18, Penguin. The title of this extract is that of the editors.

PART TWO

The Management Debate

3

An Analysis of Radical Failure

Charles Landry, David Morley,
Russell Southwood and Patrick Wright

This article consists of passages from pages 29–47 of *What a Way to Run a Railroad* – a book published in 1985 by Comedia Publishing Group and based on the authors' experiences in a variety of radical projects in the 1970s and 1980s. Their sharp critique of commercial ignorance and 'voluntary disorganization' opened up an intense debate in many co-operatives and community-based organizations. Things have moved on since then. For all kinds of reasons – not least of which has been the recognition that equal opportunities require good management practices – an overt rejection of management is no longer good currency. However, if the authors' attack on zealous, self-righteous ineptitude is in some respects dated, its central arguments are timeless. A neglect or distrust of management is endemic in voluntary and non-profit organizations. Those involved may be enthusiastic about the direct work of the organization – but no-one is much interested in 'the admin'. Professional staff are concerned to prevent 'interference' in their work. Trustees are reluctant to devote resources to anything other than direct service provision or campaigning ... and so on.

■ Introduction

This [article] is written on the basis of our experiences of working in the alternative/radical press, in publishing, in libertarian and community politics, and in the voluntary sector over the last ten years. This experience has included work with community newspapers and magazines as well as with a variety of distribution and publication projects as well as work for other kinds of radical projects. We take, on the whole, a doleful view of this recent history, but our reasons for exhuming it are positive.

Our aim is to define certain factors which, in our view, help to account for the collapse and failure of many radical projects in this sector. We offer this analysis of 'past failures' in the hope that other people – whether they agree or disagree with our specific analysis – will recognize many of the problems discussed here and feel it worthwhile to consider and discuss them further.

[...]

■ Cultural snobbery, commercial ignorance

We believe certain political and economic perspectives have played a major part in locking the radical alternative movement in this country into its own ghetto. Radical movements in France, Germany and Italy have in many respects a better developed infrastructure than their counterparts in Britain.

What is noticeable, particularly in Britain, is the ignorance in the radical movements of how 'the system' works. On the whole, people in these movements know little of commerce, accounting and other business practices. This is partly due to some very crude and irritating forms of cultural snobbery – such as the disdain of commerce and industry among the educated middle-classes. Still prevalent, this cultural rather than political contempt may well be rooted in the landed aristocracy's disdain of the nouveau-riche industrialists of the 19th century.[1]

[...]

We would suggest that the key organizational weaknesses of the sector stem from the ideological framework within which most of these organizations were conceived. The political culture from which they emerged had a number of blind spots which made it difficult to conceive of the genuine importance of skills such as financial planning, budgeting, credit control, accountancy, entrepreneurship and management. These skills were seen as 'capitalist' and therefore reactionary by their very nature.

[...]

One simple index of this problem is the widely held view of financial accounting as merely an external/legal requirement, with which an organization must comply (in order, for instance, to get its grant renewed) rather than a vital tool for the internal management of the organization itself. Without proper financial planning, cash flows and forward budgeting, an organization has no clear measure against which performance can be judged. One is navigating without a compass – invariably something of a problem. Even if this particular form of compass was invented by capitalists, life without it can be difficult.

The alternative sector displays both a general lack of understanding of capitalism's financial practices and the inability accurately to calculate costs. Everything is improperly costed. Free labour, subsidised premises and grants all disguise real costs – and this is compounded by the feeling that finance is an inconvenient truth, best avoided. This amounts to a plain lack of business sense, disguised by a political rhetoric which attempts to deny these problems are relevant. Creditors are rarely impressed by rhetoric.

[...]

■ Manager, co-ordinator or commander?

In a traditional business organization it would be the responsibility of management to develop a strategic overview which could anticipate problems [...] and develop strategies for dealing with them. However, the wholesale rejection of management theory, as part of capitalist ideology, has had the unfortunate effect of throwing the baby out with the bath water. This perspective simply fails to disentangle the role of management as a necessary administrative function within any organization, regardless of its political purposes, from the particular, 'command-structure' form of management which has developed in traditional business organizations. Many collectives have concentrated on sharing out the swabbing of the Titanic's decks but forgotten to post a lookout for the icebergs. The dominant view of management among the radical movements – as merely a command structure capable of passing orders downwards – represents a serious misunderstanding of how management works. The Left avoids the idea of management by calling people 'coordinators' – as if the skill of management was merely that of stopping people bumping into each other.

One crucial function of management in a capitalist enterprise is the clarification of organizational goals and the continuous development and monitoring of strategies to achieve those goals. The problem – of how to clarity objectives, create a strategy to carry them out and find the means to make them happen, is one that few radical organizations recognize explicitly – most just muddle through. The lack of strategic clarify can only be a recipe for disaster, as the history of failure in this sector over the last few years plainly demonstrates.

[...]

■ East End blues

Many of these problems are illustrated in the following account of what happened on the *East End News*. When it was launched in 1980 the *East End News* made bold claims that it would reach a general readership and the team who launched it were able to raise what seemed to be the enormous sum of £23,000 from a wide range of new sources, including the trade unions. Even with this degree of financial support the *East End News* suffered acute problems. A weekly publication cycle demanded getting things right quickly. With weekly production costs amounting to £3,000–£4,000, the launch capital gave the paper precious little time to establish itself. Mark Lloyd, who sold advertising space on the paper, gives an interesting account of its early days:[2]

> 'The *East End News* did no extensive market research before launching, or work on identifying a specific target audience within the three London boroughs. More importantly, little attention was given to the paper's commercial infrastructure, such as the need to fully develop and give priority to establishing an effective advertising department to generate the "financial life blood" of the paper. Within weeks not only had the launch capital evaporated but more seriously little new finance had been gained.
>
> On arriving for work in the second week of the paper's life the office was obviously full of people and busy, that is with the exception of the advertising department. All the free labour ... was involved in the more glamorous tasks such as journalism and photography. The advertising department had to share two telephone lines with everyone else and as for rate cards and vital advertising material, they had simply not been printed in time. In addition, the location of the "department" was a joke, between the telephone switchboard and the reception counter – thus hardly a professional set-up to impress advertisers. For me, the paper failed in the first month due to its inability to capitalise on all the publicity attracted in both the local and national media.'

The lack of preparation had a disastrous impact on the flow of revenue to the paper:

> 'I found myself in a position where I was selling space, collecting art work, and carrying out the entire administrative work of the department. Not the least of the tasks was the question of invoicing. No plans had been set for who was going to carry out the important task of invoicing the clients. Thus it fell on me to spend over two weeks going over the early advertisers, finding out their addresses, so as to be able to send them a bill! This oversight meant the paper never received 40% of its advertising revenue, since advertisers quickly realised the *East End News* lacked the machinery to pressurise late payers.'

Unable even to chase existing display advertisers, the *East End News* had little hope of attracting classified advertising – one of the staple revenue earners of a local paper. The failure to attend to the need for a commercial infrastructure was also matched in those early days in the area of distribution. It was some weeks after the launch before anyone was interviewed for the job of distribution manager. There were two applicants for the job. One really wanted to be a journalist on the paper and the other was a bewildered youth sent from the Job Centre where the post had been advertised. He had been led to believe the task only involved shifting bundles of paper about and was overwhelmed when its relative complexity was outlined.

Luck and money could have helped to overcome these problems in time, but the paper also faced stiff competition from two other papers; the *Hackney Gazette* and the *East London Advertiser*, each of which had a circulation of over 30,000 per issue. Both were determined to see off this upstart competitor and they deliberately undercut any rates the *East End News* could offer to advertisers. As the *East End News'* circulation slumped from a high point of 14,000 with its first issue to just 4,000 three months later, it had little competitive advantage to offer advertisers.

These problems were compounded by the prevailing attitude to advertising:

'Tower Hamlets Council placed an ad. of coming events in the borough which included a beauty contest. On this occasion the ad. was banned without any consultation with the advertising staff. This action could have been serious since the Council were potentially our biggest customer and, given the manner in which we treated them, could easily have not bothered to return to us . . . If *East End News* had taken the ad. and thus the money but *also* printed an article against beauty contests, then all people within the paper would have been happy. As it was the paper rigidly stood by its interpretation of its principles, rejected the advert and thus lost vital money and alienated an important potential client.'

■ Profiting autonomously

[. . .]

Movements in the alternative sector share many of the dilemmas of Third World countries. Deciding on a political strategy is only the beginning – the problem is how to finance such strategies: how to avoid relations of dependence on external finance which will jeopardize autonomy; how to juggle contradictions so as to create an inch or two of space in which to operate autonomously; how to ensure your long-term autonomy, survival and development. This is not simply an argument in favour of pragmatism and against idealism, but rather an argument against a form of moralism rampant in this sector – a moralism which has had the overweaning arrogance to identify itself as the 'One True Way to Salvation' and to damn all others who veer from that path.

We make this point forcefully because, on the whole, this sector has failed to pay anything like enough attention to developing its economic base. Indeed, the argument goes further – these kinds of questions have usually been relegated to the bottom of the agenda, or indeed excluded from the agenda of political discussion within the sector – as merely 'mechanical' or technical problems, to be dealt with, if there's time, after the 'policy' meeting, and otherwise left 'till the next meeting'. All too often the creditors have arrived before that meeting.

Just because capitalists are concerned with efficiency and cost-effectiveness it doesn't mean that we have to abandon these concerns in favour of good old-fashioned socialist inefficiency. We need to rescue what is valuable here: we may be motivated by a desire to develop efficient mechanisms to sell a lot of papers in order to make a lot of political impact, rather than to make a lot of money. Either way, resources being scarce, we need to be cost-effective. Of course, that raises a set of difficult questions about the criteria to be used to assess efficiency; of how to distinguish the display of 'efficient action' from what is often less spectacular but more cost-effective; but these are the issues to which we urgently need to address ourselves.

[...]

■ The collective decides ...

For ten years the political rectitude of a collective method of working has been largely unquestioned. Nevertheless, a number of problems and issues have emerged in this method of working. [...] We do not wish to decry the concern with democratic and accountable structures of organization which gave rise to collectives, but we feel that many of the problems have gone unstated for far too long.

[...]

Even though many people in such collectives will readily admit that the process is inefficient and messy, it is nevertheless often held to be more 'democratic'. From this position it is a short step to claiming that the process is morally superior to the 'bourgeois' way of doing things and therefore cannot be called into question. At this point the group finds itself trapped. A discussion of doing things differently, within the realms of the 'morally acceptable', is no longer possible.

[...]

[One] problem is the frequent lack of clear discussion over policy options: often the very notion of being clear about what your policy objectives are is tainted with all the evil connotations of machismo and 'power'. A polarized discussion will be presented in such a way as to blur differences. Moreover, this whole process (especially when merged in a 'consensus' decision-making procedure which excludes the possibility of decision by majority vote) encourages people to say similar sounding things when they actually mean the very opposite. Equally bad, it often leads to a use of language that serves to obscure sharp differences of opinion so that at least the work at hand can carry on.

[...]

Without a forum in which formal policy of any kind can be made, there will usually be, by default, a kind of *de facto* policy-making by a network of personal friendships which is able to utilize the confusion built into the process. The only formal record of the decision-making process is often the minutes of the collective meeting. Since these won't necessarily represent the necessary day-to-day decisions taken during the group's actual work, there can often be immense confusion over what decisions have been taken.

If a collective meeting is too obviously divided, a problematic issue will often be deferred to give the collective more time to reach a consensus. Such a process does not allow decisions to be taken quickly on controversial issues. This poses no problems in a self-contained discussion group, but if the collective in question is trying to produce a service or product for the outside world – a café, a cinema, a magazine – it can cause obvious difficulty. Quite simply, the outside world will not necessarily take heed of Canute-style gestures indicating that the collective needs time to arrive at a consensus. The democratic impetus behind the notion of collectively discussing and deciding things is certainly important, but in order to survive, an organization must be capable of taking key policy decisions quickly when the situation demands it.

[...]

■ Accountability and the rationality of bureaucracy

At the heart of the matter is the problem of defining responsibilities in radical projects. The present pattern is one in which undefined responsibility is too lightly undertaken without considering the nature of the job and whether, for example, a volunteer is the right person to do it. And when things start going wrong it becomes even more difficult to reallocate responsibility.

Experience shows that clear patterns of accountability are crucial if a collective is to function effectively. So if, for example, the task is to sell advertising space and after an agreed period the individual responsible has not sold any advertising space, he or she should be asked to account for their failure to do the job effectively. Then we need to discover whether the problem arose because the job was delegated to the wrong person, or whether it was because the job itself was badly defined, or whether there are external factors which mean that the job cannot be done by anyone until the circumstances have changed.

[...]

One of the strengths of a bureaucracy is that it will develop explicit rules and procedures, written down in rule books, which can be shown to newcomers to the organization, who can thus take over a new function without too much trouble. Our argument is that in relation to 'bureaucracy' (and in relation to the division of labour) the Left has, on the whole, only got *half* of the argument. Bureaucracy may have depressing aspects and ironically the Left shares some of these, but it also has some vital points on its side. For instance, it is quite normal for a crisis to occur when workers leave a community project. No one else can effectively take over from them, because all the information, contacts and criteria of decision-making are inside their heads, rather than explicitly formulated in a way that makes them accessible to others.

[. . .]

■ Are skills a good thing?

Behind the attitude that good politics will produce good works lies a particular attitude to skills. Everybody, with help and mutual criticism, is seen as capable of becoming competent at any task. The work process in the voluntary collective begins to resemble one long night-school class. Some graduate, others don't, and the exam results are often painfully clear in the results of the group's work, as it becomes impossible for a group to accumulate enough skills to take it beyond a certain minimum level of activity.

[. . .]

Skill-sharing and learning in such a context can only be given a very small amount of time and resources compared to the length of formal courses necessary to teach these skills, or to the substantial budgets available in commercial companies for in-service training.

[. . .]

Skill-sharing is often made more difficult simply because no-one can admit to having skills or knowing more than somebody else without putting themselves in an unfavourable and ideologically 'illegitimate' power relation over that person.

[. . .]

The dominant assumptions seem to have been that since capitalism produced the division of labour, then that is an exclusively capitalist method of working and not to be touched by an alternative form of organization. Some argument is needed to re-establish the premise that there are, in fact, real and valuable skills which people need to learn, over time, and that the development of specialized skills is not intrinsically bad. Moreover, anyone who wants to abandon the benefits of specialization needs to be very aware of just how much they're losing. These skills, and the professional structures within which they exist, may have bad associations, but that doesn't mean that they can be abandoned without enormous costs.

[...]

Notes

(1) See Wiener, M. J. (1981). *English Culture and the Decline of the Industrial Spirit, 1850–1980.* Cambridge University Press.

(2) Mark Lloyd, unpublished paper on 'The East End News Experience'.

4

Professional Management in Voluntary Organizations:
Some Cautionary Notes

Tim Dartington

Anyone who reads the financial press closely (or who has read the assignments of business students on management courses) will know that the private sector has its full share of waste, incompetence and failure. Nevertheless, better management is often taken to mean commercial management, and the difficulties of voluntary organizations are often assumed to reflect their own failures (rather than their successes or the consequences of external decisions). Such assumptions are not just irritating and unfair, they also overlook the strengths of voluntary organizations and undermine the confidence of those who manage in them. This article is not 'against' the private sector or its management. It simply warns against an uncritical acceptance of the notion of 'professional managers'. It is a gentle and insightful reminder of the complexity of organizational life, especially in the social economy.

Management is not a dirty word any more. With all the interest in it, it is important to think about what we mean by management, so that we do not simply take the view that professional management means giving power to an accountancy-led business approach to organizing an enterprise to meet short-term aims of profitability.

Voluntary organizations, even more than other organizations, have implicit not just explicit aims. One of these is providing opportunities for learning. Voluntary organizations are expressions of awareness and the wish to get involved in societal issues. They are the stamping ground of the active citizen. People come in with enthusiasm and concern – commitment – which may then be turned into expertise and specialist knowledge.

The structure of a voluntary organization – with a committee or board of management and a 'workforce' – can be seen as ensuring a continuing balance of commitment and expertise. In this sense management education is empowerment and, as the organization's capacity grows, it is about the continued integration of commitment and experience.

Certain principles which are increasingly acknowledged in the more progressive and successful companies in the private sector have long been understood in voluntary organizations:

(1) People value a sense of ownership of what they are doing, even or especially when they are working in a collective or corporate enterprise.

(2) Organization around task is more effective and satisfying than organization around the management of resources.

(3) Authoritarian management has limited effectiveness and potential compared with networking democratic management.

(4) Individual initiative can be encouraged within a collective or corporate structure – and small enterprises are often efficient in comparison with bueaucracies.

(5) The quality of work done is the most important indicator of effectiveness.

(6) Intuition and creativity are often more effective than going by the book.

Voluntary organizations have traditionally developed their management skills through the experience of doing and through peer support. In recent years the voluntary sector has seen the emergence of the professional manager, who is expected to demonstrate the entrepreneurial, marketing and financial skills associated with the business executive.

Many people are wary of the 'professional' manager but are concerned to support the commitment of those who take up leadership roles and who then need to demonstrate management skills. Many people understand management but do not always honour the manager. Those with management responsibility have to demonstrate an ordinary competence; that is, a competence based on their own experience. In this way they can be aware of and if necessary resist those who would like to colonize their activites.

The new emphasis on professional management is welcome, and the interest of the private sector is supportive. But we should note that some professional management, with its emphasis on management by objectives rather than mission, on job descriptions rather than roles, on financial sophistication rather than political will, could lead to the development of static and uncreative organizations, which cannot sustain the creative tension between entrepreneurship and corporatism. The private sector is now rediscovering 'amateurism', autonomy of work groups and networking, and the public sector is now breaking down some of its bureaucratic structures. It is important that, in learning from other sectors, the voluntary sector does not come to look old-fashioned and rigid in its own management thinking. There is a cycle of management learning, which means that voluntary organizations may be going the long way round to rediscover the point at which they started.

Management education in the voluntary sector is not altogether about nuts and bolts as represented by any number of basic courses in committee skills, budgeting, negotiating grants, and all the day-to-day business of harassed managers. These have their place but it is important to establish that there is a context of creativity, where the challenge is to manage from a position of moral authority, through influence as much as power. The nuts and bolts training is necessary but also a flight from the complexity. The irony is that many voluntary sector managers are more experienced in the complexity of representation in a context of multiple accountability than they are in the nuts and bolts. They have often been exposed early on to issues of autonomy and accountability that in other sectors are thought of as 'strategic' and the concern of senior management. It is crucial that management education confirms and develops understanding of the complexity and does not simply collude with a sense of inadequacy about the nuts and bolts. The accreditation or confirmation of what people already know is just as important as what they need to know.

Management education has to address the issues of autonomy, accountability and representation. We require a high level of skill in understanding how different parts of an organization fit together, often in creative tension and reflecting different pressures in the environment. In practical terms, integration demonstrates the ability to hold together disparate needs according to a common understanding of purpose.

Current thinking invests hope in the efficacy of strong leadership.[1] The myth thrives in a voluntary sector that is largely built on the efforts of inspirational and charismatic founders. There are many examples also of the struggles to break free of the mould. Strong leadership, while not charismatic, is attractive to those who are nostalgic for the energy and passion of founding fathers and mothers, and who want the strengths and not the weaknesses of a cult of personality.

In the voluntary sector, as in the much wider context of social, economic and political life, strong leadership is given credence at the expense of other kinds of management culture, including group leadership, a traditional and underrated strength of much voluntary sector management.

The inefficiencies of ideologically based organizations were well exposed in *What a Way to Run a Railroad*.[2] No doubt the unspoken assumption that management is what MacGregor did to the mineworkers is not far below the surface. It is an important assumption and we should not forget it in the current more rational discussion of the need for professional management. The fear of management as a destructive uncreative force in an organization has to be understood if we hope to overcome the resistances to ordinary good practice in budgeting, financial control and the personnel and marketing functions of any lively organization.

The fear surfaces when we are faced with the need for an us-and-them relationship – even when it does not formally exist. Ask any collective, which is organizationally designed to work as a unity, about the internal schisms with which it has to struggle. In our minds we work all the time with distinctions – what is us, what is not us – and those involved are broken down into the polarities of manager/managed. In such circumstances, having set up our leaders, we seek to destroy them.

A collective can be a very effective way of working and is particularly appropriate to certain kinds of voluntary organizations, but it is unlikely to survive unless it understands and takes on this dynamic of destructive splitting when it occurs. Hierarchical organizations – and organizations split into functional units – of course offer a ready-made framework within which we can build us-and-them relationships.

The negative image of management surfaces in other ways, most typically in the relationships between paid staff and a voluntary committee, each experiencing the other as manipulative and withholding.

In thinking about voluntary organizations and the enterprise culture, we appreciate the emphasis on increased competition and the importance of rewards and incentives of different sorts. Such 'fight' leadership is well understood in other sectors. It raises important issues in voluntary organizations. Should Age Concern be concerned about its share of the market, for example, or the vulnerability of its position as brand leader? There is also an increased interest in collaboration and inter-organizational practices which recognize interdependence and responsiveness to client need. Competition also calls for a re-examination of the powers and accountability of the director or chief executive in voluntary organizations. Are we looking for welfare entrepreneurs? Voluntary organizations often have their origins in a flexible response to need, although we recognize that this may soon degenerate into a defence of current practices. The logic of competition leads us to emphasize what we can say we have done rather than keeping in mind the common task – which is why people get involved in the first place. In reaction we become cautious about value-for-money arguments and business style performance reviews. We have to think what the caution is about and whether it is defensive.

Management is also about developing a capacity for living with uncertainty, a capacity for reflection leading to action. In the voluntary sector it allows for the possibility of direct action, providing opportunities to live responsibly in a free society. Guidebooks to entrepreneurial excellence give an impression of unlimited opportunity, energy and enthusiasm for the project. But what happens to those working with the unenterprising in an enterprise culture? Our admiration of the workaholic defies all we know about mental health. The public sector management of teachers, doctors, social workers and nurses is not a lesson to be learned uncritically. The demoralization of such professions is one of the most potent arguments for the reform of the welfare state. It would be good if the voluntary sector could achieve a better record in finding a balance between service and exploitation.

Imposed solutions have their built-in self-destructive mechanisms. In the end they just do not work. Authority, as it is understood in a non-coercive system, ultimately belongs to the individual, to do what she or he thinks is right. This is not individualism gone mad but a challenge of organization to co-ordinate all that energy and, if it is done, the individual should not have difficulty in giving authority to the collective enterprise. It follows that the right to manage is not automatic. It can be very difficult to 'let go' an incompetent member of staff, because the organizational culture values loyalty and commitment. What looks weak and procrastinating may be hard to understand, but the price of greater efficiency is experienced as too high. Everything has to be understood in context – and especially authority.

If management education creates or strengthens a new class of experts, successfully running organizations in ways which distance them from those they are trying to help, a consumer reaction will arise with increasing justification. In North America large non-profit agencies have been the target of campaigns by smaller community-based groups. We have to recognize that good business practices, marketing strategies and the development of performance indicators to satisfy funders could – if uncontrolled – tend to disenfranchise the ordinary members of the organization from having a sense that it is their organization, pursuing their ends in their own way.

Good management does not have to disenfranchise in this way. In fact many practices enthusiastically taken up in the private sector are designed to motivate and involve the workforce and to ensure that service organizations are consumer-led – exactly the kinds of strengths from which the voluntary sector should be starting.

People who are developing their individual capacities on courses or in other ways may feel frustrated by the unresponsiveness of their organization to their own learning. But their management skills may have to be tested at this stage; how are they using their knowledge and skill to empower the group? Leadership depends on appropriate 'followership'. Ideas of shared leadership have to link with ideas of shared learning.

We may think that learning in isolation is a dangerous thing. Many managers – chief executives and others – may already feel isolated. They can only work on issues of authority, autonomy and representation by referring to the real world in which they are living. Consultants and trainers can sometimes provide a safe environment for them to work on these issues: sometimes they make such opportunities for themselves through small informal networks. These networks also emerge among students of management courses, including distance learning courses. These networks are themselves laboratories for testing management ideas. The future of management learning which meets the overall needs of voluntary organizations has to be developed in this context of mutual exchange and peer support. In this sense it is as relevant to ask who are one's colleagues in a learning group as it is to ask about the tutors' experience.

Resources for management learning have to be built around the resource of people's experience, and we have to think about the context in which the learning takes place as well as the content.

Notes

(1) Little, G. (1988) *Strong Leadership – Thatcher, Reagan and an Eminent Person*. Oxford University Press.

(2) Landry, C., Morley, D., Southwood, R. and Wright, P. (1985) *What a Way to Run a Railroad – An Analysis of Radical Failure*. London: Comedia.

5

What's Different about Managing in Voluntary and Non-profit Organizations?

Rob Paton and Chris Cornforth

This book and numerous courses on managing voluntary organizations are based on the assumption that managing in voluntary and non-profit organizations is 'different'. But in what ways? And do the differences make a difference? Or are they really rather superficial, however much those involved (who often have had little or no experience of management elsewhere) would like to believe otherwise? This article examines several arguments that have been made for why voluntary and non-profit organizations are different. It suggests that, considered separately, these arguments are not particularly convincing and, indeed, are often overstated. However, taken together they do make a convincing case for the distinctiveness of the management task and context presented by voluntary and non-profit organizations.

■ Introduction

Questions about the nature and quality of management in voluntary and non-profit organizations may not be new but they have taken on a new significance. This is not just because of some well-publicized failures threatening to tarnish the reputation of the sector as a whole. Government policies mean that voluntary and non-profit organizations are becoming increasingly, and more closely, involved with organizations in both the public and the private sectors. Sponsorship, corporate community affairs programmes (that include secondments, employee volunteering schemes and donations in kind), partnerships and 'service agreements' or contracting are all the order of the day. Along with the opportunities they present, these developments are making new demands on the managers of voluntary and non-profit organizations. Moreover, those they deal with in the public and private sectors have an understandable tendency to view things in terms of their own organizational practices and experiences. As a result, voluntary organizations are increasingly being expected to imitate business or public authorities – or both.

This poses a major challenge to managers in voluntary and non-profit organizations. Most would claim that, even if things can be learned from other sectors, a wholesale adoption of business management would be undesirable and impractical; management in the voluntary sector is different. But what is it that is distinctive about the managerial task or the context of management in voluntary organizations? Unless one has a fairly clear and convincing answer to this question it will be difficult to decide which ideas and practices from other sectors are transferable or to help others to distinguish between poor management and different management.

■ Distinctive purposes

One common answer to what is different about managing in voluntary and non-profit organizations is that they have distinctive purposes. Characteristically, they pursue social goals for which meaningful measurements of performance are very difficult. There is no single underlying yardstick like profitability. This has a pervasive impact on managerial work, especially when several competing goals are being pursued: defining objectives, setting priorities and assessing progress all become much more problematic. This is indeed the case, but the extent to which voluntary organizations are distinctive in experiencing these problems is less clear.

First, these problems are obviously inherent to many areas of the public sector, too. Second, these problems are also commonplace in the private sector. Quite apart from service units like public relations or training departments, whose outputs are extremely hard to quantify, profitability seldom provides an unambiguous basis for choosing between rival strategies or resolving conflicting departmental demands (though each side will usually present its arguments in such terms). So even if more is measurable in business, albeit often with difficulty, many important issues remain well beyond the reach of any rational calculus, as operational researchers know to their cost. Third, there may be somewhat more scope for specifying tangible objectives and measuring performance in voluntary and non-profit organizations than has been realized to date; it is too early for a final judgement. Overall, therefore, this is an area of difference, but the extent of that difference has often been overstated.

■ Resource acquisition

Another answer[1] to what is different about managing in voluntary and non-profit organizations focuses on their different pattern of resource acquisition. The difference here is between trading and non-trading organizations as shown in Figure 5.1.

In trading organizations, service delivery (output) is also resource (input) acquisition. The problem of maintaining a balance between inputs and outputs is solved by setting prices so that outputs generate at least the inputs required and then varying outputs to meet demand. If no such prices are possible, the firm may avoid closure by switching to a different line of business. In non-trading organizations, by contrast, the balance between service delivery and resource acquisition can only be maintained by restricting the level of outputs – regardless of need or demand – to match the available inputs. If few inputs are available the scope for switching to a different line of business is likely to be limited; a project with ex-offenders can hardly start animal welfare or baby-saving projects just because resources are more easily acquired for these.

In many ways this looks like a more promising explanation of the differences associated with voluntary sector management. Resource acquisition and management in the voluntary sector present distinctive problems and, arguably, a rather different management task. The organization has to face two ways. Neglect of one side at the expense of the other or a schism between those committed to the clients or the cause and those concerned with fund-raising are common problems. Likewise, securing a predictable level of income poses a very different challenge, especially given, for example, vulnerability to any undermining of public confidence and the delays and uncertainty associated with governmental decision processes. Finally, the relationship with service recipients is usually quite different to a relationship with paying customers (with a need, for example, to ration, rather than stimulate, demand).

On examination, however, the distinctiveness quickly begins to fade. First, public sector organizations may not have such complicated problems of resource acquisition but they, too, are non-trading organizations and many of the points mentioned apply equally to them. In addition, fund-raising by schools

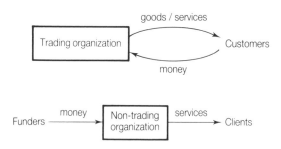

Figure 5.1 Resource acquisition in trading and non-trading organizations.

and hospitals is becoming commonplace. Second, some voluntary and non-profit organizations depend heavily or even entirely on trading income – examples are co-operatives and charities that rely on fees for their services. But third and most important, trading and non-trading are not so much types of organization as types of activity and as such they can appear in organizations in any sector.

So, a substantial part of what goes on in large businesses is done through non-trading (and non-profit) units, operating within a business environment: the managers of a wide range of service departments (research and development, management services, information support), for example, will be continually trying to identify possible client needs that can then be developed as projects to 'sell' to senior management who are the funders. In this context they face the familiar problems of maintaining or extending their operations, preserving their autonomy and demonstrating the importance of what they do[2]. Equally, trading activities have become an important source of funds for many voluntary and non-profit organizations, even if they also rely on grants and donations. Admittedly, the overall organizational context and culture still colours how the activities are carried out in each case, so it would be a mistake to say the activities were just the same, whatever the context. The point is simply that a clear-cut distinction between the sectors in terms of their resource acquisition is not really possible.

■ Stakeholders and governance

Another argument for what is different about managing voluntary and non-profit organizations starts from important differences between organizations in terms of their stakeholders (that is, those with a stake in the success of the organization and the capacity to influence it) and the sorts of relationship between stakeholders and organizations. These are shown in Figure 5.2 overleaf for the typical business and the typical voluntary organization.

The contrast is quite striking: not only are stakeholders in voluntary organizations different from stakeholders in business but also they are often very different *from each other*. Equally though, particular individuals can hold more than one 'stake' (clients may also volunteer, members may become trustees; this can usually be relied on to generate ambiguity and confusion, whatever advantages it also brings). Moreover, stakeholders in a business pay or are paid for their involvement – it is a mutually advantageous exchange. The basis for the involvement of most stakeholders in a voluntary organization is much less clear-cut.

These contrasts are expressed most sharply by comparing the ways in which organizations are governed. The typical company board has a fairly stable and homogenous membership (representing shareholders) and undertakes roles and responsibilities in relation to executive management that are fairly well understood. Management then deals with other stakeholders. In contrast, management committees of voluntary organizations often have an unstable and diverse membership (incorporating a variety of stakeholders) whose roles and responsibilities in

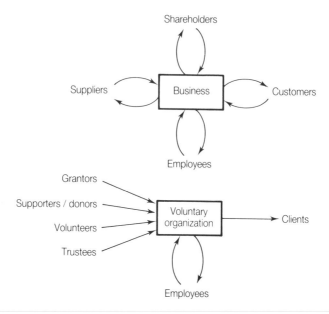

Figure 5.2 The stakeholders of typical business and voluntary organizations.

relation to paid staff are frequently uncertain or contested. Surely, therefore, this is the source of the management difference: the nature and variety of external relations, and the way these impact on the governance of voluntary organizations, poses a very different set of problems from those experienced by business managers.

Once again, though, it is not difficult to poke holes in this argument. The contrast between the two sets of stakeholders is exaggerated (businesses may be affected by trade associations, regulatory bodies and government agencies they are involved with; voluntary organizations have customers and suppliers). Companies have their share of boardroom battles and confusion. Many voluntary organizations (especially larger ones) have trustees or management committees that function just like the boards of companies. The 'clear contrast' is an illusion that arises from comparing *some* voluntary organizations with *some* companies.

■ A distinctive culture?

A fourth answer to what is different about managing in voluntary and non-profit organizations adopts a rather different approach: the difference lies not so much in what voluntary organizations do as in the way that they do it. They have a different culture which has far-reaching implications for those undertaking managerial activities. Like all cultural differences, this is hard to describe – but those who transfer to voluntary organizations from business or the public sector quickly discover that the differences are real and important. Key aspects of the culture of voluntary organizations are the importance given to participative forms of decision-making and to certain values, especially those associated with the organization's cause or mission (for example, equal opportunities, in recent years).

These features are indeed characteristic of many voluntary organizations. Staff are often committed more to the cause than to the organization itself; many are deeply concerned about how the organization goes about its work; they expect to be involved in decisions that concern them; and many organizations have elaborate democratic and federal structures. But the crucial question is should voluntary organizations be this way? Perhaps voluntary organizations would be more effective if they adopted a no-nonsense business approach that focused more sharply on specific objectives and allowed much less time for angst-ridden discussions of the most morally correct means of achieving those objectives; that enabled managers to act more decisively; and in which lines of authority were clearer and shorter.

In short, perhaps the culture of voluntary organizations is actually symptomatic of poor management. This may be called the business management critique of voluntary organizations but it is too sweeping. There are good grounds for believing that the sorts of beliefs and practices that make up this culture are to some extent unavoidable or generally beneficial to the work undertaken – or both.

The attention given to values arises partly from the strong personal commitments which many participants bring to the voluntary organization and which fuels an often dedicated involvement. Even if less committed staff and volunteers were available, it is not at all obvious that an organization would do better to recruit them instead. As for the extent of participation, this may simply be what is needed in order to generate consent and operate effectively in organizations held together as much by the common cause as by financial and career rewards – especially when a high proportion of staff are welfare or other professionals who will expect to be consulted. Volunteers who are treated like hired hands will walk out, just as members who think they are the organization will protest or resign if they feel their concerns have not been taken seriously enough.

Participative decision processes may also reflect the goals of the organization or the nature and diversity of the stakeholders to whom the organization is accountable. The most obvious case is that of community-based organizations: it simply does not make sense to expect a community development organization single-mindedly to pursue an agreed set of goals while operating through a simple hierarchy that culminates in a single leader or a cohesive directorial team. Whatever useful work such an agency did, it would not be community development – for that always involves debates about means and ends, widespread (if erratic) participation and competing bases for authority and accountability.

In community-based and many other voluntary organizations, how things are done is as important as what is done; the process is also much of the product.

For example, a professional fund-raiser may consider that an event wasted time and effort and raised far less cash than it might have. But if it drew people together, developed new competences among them, raised their confidence and brought in more members, it may properly be judged a considerable success. In such settings a conventional management logic of efficiency and control could easily destroy what it sought to improve.

So the culture of voluntary organizations is informed by its own logic of effective action and is not just symptomatic of poor management. Once again, however, it is important not to push these arguments too far. All that has been established is the appropriateness of 'the voluntary sector way of doing things' in some contexts. This does not mean that such a culture is always appropriate in voluntary organizations and never occurs elsewhere. In fact, quite a few voluntary organizations are successfully run on a fairly autocratic or instrumental basis, while parts of the public and private sectors also have strong (though different) value bases and high levels of participation.

Nor does this defence of the culture of voluntary organizations mean that intense value commitments and extensive participation do not also bring problems or get carried too far on occasions. Indeed, considering that voluntary organizations have a distinctive culture, one would expect their organizational problems to take somewhat distinctive forms. Arguably, the dominant cultures of businesses and public sector organizations each have their own characteristic ways of 'going wrong', too, even if most of the time they are generally effective in their own terms.[3]

■ Reconsidering the question

Clearly, there is no simple and straightforward answer to the question 'what is different about managing voluntary and non-profit organizations?'. No single characteristic is anything like universal in and exclusive to such organizations – and makes their management processes significantly different from those in other sorts of organization. The trouble is that the way the question is posed draws one into comparing voluntary organizations with those in the public and private sectors. Once this happens, one is using a very crude set of distinctions, not to say stereotypes, to answer a complicated question. This results in exaggerating the differences between the sectors *and overlooking the diversity within them*.

This does not mean that management is 'all the same really'. This is only true in a very abstract sense, devoid of content and context. But how to manage particular tasks in particular settings is what it is all about. Which is why some successful managers find it very difficult to move from one industy, or even job, to another – quite apart from changing to a different sector. So there are enormous differences in what is required of managers in particular contexts.

Just as managing in the private sector varies enormously between industries (compare the back-street sweatshop with a bank, the family-run corner shop with an advertising agency, a farm with a multinational corporation) and the public sector ranges from the armed forces, through the Civil Service to hospitals, schools and social services departments, so the term voluntary organization covers a diverse range of organizations, posing very varied management problems. As a result, managing in some voluntary organizations, or parts of them, is quite similar to managing in certain sorts of business; managing in other voluntary organizations is readily comparable with managing in parts of the public sector; while managing in yet other voluntary organizations does indeed have some important characteristics that do not occur, or are seldom very marked, in either of the other sectors.

■ A limited answer

The above points highlight the difficulties and dangers in trying to give a general answer to a disarmingly simple question. Nevertheless, some cautious generalizations and a limited answer are still possible.

Even if none of the characteristics of management in voluntary organizations that have been considered can be relied on to distinguish it from management in other contexts, they are nevertheless more widespread and more marked in voluntary organizations. Moreover, taken together, they certainly do make managerial work distinctive when compared with most management in the other sectors. Even if many voluntary organizations do not have all these characteristics, most have most of them to some extent, few are untouched by them and combinations of them are far less prevalent in the other sectors.

One other feature that has nothing to do with the sort of work they do characterizes voluntary organizations: they are predominantly small and medium-sized, and even the larger ones tend to operate through modest units, spread across the country. Large organizations are much more formalized and managerial roles tend to be more stratified and specialized. Smaller organizations are usually quite informal and their managers have to be generalists, concerned with more than one function and doing work that might cut across several management levels elsewhere. This probably makes as much difference to managerial roles as any of those features already mentioned.

Finally, one should not overlook the fact that, characteristically, management in voluntary and non-profit organizations does not involve the range of problems and issues associated with managing large technological systems that arise in both the public and the private sectors; for example, major risk assessment and health and safety issues.

Adding these to the points already considered gives the following list of factors that can, together, make managing in voluntary organizations 'different':

- social goals – which make it more difficult to determine priorities and evaluate performance

- particular resource acquisition and management issues associated with independent, non-trading organizations
- the nature and variety of stakeholders and their relationships with voluntary organizations
- a 'way of doing things' or culture that emphasizes value commitments and participatory–democratic decision-making
- operation through small, informal units
- the virtual absence of complex technological systems.

■ The demands on managers of voluntary organizations

The above factors in varying degrees and combinations condition the management task or the roles of managers or the context in which management is carried out. They have three key implications for the demands placed on managers in voluntary organizations.

First, a large proportion of managers in voluntary organizations need to be 'all-rounders' with a fair grasp of most aspects of the organization's activity; this often means having to take account of or tackle the sorts of strategic issues which in larger organizations would be considered the responsibility of senior managers.

Second, there is a premium on personal sensitivity and influence in situations where you cannot rely on the authority of your position or the inducements you can offer. Such situations can arise with external stakeholders and with other staff. These personal skills include the capacity to handle intense value differences when they arise and to deal appropriately with people from very different social or organizational worlds (consider an AIDS charity that must deal with and retain the confidence of showbusiness personalities whose assistance in fund-raising is crucial, government departments, drug users, corporate donors, the gay community, the media ...).

Third, managers must cope with considerable uncertainty and ambiguity. These may result from an unstructured work environment, insecure resourcing and the need to accommodate a range of conflicting principles and expectations, both internally and externally. Crucially, voluntary enterprise managers must be able to define worthwhile but limited objectives that draw in support and avoid a dissipation of effort – while still keeping their eyes on the broader purposes, or the impossible mission, that the organization exists to pursue.

It must immediately be stressed, however, that management roles making these demands and requiring these abilities occur in all sorts of organizations. Any difference is one of relative frequency and degree. Depending on the sort of voluntary or non-profit organization in question and the sort of organization one is comparing it with, the differences identified may be trivial, moderate or enormous.

■ Conclusions: distinguishing without stereotyping

So, managing in voluntary and non-profit organizations will often be different in significant ways and for good reasons when compared with many other organizations. The difficulty lies in expressing the nature and significance of those differences without getting caught up in, or reinforcing, the stereotypes, both positive and negative, of the different sectors. For every sector has its positive self-image and legendary figures – and its negative caricatures of the other sectors.

The basic problem is that most people's careers are lived out in particular industries or sectors and their knowledge of management elsewhere is bound to be limited. Faced with problems in a foreign land, the temptation is to criticize what one does not understand. Even someone who knows the voluntary sector well may find it difficult to tell if responsibility is diffused because the people involved are reluctant to exercise authority or accept responsibility and have not been prepared to tackle these issues or because the situation is complicated and it is essential to maintain the support of several key stakeholders. Or it may be unclear to what extent decision-making is slow because there is no agreement on underlying purposes (and mistrust between different groupings) and to what extent it is because an important learning process is also involved and it is vital that everyone 'owns' the outcome. And has a failure to carry through a project as planned arisen because newly appointed staff were largely left to do their own thing and there was no system for monitoring progress or because it was experimental and the work itself generated a better appreciation of what was really required? It would be silly to deny that management inadequacies sometimes explain such apparent problems even if frequently the innocent explanations have greater validity. But it is hardly surprising if those outside the situation and with little experience of voluntary and non-profit organizations sometimes oversimplify or jump to the wrong conclusion and in the process underrate the voluntary enterprise managers with whom they deal.

The problem cuts both ways, though. Many of those in voluntary organizations have had no experience of business management and instead depend on populist (and out-dated) caricatures for their understanding. Others have experience but their views may have been conditioned by dealings with firms which seem not to have heard of equal opportunities or were indeed exploitative rather than progressive employers. So, as with the business view of voluntary organizations, there is a mixture of real and imaginary shortcomings and an ignorance of the positive elements. This had made it difficult to recognize elements of business management that are relevant to voluntary enterprise management.

Viewed this way, the problem is one of inter-communal relations. In the long run there is no substitute for actual contact and interaction to erode the stereotypes, to increase understanding and respect and to reveal unexpected common ground as well as clarifying the extent of the differences. But in the meantime, the difficulties will remain and the inequalities of status and resources between the sectors do not make the dialogue any easier.

Notes

(1) Clearly expressed by Mason (1984) whose ideas influenced the discussion that follows.

(2) We are grateful for this point to one Open University student from a large company who, having attended out of curiosity a workshop on non-profit management, said that he had found it extremely helpful because he now understood much better what it was he had been doing, and had still to do, to preserve his department.

(3) Looked at this way, the business management critique highlights some of the managerial problems which tend to arise in voluntary organizations. One can accept this, and the possibility that more businesslike approaches would be helpful in some situations, without endorsing the viability of business management solutions in general.

Reference

Mason, D. (1984) *Voluntary Non-profit Enterprise Management*. New York: Plenum Press.

PART THREE

Working with People

6

Equal Opportunities Policies:
The Cuckoo in the Nest or the Goose that Laid the Golden Egg?
Problems Encountered and Lessons Learned

Jeane L. Nadeau and Sue A.L. Sanders

Those whose organizations have not been racked by contention over the implementation of Equal Opportunities Policies are sometimes bemused by, and critical of, what they see as the 'fuss' that this issue has generated in so many cases. But the research evidence pointing to substantial, systematic (if usually unintended) biases in recruitment and promotion, and in service delivery, is extensive and compelling. Which is probably one reason why those directly involved in implementing equal opportunities have known it was impossible to turn back, even if each step forward seemed to bring further difficulties. For many members of disadvantaged groups, on the other hand, progress has been a constant struggle, a matter of wringing concessions, and of disappointments, frustration, strained relations, conflicting loyalties and the pressure of high expectations. This article reviews the experience of implementing equal opportunity policies focusing mainly on race and gender issues. It explains why they have such wide ramifications and highlights lessons that have been learned about managing this process of profound organizational change. The authors point out that the approach to EOP implementation they advocate can be based on strong pragmatic justifications, not just moral exhortation, because a wide range of other organizational problems will be addressed at the same time. With the disability dimensions of equal opportunities now receiving increasing attention, it is clear this issue will pose a continuing challenge for years to come.

■   Introduction

Throughout the 1980s, the writers (previously managers in the non-profit sector) were invited, in the role of management consultants, into organizations to listen to the ways in which workers and management have been let down by their Equal Opportunities Policy (EOP) and to assist in the process of making it work.

Many people believed that designing and adopting THE POLICY would remove negative discrimination and offensive/oppressive attitudes and behaviour, or at least go a long way to discouraging their occurrence.

- '... but we're supposed to have an equal opportunities policy; *this* shouldn't happen.'

What we have been told 'shouldn't happen' includes: conflicts about maternity leave in a women-only project; pictures of nude women in men-dominated space; white staff ignoring the contributions of black staff in meetings; managers passing over disabled workers for promotions; middle class staff deriding working class values; recruitment panels avoiding lesbians or gay men as dangerous freaks.

When an agency declares itself to be an equal opportunities employer it will take time for staff, applicants and the public to find out what this means in practice. Very few of those who promoted an EOP anticipated open conflict, challenge and confrontation between staff, management and the users of the services/products provided. People have felt shocked when their minimum expectations of an agency's EOP were not met, or confused when 'tried and true' styles of management, communication and decision-making were angrily criticized. Agencies have been asking for help in developing procedures for dealing with the conflicts, complaints and discomfort experienced since adopting their EOP.

Why has all this happened? Is an EOP worth all this distress? How can these difficulties be minimized? Above all, what lessons can be learned from the efforts made over the last decade?

The aim of this article is to answer these questions in a way that will speak to the experience of those grappling with these issues on a day-to-day basis. Our perspective on equal opportunities provides no easy solution to the problems but it makes them comprehensible and it highlights the substantial and perhaps largely unexpected benefits available to organizations that are prepared to sustain their commitment. We start by considering the reasons agencies become equal opportunities employers.

■   The development of equal opportunities policies

Before considering specific areas of difficulty in implementing EOPs, it will help to look at the reasons EOPs are introduced and the way they evolve. The haphazard development of these policies goes a long way to explaining the problems that arise thereafter.

☐ **EOP as a response to anti-discrimination legislation**

To declare or not to declare the agency as an EO employer may be the first debate. The legislation may precipitate this question.

Many agency managers in the non-profit sector believe that, by and large, they appoint and promote people on merit, i.e. their ability to do the job. So opinions in the agency about the reason for adopting (or not adopting) an EOP vary significantly from:

- 'Haven't we been doing a good job up to now? Who's complaining?'
- 'We've always employed women and we have had black workers here for years.'
- 'We've done our best to fill our quota of disabled people. It's not our fault if they don't apply.'
- 'Won't having an EOP be the same as admitting we haven't been fair in the past?'

to:

- 'We have to be seen to be doing the right thing.'
- 'Everybody's declaring they are EO employers these days. It's merely stating the obvious.'

Such attitudes reflect a defensiveness against the accusation of unfair practice which anti-discrimination legislation implies. Moreover, many organizations assume that the issue of equal opportunities is merely about grass roots recruitment, a head count. They are willing to admit that certain easily-identifiable groups such as women, black people and/or registered disabled people seem to be under-represented (whatever that means) among the management or workers. But the assumption is that few, if any, of these people are eligible for the agency's jobs or interested in applying for them; otherwise, they would certainly be employed by the organization. How else can one explain the low representation in an agency which is not deliberately or formally, as a matter of policy, discriminating against anyone?

When an organization wants to be *seen to comply* with the legislation by declaring itself an EO employer, conflicts about the meaning of this statement are bound to arise. The debate starts with the priority and resources to be given to an EOP.

- 'That's all well and good, but who's got time for this and how much is it going to cost?'
- 'Don't forget, we haven't budgeted for this and we've already got more than enough on our plates.'

These worries come from a sense that the goal posts are shifting and that an EOP could compete with the agency's stated aims and objectives, particularly over the time, energy and money available.

Soon the validity of the EO employer label may be challenged by staff, users or members of the public who believe that the agency still discriminates against *them*. Once people from marginalized groups are appointed through EO recruitment procedures they can feel disillusioned and angry if their access to resources and status within the agency is blocked by the dominant group (the section of society that shapes the culture of the organization). The debate then focuses on the negative discrimination in internal employment practices such as training, career development, promotion, consultation and conditions of service. Complaints both overt and covert then abound.

Furthermore, the question of extending the policy to cover object groups such as working class people, single people with dependants, lesbians and gay men, cultural and religious minorities or ex-offenders arises. (Any section of society that has experienced negative discrimination and is under-represented in the organization is a potential object group of an EOP.) By this stage, what started as a piece of cake, a simple matter of legal compliance and public relations has become a can of worms.

☐ EOP as a moral imperative

Other organizations adopt equal opportunities as an essential goal rather than an extra burden. They see an EOP as being necessary to address the deep and pervasive effects of long-term unfair discrimination in the work place. This strong moral commitment to fair employment practices often derives from an organization's mission to help disadvantaged people.

But these agencies also encounter conflicts in implementing their policies. The inclusion of certain groups, 'prioritizing' object groups for EOP focus, allocation of limited resources and the extent of the changes needed to management structures are the subjects of conflict.

First, disputes take place over how many object groups the organization can take on all at once.

- 'It's better to tackle discrimination based on race and gender well than to try to deal with all marginalized groups and do none of it properly.'
- 'How can we ask such personal questions of people and expect them to trust us with the truth?'
- 'Offering full access to disabled people will mean finding new premises. How can we afford it?'
- 'What will people think if we mention lesbians and gay men when we work with children and young people?'

Yet it is impossible to concentrate on one group at a time as many people can identify with more than one marginalized group (disabled, working class men, black women and lesbian ex-offenders, to name a few) and so an agency soon realizes that all staff must learn fairly quickly about the way discrimination takes place for each group. Dealing with these complexities can overwhelm an organization.

Second, implementing EOP usually takes more time than initially anticipated. Expectations have been raised so there is great pressure to address and resolve every issue immediately. Deciding which object groups to include next can be fraught with tension and setting up a hierarchy of issues can provide an excuse to avoid the most challenging ones.

- 'We've been talking about anti-racism training for over a year now and nothing has been done.'
- 'No one ever mentions "class" when we talk about equal ops.'
- 'I'm the only single parent here and the only one who ever raises the issues of flexi-time or job sharing.'

Third, the organization soon discovers that it can only do so much from an altruistic motive before there arises a conflict of interests with an agency's practical needs like the boundaries of its funding, space and time. For example, one group of workers complained that, since their EOP was introduced, recruitment for vacant posts took at least six months, during which they had to cover these posts. Previously, vacancies were filled in two months or less.

When insufficient resources are given to an EOP everyone can suffer, moral imperative begins to look ragged and feel shaky and it is the EOP that gets the blame.

□ **Mixed motives and limited gains**

These sketches are, in some cases, an oversimplification. Different groups or tiers of the management structure have their own ideas about why their EOP was instituted, what it is meant to accomplish or the way it is meant to fit in with their pre-existing goals. These distinctions can lead to varying expectations about the degree and kinds of changes in procedures each will need to make to implement the policy. Addressing these conflicts has certainly not been totally unproductive.

In one institution for higher learning, the number of black lecturers that applied and were shortlisted for a post increased by 600% after one section spent three years examining and changing its recruitment procedures to remove the direct and indirect racially-discriminatory criteria and procedures that were traditionally used. The institution's personnel department had refused to advertise for a black lecturer when it was essential and legal. Two appointments were not advertised in the black press despite instructions, the excuses being, first, that they could not find the addresses and, one year later, that the advertisement did not get to the newspapers by the publications' closing date. A representative of the higher level management team decided to sit in on the interviews and commented on the first day that he had no idea there were so many suitable black candidates in the academic community: 'Why hadn't they applied before?' He also said, 'I didn't know that black people had so much more to offer the poly because of their experience in our society.' Neither did he realize the extent of the changes needed for the organization to become a full EO employer. The appointment of the institution's first two black lecturers was important progress. Nevertheless, the general experience has been that any gains associated with each step forward have been overshadowed by the new problems then encountered.

■ Problems encountered

It is obvious that the difficulties associated with EOPs are experienced in different ways by different groups in an organization. The problems outlined below are really broad headings covering the main areas as we have observed them.

☐ Interpersonnel conflict

Staff who have experienced negative discrimination or offensive behaviour may expect that an EOP should make a difference to the frequency and degree of distress they experience at work. Many have been disappointed. Confronting an offence is difficult, with many personal, political and strategic factors to consider. It may constitute a major risk to the staff member's job or whatever good will they do experience. Organizations often discourage confrontation and defend against attacks, especially on members of the dominant group. But, if it is not safe to discuss one's experience with a supervisor, reference group or directly with the person concerned, a breach begins which may widen. The staff member affected is isolated and liable to further hurt and a preventable resignation or disciplinary offence may result.

On the other hand, people who have championed the introduction of the EOP and found themselves criticized for offensive remarks or behaviour may feel betrayed and affronted by the notion that anyone could lump them in the category of oppressor, since they have shown their anti-oppression credentials. They may retire, in silence, hurt.

It is important to recognize the underlying problem in these situations: accusing people of being classist, sexist, racist, etc. attacks their identities just as labels like lazy, unreliable and 'uppity' undermine the self-esteem of those accused. Not only is it practically impossible to disprove these labels but also they are often self-fulfilling prophecies; they can easily generate rancorous attack/defend spirals that appear to confirm each side's accusation. No wonder many people choose silence.

If accusations and silence are the only options available to staff, negative stereotyping becomes enshrined in the organization's culture. Then, walking on eggshells, being conscious of every word one says, knowing one's place and avoiding criticism become the accepted norm. At this point the possibility of open communication about any difficult issue fades. Bad feelings build up while morale and co-operative working suffer.

☐ **Role/identity conflicts**

Managers who are in some sense in the middle of an organizational 'sandwich' often experience a tension between loyalty to their superiors and loyalty to their staff. However, managers and workers who are members of EOP object groups in their organization carry the added burden of being pioneers. They face choices between their commitment to the management/organization and their loyalty to the marginalized group(s) of which they are a part. The demands of their organizational role may conflict with their personal identity – hence the term a role/identity conflict. This is particularly poignant when staff members are expected to implement unfair policies or work through oppressive structures, as can happen when the EOP is new or not one of the main goals of the agency. Furthermore, they may feel pressures to disprove the stereotype of their group(s): a pressure felt within themselves, from other members of the same group(s) and pressure from the organization as a whole. So the pioneers are *trapped* by the demand 'Don't let the side down'. They must:

- constantly justify their presence in the workplace
- never be seen to make a mistake
- prove the wisdom of their appointment, that they are better than any member of the dominant group would have been.

At the same time, others of their group(s) may well expect pioneer managers to represent them at management level and force changes in the structures and procedures.

☐ **Interest groups, reference groups and cliques**

When women, black workers or others who share a life experience which has counted against them in the job or promotion stakes begin to gather together at work, members of the dominant group can react defensively. When a mandate to meet regularly and form a part of the formal structures of the agency is requested, management often replies that it would not be fair to other 'interest groups' represented in the organization and would be divisive. 'We can't spend all our time in groups. If each group that can claim to have a disadvantage were to have regular meetings in work time, we would never get the "real work" done.'

We have an example in the Labour Party where the leaders have denied permission for a recognized Black Caucus to form. This of course does not stop black members from meeting informally but it does prevent the exchange of any accountability with them. (The Party has allowed and been influenced by their Women's Caucus for several years.)

At the same time other formations may not seek recognition. The people involved may be aware of the comfort or fun they gain from these, but do they realize how some informal groupings exclude certain groups while influencing important decisions?

For example, the pub session after a women's project meeting where the black workers and management committee members did not feel comfortable or welcome and which those with dependants at home couldn't join, just happened to discuss project issues in more detail and gossiped about the workers' group from the white worker's perspective.[1]

Socializing, clubs, training courses and sports sessions can do much to bring people from all levels of an agency together, but when they are regular and involve only people from a dominant group in the organization, management may not recognize how they may pose a threat to broad consultation and accountable decision-making. And, of course, people's 'free' time and choice is all that is involved, no conspiracy!

☐ **Organizational inertia and questions of power**

Although most large non-profit organizations are in the business of instigating and sustaining societal change or at least positive changes in the lives of their users/clients/constituents, they are seldom geared to or experienced in managing extensive internal changes. On the contrary, most have been designed to be stable, consistent and predictable and consequently are resistant to change. They achieve both by establishing the control of resources, decisions and the ethos of the agency with a relatively small number of people. The functions of monitoring, evaluation and reviewing the organization's effectiveness are patchy, while the accountability of management to the managed is often ignored.

At the same time informal structures, those unowned patterns, tend to take preference over the formal, declared systems, policies and procedures simply because they are more effective. New staff glean these by observation or tip-off over time. For example, in larger agencies formal lines of communication and consultation are set up but an idea presented to someone three levels up the hierarchy at a party has more influence.

In smaller agencies formal team meetings make certain decisions on practice while, often, some of the team meet informally in the pub beforehand, discuss the issues and form their opinions before hearing the others' views and information.

Many of these informal processes reflect desires to exercise control (and reciprocal fears of losing control). When a section of an organization is driven consciously or unconsciously by the informal goal of consolidating the control of the dominant group, the systems and structures developed tend to sanction the traditional stereotypes, block the flow of power and encourage a narrow pecking order and desperate competition. Energy is diverted away from the stated goals and towards alleviating insecurity. EOPs challenge some informal systems and raise searching questions about the meaning and use of power.

Recognizing power in its many guises and disguises is not as easy as people assume, especially when it comes to recognizing one's own power. For example, scores of radical, white, able-bodied, middle-class managers and supervisors deem themselves to be 'powerless' to change their agency's racial discrimination and oppression, which as far as they are concerned reside in power structures beyond their influence. At times, we too have felt this way. 'What can *we* do if *they* won't let us advertise for a black lecturer?'

In hierarchies, middle and lower managers often perceive themselves as different from the reactionary upper levels from whom they keep a 'healthy' distance. Those in small, non-hierarchical projects may believe that an EOP should give all employees 'equal power' but that conditions will become equitable only if the management committee, executive council or the funders (the next level up and beyond) will let go of the real power.

Any power that staff from the dominant group in the middle have may be treated by them as either token or a 'hot potato', dangerous to hold, so it is thrown up in the air and directed to staff who are members of object groups at peer level and below. They are then expected to take it and eat it without getting burned, the dominant group in the middle apparently having no appetite for it: 'I agree, the management is sexist, so why don't you form a women's group?'

But, *is* power a corrupting influence or is it an energy source? Do people abuse power or is power abusive in itself? If power means control over others' actions, thoughts and feelings in one or more aspects of their lives or getting one's own way at the expense of others, then power is abusive. Why then should people supporting an EOP want to *have* it, *own* it, *share* it, *offer* it or *take* it? Would spreading power dilute it, make it less harmful? Will power sharing make an organization indecisive and less effective? Is power a limited commodity, so that one person's gain is another person's loss? Is an EOP just about shifting the power base, toppling one powerful group to replace it by another? If so, why not call it a revolution policy?

These are big questions, but an EOP is bound to raise them.

■ Lessons learned

In the process of developing EOPs as both managers and consultants in the non-profit sector over the last decade, we, our clients and our colleagues have learned from research and both bitter and joyful experience many lessons about the strategies, skills and structures needed to progress towards the goals of a well-designed EOP. We start with some general points about the rationales for EOPs and the way they are presented and managed.

☐   Rationales

If simply telling people with less power to 'change or else' were effective, the anti-discrimination legislation would have succeeded by now and equal opportunities would be enjoyed by a significant majority of the population. So when management is responding defensively to pressure applied externally, the workforce is apt to react similarly when told by the bosses that they must implement an EOP in compliance with the law. Therefore, it seems practically impossible for an EOP to have the stated effect when it is put in place merely to comply with the law.

Moreover, the legislation places the bulk of the responsibility for challenging oppressive employment practices on the victims and reflects the hypocrisy of a legislature which does not model the behaviour and attitudes it proscribes to those it governs. Likewise, if an EOP is applied first to the levels of an organization with the least power/control, the example set by upper management undermines and sabotages the policy. It is the old 'Don't do as I do, do as I say.' routine, first from the government, then from upper management.

Are the law makers unaware of the advantages which full implementation of a well-designed EOP bring to an organization, we ask ourselves?

Those organizations which introduced an EOP to respond to a moral imperative anticipated benefits to the quality of their service delivery and the accessibility of their services to the community, if not necessarily to their modes of operation. To achieve a measure of success in both recruitment and conditions of employment they have incorporated their EOP as one of their major goals (albeit a *process* goal, concerned with the way they operate).

However, a moral commitment on its own is not enough. Resources and realism are essential. The dilemma of setting priorities is eased by conducting a review of the organization's aims and objectives to devise an action plan for the changes needed in the short, intermediate and long terms. This also enables budgeting targets for EOP implementation to be set on an annual basis, in the light of experience.

Above all, one has to be recognize that, as a new major goal, EO has far-reaching implications for all aspects of an organization's systems of management and methods of practice.

Many managers recognize that the only viable impetus for such a major overhaul of the structures is the advancement of the agency's mission through changes which all staff identify as having the potential to improve their effectiveness and stimulate their energy. What this means, therefore, is that becoming an EO employer is tantamount to a full-scale organizational development process.

☐   ## Organizational development

> 'It [organizational development] means development of the entire orga-
> nization or self-sustaining parts of an organization from the top to the
> bottom and throughout. True organizational development is theory-based,
> team-focused and undertaken by means of self-help approaches which place
> a maximum reliance on internal skills and leadership for development acti-
> vities. It is top-led, line-managed and staff-supported. Development acti-
> vities focus on the "system", those traditions, precedents and past practices
> which have become the culture of the organization. Therefore, develop-
> ment must include individual, team and other organization units rather
> than concentrating on any one to the exclusion of others.'
> (*Blake and Mouton, 1989*)

> 'It would appear, then, that the purpose of organizational development
> efforts should be to effect a perfect correspondence between organizational
> goals, purposes and values on the one hand and the satisfaction of such
> human needs as belongingness, achievement, affirmation and self-esteem
> ... Generally as these needs are met, productivity for the organization
> increases.' (*Bradford, 1989*)

Internal developments which ignore what systems theory says about the role of
change agents and tack on new initiatives at the edges often cause confusion and
frustration. For example, many large organizations have added an equal opportunities monitoring unit to the centre and EO liaison officers to the satellites by
way of implementing their EOP. Without consultation and proper delegation
procedures it is left to the staff in these new posts to educate their colleagues on
the purpose and scope of the new jobs and to sell to the rest of the management
and staff the wisdom of co-operating with what is most often seen as their critical
and policing role. EO posts are usually set up to fail, having no remit to influence
highest management, little or no money or resources to effect change and no access
to formal support/supervision. In creating such a post, management and staff may
assume that the EOP will be effective with little or no input from them.

In the course of organizational development, structural reviews involving all
staff address the informal as well as the formal versions of the following:

> statements of intent, policies, timetables, contracts of employment, job
> descriptions, personal specifications, specified procedures, communication
> protocol, information systems, methods of working, decision-making pro-
> cesses, budgets, deployment of staff, meetings and groups, and the physical
> environment.

The EO employers we have worked with have commonly identified the need for
certain structural changes. An example will illustrate the issues with which they
dealt.

> Contracts of employment including job descriptions – Many contracts are
> designed assuming that the post-holders will be able-bodied, have close

family living in this country and have little or no responsibility for children or other dependants. Therefore, when people are appointed whose life experiences do not fit these assumptions there can be inequities of conditions of service in the areas of holiday entitlement, maternity/paternity leave, job-sharing, flexi-time and compassionate leave. If the contract does not require a commitment of every employee to support the development and implementation of the EOP, staff cannot be disciplined for infringements of the policy. Also, a clear definition of harassment, a major transgression of EOP, is important and complex. One model which is used is: if a staff member has been told that a certain remark or act has been found offensive by a colleague and yet she or he continues to use that language or behaviour with that colleague, she or he is harassing the offended colleague. If, however, the remark or act is indicated by the 'offending' staff member's job description and the remark or behaviour is being fairly addressed to all staff members to whom it applies, then it is not harassment, even though the colleague feels offended.

For example, referring to a woman colleague as 'girl' when she has asked to be referred to as 'woman' is harassment. Calling attention to a colleague's time-keeping is not harassment unless that colleague is being singled out, while other late-comers are not called to account. This example shows that EOP implementation and maintenance provides a strong motive for addressing problems which have actually affected working relationships for ages. Difficulties, such as personal conflicts between individual staff which have seemed beyond positive solutions, become the focus for renewed efforts and creative approaches.

☐   **Interpersonnel conflicts**

Establishing an open, respectful and challenging culture within the agency, where everyone admits to the possibility that they could offend a colleague, deliberately (in anger) or by accident is the key difficulty. Do people want to know when or if they have offended someone they work with? Often they don't. We all would prefer to blame the other's behaviour or attitude when we feel in conflict. Establishing our innocence and the other's guilt becomes crucial and so people often resort to accusations and labels when they feel aggrieved and in pain. And of course, sometimes offensive behaviour is an issue for which the 'other person' is responsible.

But how can we deal with offence without perpetuating this system of put-downs?

Seeking the answers to these dilemmas must involve management in a study of the *culture of the agency* at every level of the organization, the *communication styles* and *procedures for confrontation* (stating honestly what one thinks and how one feels).

When the organization's culture sanctions sweeping generalizations about staff, conflicts become entrenched in a series of acrimonious name-calling. Summing anyone up in one or more labels is never accurate and is indeed the very process which EOPs have been set up to challenge. Either people can be accurately described by a stereotype or they can't and EOP is depending on the principles that:

- stereotyping of individuals and groups is inaccurate and unjust
- people can function well without stereotyping others; they can challenge and replace the *process* which most of us learned in childhood of assuming a whole host of labels about someone once their gender, race, class or certain other characteristics or identities are known.

Labelling the offending behaviour is preferable to labelling the person. Furthermore, caring interpersonal behaviour requires a particular perspective on feed-back which concentrates on the effect of the behaviour experienced, while leaving the intellectual debate on what is sexist, racist, classist, etc., to the labelling of institutional oppressions.[2]

When high value is placed on the feelings and thoughts of each person then labelling the behaviour becomes less important and people do not feel the need to prepare a signed petition to the effect that they are 'right' to feel offended.

As regards communication styles, many agencies have found training and guidelines for the use of constructive criticism and feedback valuable. When the techniques of assertive communication, attentive listening (acknowledgement of what one has heard/seen/felt) and asking open-ended questions, become part of an agency's way of working they facilitate participation and confrontation without rancour. Dangerous issues can be acknowledged and discussed at last!

Procedures for confronting conflict are also essential. As an EOP becomes effective, conflicts surface which previously would have been withheld by those who feared the loss of their jobs if they complained about inequities or harassment. The support structures available to staff and managers (supervision) and the accessibility of reference groups help the individual who wants to confront behaviour she or he finds offensive. Skills in negotiation, collaborative techniques and neutral arbitration at management level are all useful. Managers must, when appropriate, seek win–win resolutions, where each side's view is accommodated. Although finding the collaborative solution is often the most difficult goal to achieve, the reward for success is the proof that for every winner there does not have to be a loser.

Some individuals in the agency are particularly vulnerable to interpersonnel conflict because of the personal and professional roles they have in the organization.

☐ Role/identity conflicts

Pioneer managers/workers are often more aware of structures and processes which undermine the EOP and when 'trapped' are even more reliant on fair and equitable systems than managers/workers from the dominant group. They are often watched and depended on by members of their object group(s) to challenge any sabotage or backsliding regarding the EOP. The following example illustrates this point.

> A black woman manager decided she had to implement disciplinary procedures against a black staff member. Other members of both management and staff pressed her to ignore the worker's bad practices, fearful of being called racist and hoping that the problem would solve itself. Some black staff formed an alliance with their colleague and challenged the manager to support them in their view that the worker's behaviour was justified by 'racist' management. Other staff, both black and white, were also afraid of the 'racist' label and the anger of the disciplined worker and his support group, but they were more concerned about the failure of the project to deliver the service promised and so supported the manager. The discipline procedure, in this case, ended (unfortunately) with the termination of the worker's employment. However, the manager could carry out her responsibilities in an equitable way due to several factors. The job description was clear and detailed, so management could evaluate staff performance fairly with concrete evidence of compliance or non-compliance with the organization's demands. The disciplinary procedures had been designed in consultation with the staff group. They included the provision for a hearing held by a panel made up of a majority of management committee members with life experience similar to that of the staff member (from a marginalized group) who was to be disciplined.

In general, pioneer managers must be expert in dealing with conflict in a collaborative way and in negotiating with either side of the 'sandwich' on behalf of the other. But organizations must also support them in three specific ways.

First, training in anti-oppression strategies should be provided at all levels. Learning to recognize the forms that negative discrimination takes in the workplace and the methods of preventing inequitable practice for each object group addressed in the EOP enables all staff to share in the responsibility of implementing and maintaining the policy.

Second, devising procedures for monitoring and evaluating the EOP is the responsibility of the organization. Unless these are detailed in the policy's action plan, the pioneer manager may be singled out to answer to the other members of the agency's object groups for the progress or lack of progress of the policy's implementation.

Third, supportive supervision throughout the organization is essential. The aim is the development of each employee as a person and within her or his role. Regular supervision sessions provide a forum where employees can address instances of offence which they have experienced or of which they have been accused. If this is not available to managers and staff alike, grievances may quickly escalate to formal procedures. Members of the dominant group usually have access to at least informal consultation and support from members of their group. When the agency takes responsibility for ensuring that members of EOP object groups receive fair treatment, it will provide access to supervision or external consultancy from someone qualified from the relevant object group, should that be requested. Similarly, it can be valuable for pioneer managers to meet formally with other managers in a similar position from other agencies. Support groups among staff and between agencies often form without the knowledge or sanction of the agency and yet have a significant influence on its work.

☐   **Interest groups, reference groups and cliques**

The lack of accountability of informal groupings or networks within an organization to management, agency goals or constituents can lead to either more or less influence than formal groups have on the decision-making processes. Some alliances may ask for formal status to improve their influence, while others have power which they can more easily sustain by remaining casual or hidden as in the example above of the group which unofficially met in the pub before the team meeting.

Formalizing some interest/reference groups makes effective management sense when the aims are one or more of the following:

- to provide staff with peer group support (peer meaning similar life or role experience)
- to prevent isolation of staff who are in the minority in some sense in the organization
- to provide the organization with certain life experience perspectives and wisdom which are under-represented at the management level
- to share power (influence, control) with sections of society which are under-represented in the staff group
- to use consultative and democratic styles of management
- to delegate decisions to the staff most directly involved and affected by that decision
- to provide equitable conditions of employment to all staff.

The following illustrates some of the benefits of recognizing informal groups.

In one medium-sized, multi-site project, the women began to meet casually for lunch. The managers, all men, met formally as a management team and informally in the pub. The women felt resentful towards and alienated from the management and dissatisfied with the dynamics of the staff meeting where their influence was minimal. They decided to ask for external help and requested that the staff group work with a woman consultant. The men agreed and in the consultancy sessions all agreed to try a combination of a monthly men's support group, women's support group and joint group dynamics sessions with the consultant. The aims of each session were outlined and the reporting-back expectations were clarified. The men learned that they were playing a very important part in undermining and devaluing the women's work. For example, the men's group was never interrupted because women workers were on the front line, whereas the women's group was frequently interrupted by telephone calls and the doorbell. The men were surprised by this and agreed to cover the front line while the women met. Thereby they began to realize how little they knew about the women's jobs. Over time, the women's confidence and influence at staff meetings improved and two of the women applied for management posts and were appointed.

When the organization cannot provide a peer/reference group internally, management can explore external networks. For example, a group for administration secretaries (who worked singly in similar small voluntary sector projects) proved a very important adjunct to their supervision and improvements in their conditions of service, morale and work quality were experienced by all the members.

However, many agencies can recount painful experiences involving formally-recognized interest/reference groups related to feelings of betrayal reported by both management and the group(s). These breakdowns involved unfulfilled expectations so the terms of reference for the group must be negotiated, clarified and agreed by both management and the group in the early stages. The terms of reference should include:

- the aims of the group
- the degree and scope of influence the group will have over decisions made at managerial level
- the level of responsibility management will maintain for its own and the rest of the agency's education about the issues facing the group in the organization
- the methods of reporting back and the type of information to be reported to management and the agency as a whole
- the level of confidentiality to be offered within the group
- the methods of response to be given by management to issues raised by the group
- the support needed and to be given so that members can attend the group regularly
- the membership rules, such as who, how (voluntarily or compulsorily), when, where, how often and how long the group will meet.

The above list is a detailed example of two parties setting out how they will be accountable to each other over the implementation of a formal structure in an organization.

The big pitfalls for management are failing to recognize the difference between sharing responsibility and dumping it; assuming that giving a group permission to meet regularly is doing the group a favour, without realizing the investment this entails for both parties; and, likewise, expecting that the group should be grateful and make no more demands (tokenism).

So structures which enable respect, accountability and information to flow throughout the organization are essential if equal opportunities are to become a reality. In a sense, these are all euphemisms for power.

☐ **The question of power**

Informal hierarchies have traditionally been justified by assuming and assigning to each person a level of importance based on certain descriptions which quickly and conveniently define who deserves high and low value.

Therefore it is not surprising that certain practices which assign and maintain inequities of value crop up unrecognized or declared in most organizational structures. For example, initiations, rites of passage in the workplace, notions of earning the respect of colleagues, assumptions that management is wiser or seniors know best are found in collectives and co-operatives as commonly as in hierarchies.

The establishment defines the culture without consultation and the culture encourages all the participants to minimize or hide their differences, to conform, at least on the surface. Consensus, consistency, image and ethos are promoted to discourage differences of presentation, open conflict and challenges to traditions, while maintaining the control of the dominant group.

EOPs challenge organizations to recognize and own the indicators to the obvious power points (individuals or groups), such as those with authority over rule setting, staff and budgets as well as the subtle ones that have to do with value, independence, getting away with breaking the rules, attention paid and physical comfort.

Power-sharing habits can be creative and involve acknowledgement, encouragement to take risks, responsible consultation and delegation, training (on and off the job), plain language and getting everyone's name right, including the spelling.

The concept of power as energy has largely been ignored at great cost to organizations. It brings a whole new meaning to the phrase *power sharing* and accentuates the need for agencies to take their use and abuse of power seriously, from a purely practical perspective. Staff who are drained of energy cannot do their best work. Private industry is taking this lesson to heart and in some instances is way ahead of the non-profit sector.

Energy, a cornucopia, is no 'hot potato' but quite the reverse; it can be held without pain and shared without fear.

Sharing and taking authority responsibly involves looking for ways of exercising control which are not expensive for some and a bargain for others. The possibility of win–win solutions is often not anticipated and must be introduced and explored or they will never be found. The belief is that one person or group's power gain is another's loss. An organization's induction procedures are a good indication of its attitude to sharing power.

For example, when new employees start work in an agency their access to many aspects of power is very low. The inability or unwillingness of the incumbent staff to own their power leads to ineffective induction procedures. When the staff and immediate management believe they are powerless, the first months or years in an organization can be like landing on another planet without any knowledge of the terrain, climate or language of the inhabitants.

In very small projects, new posts can change the nature of the agency from one where informality works well to one where informality blocks new staff from participating as fully as possible, as quickly as possible. Having regular staff meetings and recording them may become necessary when the task of co-ordination and self-management becomes more complex. Informal filing and other administration systems are positive barriers to new staff and their assimilation into a working group, department or the agency as a whole.

So what is the sense in an agency slowing down this process? Inhibiting effectiveness is inefficient, costly and debilitating to the morale and motivation of new employees. Sometimes the belief is that a tough initiation period will sort out the wheat from the chaff, or the view is that 'I had to go through it, why shouldn't she or he?'.

Dealing with the informal structures in induction can also be disconcerting. Letting a new worker in on the way the system really works can be embarrassing and destructive to the organization's image; it can be painful to admit that informally the organization betrays its own mission. Equal power is almost impossible to achieve and even harder to maintain, rather like trying to keep hanging scales balanced in the wind. The concept that in a healthy organization power is not static, hoarded or stagnating but flowing between and among individuals and groups is key to equal opportunities and must be given a chance if the policy is to live long enough to prove its merits.

■ The future – equal access

For some non-profit organizations, improving the access of marginalized groups to their services began in the early 1980s, and since then other agencies have focused on their accessibility to the *whole* community. Concern with 'customer care' and 'user involvement' are indications that more organizations are becoming aware of their accountability to their constituency. Marginalized members of society are becoming more demanding of their rights to courteous and accessible services for which they pay, directly or indirectly.

When recruitment of object group members is working and they are well represented at management and staff levels, EO employers give the most important welcome sign to the whole community. However, users from marginalized groups may encounter offensive behaviour from other users as well as staff and so the agency must take on an educative role with clients (in addition to staff training) if all users are to be protected from abuse.

To be sure that an agency's provisions are reaching the entire community it is meant to serve, research into the demography of the constituency and monitoring of the user group are necessary. The information yielded by these processes will need analysis to discover whether developmental changes are indicated.

Developing equal access is to be distinguished from that well-known pitfall of trying to become all things to all people. In the course of researching the needs of those who are not using the service, the agency can become better resourced to offer information about the facilities available through other organizations (when appropriate) and to decide which needs it should add to its provisions. Consulting the experts on improvements to the provision means starting with the current users and agencies which represent object groups which are not using the service.

But what does an organization do when it finds that its already over-stretched services will require expansion? The implications for fund-raising and devolution can be great. Regular reviews of an agency's overall objectives will help in making crucial decisions about the developments required to ensure equal access.

■ Conclusions – the golden egg

An equal opportunities policy (EOP) is not, as some feared, a disguised attempt to exchange the names, gender, race, class or level of disability of the dominant group with those of marginalized groups. An EOP is an open challenge to examine closely the way power is wielded in an organization's systems. And beyond this moral imperative, adopting an EOP provides the impetus for dismantling a whole host of barriers to staff self-esteem, motivation and effectiveness by developing an organizational culture based on open communication, power sharing, valuing the differences among people and supportive structures.

The operational benefits of implementing an EOP by using organizational development principles to manage change start with providing management with the methods and skills needed to implement sustainable innovations with the involvement and support of the staff. Then flexible structures can be designed which are instruments of two-way accountability and management is equipped to perform its enabling functions. Organizational development makes use of efficient consultation and delegation to encourage the flow of ideas, opinions, information, responsibility and power. Following from that, organizations can make quality decisions based on high-value information accrued by appreciating differences and using more collaborative and co-operative methods of problem solving. When everyone is involved in an organization's successful achievements, the respect is mutual. No one *has* to lose while working for an equal opportunities employer.

Notes

(1) People who are members of a marginalized group in one agency may be members of the dominant group in another. Often it is easier to see what others are doing to offend and oppress than to recognize one's own discriminating behaviour.

(2) Discrimination or oppression by a dominant group aimed at people identified by one or more characteristics is what is meant by the words sexism, racism, disablism, classism, heterosexism, other *'isms'* and combinations of them. Individuals can express oppressive behaviour or implement an institution's oppressive policies. Institutions can oppress.

References

Blake, R. and Mouton, J. (1989) quoted in Mee-Yan Cheung Judge, L. *Organisation Development Consultancy*, Quality and Equality. Oxford: Organisation Development, Consultancy and Training Services.

Bradford, L. (1989) quoted in Mee-Yan Cheung Judge, L. *Organisation Development Consultancy*, Quality and Equality. Oxford: Organisation Development, Consultancy and Training Services.

7

Remuneration Policies and Employment Practices:
Some Dilemmas in the Voluntary Sector

Chris Ball

This article by Chris Ball draws on his experience as a trade union officer to examine some of the distinctive constraints and conflicting pressures that voluntary organizations face when deciding remuneration policies and employment practices. Using the results of a survey by the Manufacturing, Science and Finance Union he compares pay and conditions in the voluntary sector with the national picture. He discusses the common practice of setting pay rules by drawing 'analogies' with the public sector, highlighting the strengths and weaknesses of this approach and examining pressures for change. Conditions of employment offered within the voluntary sector vary widely. In some areas, such as paternity leave, it is ahead of other sectors; in other areas, such as pensions, it often lags behind. Various options are discussed for improving this situation.

■ Introduction

Voluntary organizations may exist as the result of altruism or philanthropy but the practical problems they face in managing their affairs are likely to have more to do with the harsh world in which small organizations struggle for survival. Yet – and here is a big source of contradiction – they must strive to retain their commitment to the ethical values that make them different from the business world outside the voluntary sector. They need to recruit and retain employees in the market-place and to motivate them to function well. Voluntary organizations also need to maintain their credibility with their client groups and potential financial supporters of the causes they espouse. Demands from these different groups may sometimes pull policies in different directions, particularly over issues of pay and conditions of employment. The voluntary sector cannot be a law unto itself. Its values may be more humane and philanthropic than in the private sector, or more spontaneous and informal than in the public sector, but the political and economic influences in society at large emerge here just as they do elsewhere.

The success or otherwise which voluntary organizations have in reconciling these conflicting demands is likely to have an important bearing on their overall impact and effectiveness as providers of services, formers of public opinion, givers of advice, etc. For example, lack of attention to the conditions of paid staff may create (or exacerbate) a tense relationship between employees and an unpaid management committee. Dual standards on equality of opportunity may lead to cynicism about the organization by both the employees and the clients. Measures such as positive action programmes may be seen as a potential cost burden which the organization can ill afford. Lack of funding may preclude the possibility of a voluntary body meeting the sort of standards that everyone involved with it believes are necessary. The type and security of funding may have a direct bearing on the people employed to deliver services, for example whether or not posts are offered on a permanent basis, or on the form of fixed-term contracts. Involvement in government programmes can have a bearing not only on the nature of the organization (including the public's perception of the work it does) but also in setting the conditions of employment of staff engaged to implement the programme. On top of this there is the question of the relationship between volunteers and paid workers in voluntary organizations. This impacts on the *roles* of staff and may be a factor when conditions of employment are under consideration. It is as well, then, to remember that voluntary organizations and their managements do not have a free choice in deciding personnel and employment policies. Yet they do have *some* choice and it is interesting to note how the distinctive values and dilemmas of the sector often emerge in the policies adopted in the personnel sphere. Let us consider this, by looking in the first instance at questions of pay determination.

■ Pay policies and practices

One of the most important aspects of personnel management in any organization is what kind of pay policy should be adopted. How should the different demands and responsibilities of employees be reflected in pay differentials? Indeed, does the organization want to adopt a hierarchical structure at all, or is there a case for a more egalitarian system? Some voluntary organizations adopt common pay scales for all employees irrespective of the job done (for example some law centres offer advice workers the same pay as solicitors). Pay policy is used generally as a means of providing incentives and controls for staff. In the voluntary sector this may be linked to a view of alternative forms of society or political values that do not generally find expression in the world of business. To put the issues in this way, however, is to gloss over the fact that many organizations have grown up with systems of some sort. What they have is often more a legacy of history than a policy which reflects current thinking. What may once have seemed a worthwhile policy may become a source of tension with some staff, or may lead to difficulties in recruiting people with the necessary skills. However, it may be considerably more difficult to make changes than it would have been to adopt a different policy in the first place. Organizations can sometimes be stuck with practices that have outlived their usefulness.

A picture of voluntary sector policies is given by the results of a survey conducted in 1989 (Manufacturing Science and Finance Union, 1990). The survey provides a snapshot of a particular period in time and, although in the real world conditions are constantly changing, it is helpful in making comparisons with other industrial sectors. Of the staff covered by the MSF survey 25% earned less than £9,000 and 25% earned more than £13,000. The pie charts in Figure 7.1 compare this distribution with the national figure for all non-manual employees.

Two main points emerge. First, pay in the voluntary sector is lower than elsewhere. Second, pay structures are flatter, that is pay differences are less pronounced. What does this mean about the voluntary sector and how might one explain such differences? One obvious point is that voluntary organizations' size and finances may be directly related to the pay levels of senior staff. In other words, voluntary sector jobs may be lower paid than elsewhere quite simply because senior jobs in other sectors carry more responsibility. It is difficult to test this argument because of a lack of comprehensive data relating pay to organization size, etc. Whilst we might presume that organization size would be a likely influence on senior executives' salaries in all sectors and that small voluntary organizations might simply reflect this general rule, there are grounds for believing that this is by no means the whole story. Taken as a whole, it seems that jobs in the voluntary sector are lower paid than similar jobs elsewhere. Another explanation could be that in the voluntary sector occupations are less hierarchical and less differentiated than elsewhere in terms of demands such as skill and responsibility. By this yardstick the flatter pay structures reflect more collegiate organizational structures. Another possibility is that those who manage voluntary organizations self-consciously set out to achieve narrower differentials in pay. The example of law centres has already

Figure 7.1 Distribution of salaries. (Source: MSF Survey 1990)

been mentioned, but this type of practice is by no means restricted to the smaller organizations in the voluntary sector. (The charity Oxfam falls into this category.) Even if pay parity policies are relatively rare, there is, in some bodies at least, a belief that low pay should not coexist with high salaries for senior executive staff. Both policies (egalitarian work arrangements and reduced differentials) have their origins in a measure of belief in equality and fairness. But in either case it seems that compromise is often found. Work is only *relatively* more equally structured. Even in organizations where pay differentials are kept to a minimum, there may well be a fairly conventional separation of work tasks and lines of authority.

On the other side of this coin are some of the old established household-name charities, steeped in traditions of Victorian philanthropy, which have adopted policies of engaging people of independent means to their key positions, so that relatively low or even token salaries have sometimes been paid to senior staff. This practice may be motivated less by a desire to create an egalitarian work environment than by a desire to minimize costs to the organization. (The low pay of the chief executive may depress the salaries of support staff who are less likely to be able to subsidise the body for which they work out of their private means.) This practice seems to be dying out as charities have become more professional in their approach and chief executives are now more likely to be career people, but salaries for senior jobs are still much lower than they would be in other sectors. The MSF survey, for example, reported relatively low salaries in a 'top job' analysis and a survey by the Reward Group showed that charity chief executives are on average at least 25% lower paid than their counterparts in the private sector (Reward Group, 1990).

It is important too not to lose sight of the fact that voluntary sector salaries are *generally* lower than those in the private and public sectors. Based on 1989 figures, the average salary for all employees in the voluntary sector was £11,542 per annum – over £2,000 less than the figure of £13,764 given by the Department of Employment's New Earnings Survey for the same period and a gap of some 19%. Staff in the voluntary sector may experience somewhat less relative deprivation compared to their immediate work colleagues, but it seems that this is more than off-set by the contrast with employees doing similar jobs in the other sectors. External comparisons, however, do not show that all voluntary sector workers are worse off. At junior management level they are on average actually 2% better paid than in similar jobs in the private sector, although 11% lower paid in London. Clerical workers are also usually paid fairly close to the market rate. This may again be a reflection of the desire for more egalitarian pay structures or it may reflect market pressures. If there is a trade-off of salary against the satisfaction of working in a voluntary organization, this may not apply to all staff and is unlikely to be a complete bulwark against the market in setting pay rates in the sector.

■ Pay analogue policies

One feature of pay policies in the voluntary sector is rarely encountered elsewhere. This is the practice of adopting some form of link with either local government scales or the Civil Service. (About two-thirds of organizations in the MSF survey were linked to local government scales and a smaller number – 5 out of 73 – were linked to Civil Service settlements.) The reasons for this tendency need to be understood. First, it avoids the time, effort and controversy of working out pay from first principles, which can be an onerous responsibility for management committees and employees, particularly in small organizations without specialist personnel officers. Second, if the voluntary organization depends on funds from a local authority or government department, it may be important to provide a ready means of comparing salaries of staff with those operative in the public sector. Adopting an analogue pay system in which the pay scales of local government are quoted in this way might be thought to provide the answer to difficult questions about whether salaries are justifiable, etc.

There are several problems with this approach, however, which also need to be noted. If, for example, the local authority Administrative Professional Technical and Clerical Scales (the APT and C Scales) are used, how do we know that staff are being slotted in at the right points in the 'spinal column'? There are some guidelines in the form of 'benchmark jobs' (such as social workers) which are given defined points on the scales. But, with the infinite variety of specialist jobs in the voluntary sector, broad grading definitions which amount to little more than a 'rule of thumb' approach are the only measure which is available.

The public sector where the APT and C scales are negotiated has its own means of overcoming these problems through strong trade union representation throughout local government. This undoubtedly provides a means of 'policing' the national agreement, and sometimes succeeds in establishing conditions that are sometimes better than the minimum provisions it lays down. The voluntary sector, however, is relatively weakly unionized and hence this 'policing' function does not exist in many organizations. It may be, then, that those employed within the voluntary sector have salary scales which are lower than they ought to be according to any really fair assessment of the jobs.

Of course, one consequence of the relatively lower pay that operates in the voluntary sector is that it probably offers better value for money than the public sector *per se*. Undoubtedly this possibility is not lost on the government and probably contributes to the favourable attitude which it seems to have towards the voluntary sector in certain social policies of recent years. Many leaders of voluntary organizations are genuinely concerned to avoid the process of job substitution between the public and voluntary sectors. It could be argued that eliminating the low pay and lack of union representation within the sector would be one way of overcoming this undesirable tendency. How to achieve such an objective is quite another matter and, clearly, it has major cost implications which those managing voluntary organizations need to consider.

■ Pressures for change

From the point of view of decision-makers in voluntary organizations, there are disadvantages in analogue systems. This is particularly the case where an organization offers a range of services and attempts to operate some sort of 'parity with the public sector' policy by giving each staff group the 'rate for the job' that would be applied outside. The problem here, however, is that pay scales are completely different according to the various professions and bargaining groups in question, and there is really no way of converting one grade into an equivalent on another set of scales. So, if we consider a large or medium-sized organization which delivers health care and therapeutic services, plus elements of education or training, we are likely to be faced with a multiplicity of scales – teachers', NHS professionals', administrators' and so on. The question of how staff might react to differences in the settlement levels of these pay scales is just one aspect of the complex and untidy impact they are likely to have on salary administration.

A potentially more far-reaching consideration is the disruption that would be caused if individual members of staff were to seek to compare their jobs with those of the opposite sex under the Equal Pay Act 1970 (for example, see *Waddington v Leicester Council for Voluntary Services* [1977] IRLR32 EAT). Under the provisions of the Act it is possible to compare jobs which: are 'the same or broadly similar', have been 'rated as equivalent' under an analytical job evaluation scheme or fall into neither of these categories but are nonetheless held to be of 'equal value' in terms of demands made under such headings as effort, skill, decisions, etc. (Equal Pay Act 1970 S.1). The amount of time and effort involved in defending claims of this kind would alone seem to justify their avoidance, quite apart from the stigma associated with a finding that a voluntary organization, committed to the pursuit of equal opportunities issues, could be in breach of the Equal Pay Act. However, an organization which follows several *ad hoc* pay analogues for different professional or occupational categories of staff could be at risk of such claims being pursued, in particular under the 'equal value' provisions of the Act. Essentially, these provisions require organizations to introduce a form of analytical job evaluation if there is to be a secure defence against such claims. The problem is that this type of provision requires a considerable amount of time and effort to introduce. Small organizations would probably not want to embark on such complex exercises unaided. 'Off-the-shelf' consultancy schemes would not necessarily be appropriate either, for the same reasons, and a further problem might be that some of these schemes could be criticized as containing elements of 'sex bias'. Given the awareness of many of those who work in the voluntary sector of equality issues, one would hope for creative solutions to these sorts of problems as, for example, in the Save the Children Fund Job Evaluation Scheme (Save the Children Fund, 1987). This set out to be explicitly 'non-sexist' and is often held up as a model by those interested in these matters. However, some organizations will probably encounter difficulties in this area which might encourage them to continue with existing pay structures.

Another factor to consider is the future effect of policies encouraging region-ally differentiated pay settlements and performance-related pay (PRP). Whatever the merits of these policies in the public and private sectors (and there is a paucity of evidence on which to base assertions that they will lend greater efficiency and incentive where introduced), there are special considerations that might apply in the voluntary sector. Take the issue of PRP systems first. How does the underlying rationale of such approaches to rewarding people square with the employment culture which one might expect to find in a voluntary organization? The (perhaps excessively simplistic) idea behind PRP is that if one rewards the high performers in an employment context, by giving them additional payments over and above those granted to people who perform at an average or below average level, everyone will be spurred on to greater efforts.

Experience of 'merit' based payment systems in the private sector leads one to adopt a cautious, perhaps sceptical view. Where such systems operate, it is accepted that in only very rare circumstances do individuals receive other than a 'normal' merit increment. Where increments are withheld great bitterness often ensues, leading to grievances or disciplinary action. Some advocates of PRP freely admit that it has the effect of encouraging 'low performers' to 'get out' or 'move on'.

For those working in the voluntary sector, this type of reward system seems likely to be more damaging than helpful. Staff who work in an organization that has 'not-for-profit' objectives will probably be more unsympathetic to such 'carrot-and-stick' incentives than others. Indeed, it seems that there is a strong measure of *personal* conviction among those who choose to work for charities, etc. How then are they likely to respond to a system of cash-based incentives which by definition leave some of them unrewarded? A scheme of personal performance assessment introduced by a consultancy firm in one major charity was linked to such a reward structure and caused great consternation and dissent among staff. PRP may not be quite the good idea it is held up to be, at least as far as the voluntary sector is concerned.

Regional pay settlements present a different problem. Small or medium-sized voluntary organizations that once followed a set of nationally agreed pay scales in the interests of simplicity are likely to find their policies in disarray if there is ever a proliferation of local bargaining in local government or the National Health Service. Nothing is straightforward, however, and problems of a similar kind will probably be faced by some bodies if analogue pay systems are abandoned. The difficulties are easy to see: scales may in some cases rise as organizations com-pete for the scarcer skills in the market-place. The need to contain costs when funding difficulties arise might well lead to some salaries being forced down. The voluntary sector (now relatively egalitarian if lower paid) could become a more stratified place of work. There is, however, no reason to suppose that if this happens there will necessarily be any closing of the gap between voluntary sector pay and that on offer elsewhere and, just as disturbing, the very thing that would seem to compensate for the poorer pay and conditions in the voluntary sector might easily be lost in the process.

The question arises about what course of action might be taken to deal with pressures such as those described above. All voluntary organizations need a pay policy. Some of the larger charities' personnel managers have meetings, so a mechanism for a concerted approach to the problem should not be impossible to devise. However, given the relatively weak nature of the links established between voluntary bodies for dealing with employee conditions in the manner of the traditional employers' association, this seems to be the least likely of scenarios for the voluntary sector. Whatever form an organization's policy might take, links with the public sector may well be retained, although possibly in a less literal form. The advantages of adopting an approved yardstick of 'fairness' will not be readily abandoned. However, the policy should also allow jobs to be compared with each other throughout each organization by analytical forms of job evaluation. Ideally, such schemes should be introduced co-operatively and there should be genuine staff involvement. None of this is very likely to happen, however, if trade union organization is not established among the staff. Managers may want to control the evaluation system, and no doubt staff will be ill-equipped to challenge this in the absence of union support. On the other hand, even if larger organizations like Save the Children together with staff represented by MSF can produce an innovative scheme there is no guarantee that smaller organizations with fewer resources will be able to follow suit. Perhaps the least attractive prospect for the future is that charity staff will find themselves being offered basic salaries that remain on the low side but are supplemented by divisive bonuses and PRP.

■ Other employment benefits

The above analysis suggests that, in matters of pay structures and salary levels, voluntary organizations are likely to be hemmed in by market forces on one side and funding insecurity on the other. The trends seem to point to fewer options being available in the future, although there is scope for internal consistency and fairness. Pay levels and policies provide little scope for voluntary organizations (or those who manage them) to express their caring, humanitarian values in matters affecting the employment of staff.

The same need not necessarily be true of other employment benefits. Whilst it is difficult to compensate for inadequate pay levels, most people accept that the rewards and benefits of any job consist of more than the salary offered. Working hours, overtime, sick pay, pensions, leave arrangements for maternity, paternity or other family-related reasons, child care support, etc. can be very important in creating a feeling of fair treatment and a sense of well-being. For voluntary organizations these aspects of the employment package are important for other reasons, including the fact that 71% of the workforce is female. How then do they deal with policy issues in this field? As in other sectors of employment there is much variation in the voluntary sector. Figure 7.2 shows the percentage of organizations making various provisions.

Percentage of organizations with:

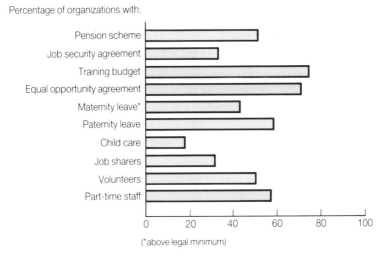

(*above legal minimum)

Figure 7.2 Employment benefits in voluntary organizations.
(Source: MSF Survey 1990)

Over 30% of the organizations in the MSF survey provided for job share arrangements. Nearly 60% employed staff on a part-time basis and 18% had some sort of scheme to assist staff with child care arrangements. Nearly 60% of the organizations had arrangements for paternity leave (a high proportion compared to the private sector where such schemes are still quite rare). Maternity leave provisions better than the minimum laid down by law were provided by 45% of the organizations.

■ Maternity leave and child care

Although organizations involved with women's and children's issues are generally leaders in providing maternity leave and child care, this is by no means universal. Small organizations in particular seem to fear difficulties in coping with unexpected financial or organizational demands arising from maternity leave. Sometimes, however, they manage to go further than larger charities which are in some cases unwilling to exceed the standards set by state legislation. There do not appear to be any generally adopted strategies for dealing with these sorts of issues, although several obvious possibilities exist. One approach would be for small organizations to establish maternity schemes in conjunction with their local councils or Councils of Voluntary Service. A percentage of employee costs could then be regularly set aside to cover the fluctuating demands of maternity leave cover. The difficulty however for many voluntary organizations is that they receive funding for posts from a wide variety of sources and it might not always be possible to cover such extra overheads. Nonetheless, if such schemes were established, the maternity leave contribution could always be incorporated into grant requests from the start, thus identifying it as a normal part of the total overheads to be covered in the cost of employment. For larger organizations there are fewer practical difficulties. Moreover, maternity leave and child care arrangements may become essential as it also dawns on private sector employers that demographic changes are leading them to require a more economically active female workforce. In the voluntary sector, employers who adopt policies of minimalism will stand the risk of losing out in the labour market as well as in their store of credibility as 'equal opportunities employers' with caring policies.

■ Job security

Just over 30% of the organizations in the MSF survey had forms of 'job security agreement'. In practice, these agreements rarely enhance 'security' *per se* but rather lay down arrangements to compensate staff in the event of redundancy. Such schemes have been a feature of employment in the private and public sectors for many years – long before the Redundancy Payments Act 1965 laid down a minimal level of statutory provision. Given the high degree of insecurity of jobs in the voluntary sector, and their particular vulnerability to termination when short-term funding runs out or when grants are cut because of Poll Tax capping, etc., it seems remarkable that such a low proportion of organizations had made specific provisions for compensation. No information is available on the size of compensation but anecdotal evidence suggests that it may be on the small side and probably does not meet the levels which are typical of private or public sector employers.

On the other hand, examples have been found of interesting approaches to the problem of providing job security in a more genuine sense than mere redundancy compensation. In one organization there was an agreement providing staff with the chance to be given 'outplacement' when facing redundancy. This effectively kept them in employment for an undefined (and theoretically unlimited) period, whilst they were given career counselling, training and support to seek alternative employment. In another voluntary body the question of hand-overs of projects to local management committees was addressed. Very long periods of advance notice were provided and commitments were given that employment conditions would as far as possible be preserved. Nonetheless, the closure of projects and the dismissal of staff would seem likely to be an especially fraught area for some voluntary organizations, especially those which depend on direct or indirect sources of government funding. Moreover, there seems to have been little searching analysis even in the bigger organizations about the nature of an employer's legal obligations to staff when 'ownership' or responsibility for a project is transferred. Certainly, there have been several examples of projects being transferred to new 'owners' – that is, different charities or local management committees – and being given new (often worse) conditions of employment. In the private sector it is clear that such arrangements would be unlawful, either because the legal entity of a company remains the same when it is transferred by an acquisition of shares or because the provisions of the Transfer of Undertakings (Protection of Employment) Regulations 1981 would apply. British labour law may well provide a loophole for some voluntary organizations which are not commercial ventures but they might nonetheless be in breach of the EEC Directive 77/187 (the 'Acquired Rights Directive') which calls for legislation to safeguard employees' rights in the event of a transfer of a business. UK law will probably increasingly be interpreted as falling into line with EEC Directives where there appear to be deficiencies in domestic legislation that fail to give EEC law its intended effect (see *Pickstone v Freemans Plc* [1989] A.C. 66). One effect of this could be to prevent voluntary organizations terminating employment contracts or offering different conditions when transfers occur. In the circumstances, one might hope for a general tightening-up of policies on job security and redundancy issues in a sector where jobs are often less secure or stable than their counterparts elsewhere.

■ Pensions

One area where voluntary sector staff seem to fare especially badly is pension provision. Only 50% of the organizations in the MSF survey made any provision at all in this area. Many of them were 'money purchase' pension schemes, which are generally regarded as being inferior to the 'defined benefits' or 'final salary' schemes offered by most organizations in the private or public sector to their employees. ('Money purchase' pension schemes do not define benefits, including the eventual pension, in any way that allows one to predict what their value will be at the time of eligibility. 'Defined benefits' schemes, on the other hand, state the value of pension, death benefits, dependents' benefits, etc., according to some established formula; for example, pension on retirement $= n/60 \times$ final salary, where n = the number of years of service in the scheme.)

There are a variety of strategies available for reasonable pensions provision for staff in large or small organizations. None of them is cheap, however, and everyone concerned needs to appreciate that direct provision must be made in funding applications if voluntary sector employment is to move away from being both low paid *and* non-pensionable. The consequence of a failure to address this problem will inevitably be a drain of good people seeking better conditions in 'real jobs' elsewhere. As in the case of maternity benefits, the problem is greatest for small organizations. Even if they have the funds, it may not be easy to find a scheme that offers defined benefits to a small number of employees. (Pension funds and actuarial calculations work on the basis of many employees contributing to a scheme, and payments of benefits averaging out according to the normal individual variations within a demographic pattern.)

Organizations sometimes deal with this problem by attempting to gain access to the local government superannuation scheme. Also there are several schemes run in conjunction with 'umbrella' organizations in the voluntary sector that offer small organizations the chance to share in a 'final salary' scheme on a group basis (The Pensions Trust/National Federation of Housing Associations Scheme for example). The Manufacturing Science and Finance Union and The Pensions Trust have been working to develop a 'group scheme' for small and medium-sized organizations which recognize the union for bargaining purposes.

The technical details of pensions benefits are too intricate for further discussion here. It is sufficient to note, however, that this area has been bedevilled by unequal treatment of men and women employees because of distinctions made by pensions actuaries. Some of these distinctions are in the process of being outlawed by decisions of the European court (for example *Barber v Guardian Royal Exchange*, ECJ, 1990) but other areas of discrimination will no doubt persist. For example, on the question of discrimination against lesbians and gays, it might be asked whether widows', or partners', death benefits may be enjoyed by people of the same sex as individual pension fund members. The sensitivity of voluntary organizations to issues such as this will be one way of carrying through a commitment to equal opportunities. Their choices may contribute to the adoption of socially aware practices that can distinguish them from other employers in the public and private sectors.

■ Policies on unions

The voluntary sector is by no means homogeneous. Parts of it will continue to provide employment which, if rarely well-paid, will at least compare reasonably with that on offer in other sectors. For people who value the prospect of doing jobs that they believe in, it will be a stimulating and satisfying work environment. Among the multitude of voluntary organizations, however, there will inevitably be a substantial number that provide employment that is stressful, sometimes unsafe, and often unfair and badly paid. The insecurity of funding of many voluntary organizations will continue to be a source of worry to staff. Cash crises brought about by such factors as restraints on government expenditure will force more organizations to close or resort to other cost-cutting measures. For many people, employment in the voluntary sector will have greater tensions and disappointments than in other less value-based sectors. From time to time frustrations will explode as people cope with difficulties brought about by poor management and unrealistic expectations. Inevitably there will be occasions when individuals become the subject of disciplinary enquiry and action or raise grievances that are equally difficult to manage. Some organizations at the present time seem to deny the existence of these pressures and difficulties. When staff respond to them by joining unions, members of management committees or senior staff interpret this as disloyalty. Occasionally there are difficulties in getting organizations to recognize a union for bargaining purposes. This is not often the case, but a lower more discreet form of disapproval of union organization is more common.

Union membership and representation of staff is of course a development intended to safeguard employee interests. However, it may also be of considerable value in an organization which is seeking to project a caring image and provide a fair employment environment in which to motivate staff. Organizations which remain passive, which do not respond to the pressures and changes in contexts around them, may muddle through without encountering any particular crisis. This, however, is an uncertain if not dangerous scenario. Fortunately it does not typify the majority of the voluntary sector which in the main is innovative and open-minded as well as imbued with 'fair play' and 'social justice' as motivating ideas. But there is for all that a tendency for head people in value-based organizations sometimes to compartmentalize their values. What is worthy and important in one area, in the interest of 'the cause', may hardly be considered in another area. It is a tendency that staff in the voluntary sector who are joining unions for the first time often find offensive. They see it as demeaning the professional selflessness that *they* bring to their work. They feel unappreciated and let down, and turn to union membership in the hope of a fair remedy.

■ Conclusions

In considering remuneration policies and employment practices in the voluntary sector then, it seems important to note that staff often approach these matters by looking at what help and advantages they can get from union membership. Increasingly they are turning to unions for assistance. If managers and management committees are considering policies in this area, it is important that they too should seek to understand what roles unions might perform. If voluntary organizations are to examine their policies on employment issues, I would not want to suggest that they should begin *and* end with assessments of the role that unions might play, but they might begin *or* end with such a consideration. Ultimately of course, the employees must make their decisions clear in this respect, although management can stimulate or stifle this process as the case may be. Management's actions will represent a public expression of the organization's values and standards, alongside the explicit statement of its charitable purposes and objectives.

References

Manufacturing Science and Finance Union Voluntary Sector Salary Survey (1990), London.
Reward Group Charity Salary Survey (1990), London.
Save the Children Fund Job Evaluation Scheme Manual (1987), London.

8

Managing Volunteers

Elaine Willis

Volunteers play a crucial role in many voluntary and non-profit organizations. Yet, particularly at a strategic level, management often fails to consider volunteers in their plans. Elaine Willis argues that the effective management of volunteers involves four interrelated tasks: strategic planning; the face-to-face management of volunteers; managing volunteer participation; and the information management task. By examining these different tasks in turn she extends our understanding of the management of volunteers beyond the usual focus on face-to-face management and presents some guidelines for developing good practice.

■ Introduction

I have met people who seem to believe that volunteering happens as if by magic. As they see it all that has to happen is that someone somewhere offers to give some time, usually, 'to help others' and that somehow this all happens to the satisfaction of everyone involved.

The process is much more complicated. It requires an astute awareness of individuals and their needs and motivations, a capacity to make *clear judgements* about how and where to involve them and an organizational capability which is responsive but clear about overall direction. The process of managing volunteers effectively is of concern to many organizations, both statutory and voluntary, and about which there are often confused and ambivalent views. Somehow, it is thought that the free-will offer by individuals to give time and skills to activities which they are not paid to do requires a more spontaneous (read inefficient), free-flowing (read chaotic) response by those who want to organize these activities to best effect. However, it is only where such offers are scrutinized, matched with an appropriate task relevant to the individual's motivations and supported and evaluated that volunteers' contributions will be effectively used to their own and others' benefit.

Management theory and practice, although shunned for many years in the UK by those who involve or organize volunteers, is now giving a new context for talking about organizing volunteers. Management skills have been given recognition in the past in face-to-face work with volunteers – recruiting, matching the person with an appropriate job, offering support and training where relevant. However, the changing external environment within which volunteering is taking place has led to an increased emphasis on effective service delivery, the cost effectiveness of volunteer involvement and the evaluation of volunteer achievement, with the consequence that other aspects of managing volunteers are becoming increasingly important.

In the 1980s the volunteer organizer's role and volunteer organization gradually became more professional. This is true for both the voluntary and the public sectors, where volunteers are increasingly affected by the changes in local government funding and management. Issues of strategic and corporate management, resource planning and human resource development all impact on volunteer involvement and vice versa. So, managing volunteer activity should be the responsibility of those who *manage the organization as a whole* as well as of those who manage the face-to-face work with individual volunteers. Unfortunately this is not always the case.

Volunteer activity is managed in small voluntary organizations by the management committee and in the larger ones by senior management. Often problems emerge when those with overall responsibility for an organization's management assume that the (usually) low paid, (often) part-time volunteer organizer is taking care of all things affecting volunteers; or they assume that the management of volunteers is looking after itself somehow or other. Where these attitudes prevail, the volunteer organizer often has difficulty making her/his voice heard and has little or no access to key decision-making processes which affect the resourcing and support of volunteer activity within the organization. I have witnessed this phenomenon in small, intimate groups and associations, in larger, more bureaucratic voluntary organizations and in parts of the public sector, such as hospitals or museums. In part it appears to be due to the attitude of those with overall management responsibilities who tacitly assume that volunteers will continue to play their role under any conditions; and in part it is due to the lack of tradition in such organizations regarding the need to consider volunteers when formulating policies and strategic plans.

In this article I will describe several management tasks which are necessary for the effective involvement of volunteers – the strategic planning task; the face-to-face management of individual volunteers; managing volunteer participation in the organization and the information management task. I will not address the role of volunteers on management committees as this is discussed in the article by Margaret Harris.

■ The strategic planning task

Some people argue that for many organizations the involvement of volunteers in their work grows 'organically' in response to an identified community need. This may be anything from caring for older people to conservation work or advising on consumer rights. The reasons for involving volunteers, it is said, flow 'naturally' from this need and the motivation of volunteers is 'obviously' linked to getting the job done or promoting a specific cause.

Research has shown that all these assumptions can be challenged: there is nothing natural about the particular form a response takes. It is always constructed, with particular personalities organizing people and tasks in particular ways according to different emphases and ethos. The work of volunteers can be responsible and demanding or relatively trivial, and the motivation of volunteers is as varied as the individuals concerned, probably only a minority being involved for purely altruistic or concerned reasons.

At some point in its development every organization has to take these realities on board where volunteer involvement is concerned. The management task involves examining the value base from which planning and practice derive their form. It is surprising how often management does not consider the principles on which its organization involves volunteers. It is assumed that such principles are self-evident and that everyone agrees about the primary purpose of volunteer involvement in the organization's work. However, research shows that even among volunteer organizers there is little consensus about the principles underlying volunteer involvement.[1] This lack of consensus may explain the reluctance of many people to consider volunteers when formulating strategic plans for their organization.

Perhaps the first and most important strategic task for management committees or senior managers is to develop a clear policy for the involvement of volunteers in their organization. This policy should include a discussion of the purpose of volunteer involvement and a code of practice governing the relationship of the volunteer with the organization.

The discussion of purpose may include statements on the following issues.

- *The philosophy/ethos of the organization and the volunteer role in relation to it.* For example, a service delivery organization will hope for different benefits from volunteers to an advocacy scheme. The former will want the volunteer to deliver a particular service on its behalf; the latter will see the volunteer's primary loyalty and role being to the user of certain services. In some cases, an organization may expect volunteers to perform both these functions, in which case they need to be aware of this.
- *The value of volunteers to the organization.* Volunteers bring a positive or added value to the work of the organizations that involve them. It is vital that organizations state as clearly as possible their value base for involving volunteers and the ways in which they see volunteers being valuable in their

work. For example, volunteers may bring independent assistance or view points, skills complementary to those of paid staff or an enthusiastic knowledge of detail which cannot be obtained elsewhere. Whichever, their value cannot be based on cost alone as there is little research evidence available to estimate what cost savings volunteers actually do bring to organizations and their work.[2]

- *The function of volunteers in the organization.* Some organizations have a set of guidelines or principles which lays out the reasons why volunteers are important to them. These assist in preventing misunderstandings about the value and function of volunteers as opposed to paid workers. The guidelines or principles can also lay out quite fully what the organization expects of its volunteers and what volunteers can expect from it.

The code of practice should include comments on, among other matters:

- out-of-pocket expenses
- health and safety observations
- training and support for volunteers
- insurance for volunteer activity
- involvement of volunteers in decision-making
- grievance procedure for volunteers
- relationship of paid staff and volunteers
- development of recruitment and selection policies
- status and training of volunteer managers.

The American Red Cross published in 1988 a most thorough example of such a policy towards volunteers, which included the following topics.

- Mission statement and principles in the organization
- Volunteerism – philosophy and practices
- Roles and functions of volunteers
- Definition of a volunteer and retention of volunteers
- Recruitment methods
- Support for volunteers
- The costs of volunteer participation
- Relevant external trends affecting volunteers
- Career development for volunteers
- Volunteer performance standards and evaluation

At this stage it is important to recall that some voluntary organizations will have been founded and developed by the activities of their volunteers; others will have paid staff and may have no tradition of volunteer involvement. These historical beginnings and practices of an organization will inevitably affect its view of volunteer involvement. The issue is not which is the right or wrong view but to be clear about which view the organization adopts and why. This should then be clearly communicated to all in the organization – management committee, managers, paid staff and volunteers alike. If this is done, managing the volunteer relationships within the organization becomes part of the corporate strategy.

■ The face-to-face management of individual volunteers

The organization and the individual worker (paid or unpaid) within it will have an implicit view of the nature of the volunteer's relationship to the organization. There is a tradition, still alive and well in many organizations with a philanthropic ethos, that what the volunteer brings to an organization is a 'gift' for which nothing is required in return. This is different to the role of the paid employee in which payment is expected in return for work done. However, it is clear from research into volunteer motivation that most volunteers do not see themselves as bringing a gift to an organization but more that they come to make an 'exchange'. The Volunteer Centre UK's study[3] on the motivation of volunteers showed that the 'exchange' which volunteers envisage included the following returns:

- social contact with others
- personal development
- skills acquisition and learning
- challenge and achievement
- making a contribution to society.

This clearly affects the management task in that the managers of volunteers will need to ensure that volunteers gain at least some of the 'returns' or benefits that they expect in order to secure their continuing commitment so that the work of the organization is achieved.

In face-to-face work with volunteers there are three recognizable management tasks: the recruitment of volunteers; the selection and matching of volunteers to a job which meets their motivational needs and the organization's goals; and the support and development of volunteers.

☐ Recruitment of volunteers

While a volunteer organizer or manager may have responsibility for co-ordinating a recruitment plan the task can never be done by one person alone. The recruitment of volunteers has to be seen as the responsibility of all within an organization. It relies heavily on communicating messages to outsiders about the organization and its work; for example, maximizing the opportunities that paid workers and existing volunteers have with their external contacts to promote volunteer opportunities, and building alliances with other organizations to co-ordinate recruitment or develop new opportunities for volunteers.

The recruitment plan will need to take into account the following factors during its design stage.

- The overall policy of the organization regarding volunteer involvement (discussed earlier).
- Any equal opportunities policy the organization may have. What is the composition of current volunteers? Does it reflect the 'local' community? Are there barriers preventing certain groups of people from volunteering? What can be done to overcome these barriers?
- The current and projected needs of the organization in meeting its objectives. How many volunteers will be needed? To do what? At what times? In what stages?
- The current activities of paid and unpaid staff. Planning should not undermine the position of paid workers and should take into account any changes that are envisaged in the roles of paid and unpaid staff.
- Development opportunities. Will there be new needs or changes in legislation which may open up new opportunities for volunteer involvement?
- The work of other organizations with volunteers. An organization should not aim to duplicate work that others are doing and will need to identify ways of linking up with other organizations to share training, support and information for volunteers.
- Resources available (both human and financial). Is the organization in an expanding, contracting or unchanging situation? How will the necessary resources be found to support volunteers in their activity?
- Strengths and weaknesses of the organization's reputation, location and interest in the eyes of potential volunteers. Every organization is attractive to some people and not to others. An organization in planning its volunteer recruitment will need to be aware of its own strengths as far as attracting potential volunteers is concerned; for example, an attractive environment or a good mileage rate for expenses. It also needs to prevent its less attractive attributes becoming obstacles to volunteer involvement. For example, one-to-one work by volunteers in others' homes is not very attractive to many but if this is balanced by regular volunteer group support meetings or social events it may appear more so.

The recruitment plan will need to be discussed with and take into account the views of various 'stakeholders' in the organization; for example, funders, clients, the local community, colleagues and management committee members.

The building of the plan is also an opportunity to involve those who will later have some responsibility in part for implementing it. The plan itself should include the following.

(1) The purpose for which the organization is recruiting volunteers. This is likely to result in a set of job descriptions and/or a portfolio of activities.

(2) The ways in which the organization will go about recruiting. This should include what message is to be given, to whom, where and how. Research has shown[4] that the most effective method of recruitment is by word of mouth but a significant number of volunteers are also recruited via the work place or through membership of an organization. General advertising, for example leaflets or local radio, accounts for only around 10% of recruited volunteers.

(3) What will happen when potential volunteers approach the organization. It will need to establish contact points for volunteers and be clear about processes for their interview, selection and placement. Volunteers may need information about the organization, its views of volunteers and its expectations of them if they 'join up'. This information may be given orally or in writing. Will opportunities be available for volunteers to sample the work and atmosphere of the organization, for example through open days or evenings? The recruitment plan must take these needs into account and plan for them.

(4) The introduction of new volunteers to the organization and vice versa. Once volunteers have been selected and agreed to become involved the organization will need to establish a means of introduction. Many organizations have a volunteers' induction process which introduces volunteers to others, explains some internal systems of the organization and possibly involves some initial training. At this early stage the organization will want to help volunteers feel that they belong and provide as much information as they feel is appropriate. Information overload is not a good idea at this stage. Managing this part of the process requires sensitivity to the informal as well as to the formal aspects of the volunteer's introduction. A volunteer's first impressions in the initial few weeks in the organization will set the tone for her/his involvement on a more long-term basis.

Some organizations will have recruitment drives periodically; for others recruitment is a continuing task. In both cases the process has to be planned for effective implementation rather than left to chance. To recruit without having a planned response to enquirers is a waste of both their time and the organization's. It may also mean that potential volunteers are lost not just in this instance but also to other organizations – their poor introduction to voluntary work may well affect their general attitude to considering volunteer opportunities in the future.

☐   **Selection of volunteers**

There are two ways of managing the selection task: in the first, an organization has a list of jobs which it wants volunteers to do. It recruits people on the basis of their suitability to undertake a given job. This approach may allow all sorts of hidden assumptions to creep in about the ability of an individual unless clear job descriptions are available and volunteer specifications carefully agreed. Even then, the expectation that any one individual can fulfil all the elements of the specification is often unrealistic. Many volunteers may then be rejected because they could only undertake some aspects of the job. Volunteers may also reject the organization on the basis that it does not allow them to state what they feel they can offer and mechanically (or so it appears to them) sorts new volunteers into pre-defined roles. This approach is most appropriate when the job demands special skills and/or responsibilities and so it is particularly important to ensure that the person has the right skills and qualities to do the job.

The second approach to selecting volunteers is best described as managing a matching process. The organization will have a portfolio of possibilities for the volunteer role which may be combined in any number of ways. A potential volunteer will be interviewed to ascertain her/his skills, interests, intended time commitment and to probe her/his motivation for involvement. A job description may then be constructed from the portfolio which matches the individual volunteer's requirements with organizational needs. This has the added benefit of involving the volunteer in defining the task with which she/he wants to be involved but within the bounds of a framework setting out what the organization wants.

☐   **Support and development of volunteers**

The selection of volunteers is the beginning of a long-term management task, that of supporting and developing volunteers. Various models have been put forward to describe the ways in which volunteer involvement in an organization develops. One model describes the life cycle of a volunteer (Figure 8.1 overleaf).

The management task is to try to ensure that the volunteer achieves a successful life cycle during her/his time with the organization. However, not all volunteers will achieve this and they may leave at any point, sometimes because they feel that the work does not suit them but also because of other factors such as moving from an area or an event in their personal life.

Stage 1 of the life cycle is an exploratory stage for the volunteer where she/he is examining the worth of the organization and of what she/he has to offer and whether or not she/he likes the people with whom she/he will have to work. To give assurance is important at this stage and to spend time communicating directly with the volunteer, exploring expectations, uncertainties and the level of need for information. During Stage 1 the volunteer may well have second thoughts. It is important to reassure, explain and persuade. Many volunteers later look back on

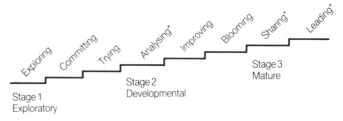

(*points of renewed commitment)

Figure 8.1 The life cycle of a volunteer. (Taken from 'Supporting the volunteer life-cycle' by Paula J. Beugen in *Voluntary Action Leadership*, Fall 1985, pp. 17–19, New York.)

this time as being when they were managed particularly well or particularly badly because they themselves were at their most vulnerable.

Stage 2 is a developmental stage for the volunteer. Having decided to stay and get involved, the volunteer will be introduced to new people and situations which hopefully will bring out her/his skills and qualities, enabling her/him to help the organization pursue its goals. There will be learning and fun on the way. Towards the end of the developmental stage the volunteer's confidence may be such that she/he begins to feel undervalued and unappreciated. Having needed more intensive support during the exploratory stage, a manager may leave a volunteer to 'get on with it' on her/his own much more at this stage. Although this is a sign of trust and respect, it can also lead to a lack of communication between manager and volunteer. Recognizing volunteers' achievements and listening and responding to their personal aspirations for the job they do and the part they play go some way to valuing and affirming volunteers' participation.

Stage 3 is the mature part of the cycle when a volunteer is making a maximum contribution, is happy to carry the responsibility for her/his particular task/role and perhaps is ready to advance participation even further. A volunteer at this stage in the cycle may be ready to share skills and experiences with others or to take on a position of leadership in terms of greater visibility or a training/support role for others. The manager's task is to ensure that the organization draws on the qualities and skills that the volunteer can now give because otherwise the volunteer will begin to lose interest and motivation.

The management task is therefore to identify stages in the life cycle for any one volunteer and to facilitate her/his successful development within the cycle. Another approach to the development of volunteers is based on Herzberg's Motivation–Hygiene Theory[5] which says there are two sets of factors to think about in managing people.

- *Hygiene factors*: policies, administration, supervision, working conditions, interpersonal relations, security

Herzberg noted that, while these things in themselves do not necessarily motivate, their absence demotivates. Indeed, research shows that at least 25% of volunteers leave their voluntary work because they feel that organizations are not clear about or do not provide these things in their working environment[6]. On the other hand, these factors in themselves will not generate the high motivation and commitment that can arise from other factors.

- *Motivators*: sense of achievement, recognition of accomplishment, challenging work, increased responsibility, personal growth and development

The management task here is to ensure that volunteers see benefits accruing to them in the course of their voluntary effort and that these are given due attention alongside the achievement of organizational tasks. The manager's means of achieving this are various: volunteer award schemes, job development, support groups with other volunteers, training events designed to meet volunteers' needs and appropriate supervision. However, they all require an allocation of organizational resources for the task to be performed effectively.

Effective face-to-face management of volunteers is crucial to any successful volunteer programme. An organization ignores this fact at its peril.

■ Managing volunteer participation in the organization

It is important to distinguish between two organizational views of volunteer involvement. One view is more task-orientated – the volunteer becomes involved in completing a task on behalf of the organization, even if the task is ultimately 'matched' to the individual volunteer's interests. The other view sees the volunteer as performing a more central role in the processes at work in an organization; that is, in assisting with planning processes, developing campaigns or other initiatives and acting as advisers, envoys or advocates.

Some organizations aim to keep volunteer involvement 'at arm's length', never allowing volunteers to become involved in the decision-making or policy work of the organization. There is some limited evidence to suggest that the effective management of volunteers in this context is constrained by this approach. Volunteers may feel that they are distant from the organization, uninvolved in its main work and that communication with them is poor. All these factors can contribute to the demotivation of volunteers. For example, an organization which delivers a public service mainly through its volunteers may not involve them in key decision-making at branch or regional level. It may consult only the paid workers and not the volunteers about key policy issues with the effect that volunteers feel excluded from the service formation. An organization may consider it unnecessary to communicate with volunteers regarding changes or proposals for change within it. The consequences will be borne by volunteers who may feel they are passive recipients of decisions made by others without regard for the day-to-day tasks with which volunteers are involved. This may lead to lowered morale and disillusion with the organization.

On the other hand, the organization which sets out to involve volunteers at its heart and achieves greater participation by them in key decision-making procedures is better placed to manage its volunteers more effectively. Volunteers who are consulted, informed, given responsibility and invited to make a contribution will be more convinced protagonists for the organization and more likely to offer their unique contribution for a longer time.

Again the overall organizational policy on the involvement of volunteers will influence the style of volunteer participation adopted.

■ The information management task

Making the management of volunteers more professional requires improved administration skills and has also created the need for effective information management.

In some areas of voluntary activity detailed record-keeping, often computerized, of volunteer profiles is necessary and useful. Names and addresses, interests, length of service and method of recruitment give the volunteer manager and the overall management personnel data which help build a picture of the volunteer workforce. Assumptions are often wrongly made about volunteer numbers, gender and ethnic balance, means of recruitment and tasks they are completing. This misinformation can lead to poor planning in areas such as volunteer recruitment and training.

Relevant quantitative information about volunteers can be a useful management tool in assessing and evaluating the volunteer contribution to the organization. Information about qualitative issues such as volunteers' satisfaction with their role is also important as an indicator of management success. Such information needs to be routinely or regularly gathered, stored and, more important, used by volunteer managers with clear policies about who can have access to it.

Information about volunteer outputs, benefits to individual volunteers and the ways in which volunteer activities in different parts of the organization contribute to the whole can all be used to improve management effectiveness. Such information can be used externally, for promoting the organization to new volunteers or to demonstrate to funders the effective use of resources, or internally, to improve recruitment, widen the volunteer role or gain more resources to support volunteers. Without this management information the organization's policy on the involvement of volunteers cannot be effectively monitored or implemented and all strategic planning will be seen as a paper exercise only.

■ Conclusion

This brings us full circle. The management tasks of those who work with volunteers or whose decisions affect volunteer effectiveness are interrelated.

Face-to-face work with volunteers requires a context, that of policy guidelines and effective strategic planning. To be effective strategic planning must encourage good practice in the involvement of volunteers and provide the relevant resources to achieve this. To know that volunteers are being managed effectively, data must be collected to build up pictures, make critical judgements and improve management practice.

To conclude, therefore, I have to return to where I began: the management of volunteers is a complex set of tasks and processes requiring a range of skills and sensitivities on the part of the organization's management. Successful volunteer involvement relies on the performance of these functions and roles at a strategic and face-to-face level whereby volunteer motivation can be encouraged, maintained and maximized to the benefit of the organization's overall objectives.

Notes

(1) In 1989 The Volunteer Centre UK published *The Promotion of Volunteering* which laid out the main principles on which consensus could be obtained regarding the values of volunteering. These principles were obtained through a series of consensus exercises with those involved in managing volunteers. It became clear that there is little agreement about these values thus making it important for managers not to assume that such values are self-evident.

(2) The evidence is surveyed in *Time is Money: The Costs of Volunteering in Britain Today* by Professor Martin Knapp (Voluntary Action Research Paper 3 published by The Volunteer Centre UK, 1991).

(3) In 1990 The Volunteer Centre UK published *On Volunteering: A Qualitative Research Study of Images, Motivations and Experiences* (Voluntary Action Research Paper No. 2) which described the main motivations of volunteers. The research revealed clear differences in the perception of voluntary activity between those who have been volunteers and those who have not.

(4) *Voluntary Activity: A Survey of Public Attitudes* (Voluntary Action Research Paper No. 1 published by The Volunteer Centre UK, 1990) gives more details regarding recruitment and type of activity.

(5) Herzberg, F., Mauser, B., and Snyderman, B. (1959) *The Motivation to Work*, Wiley; and *The Effective Management of Volunteer Programs* by Marlene Wilson (Volunteer Management Associates, 1978, Johnson Publishing Company, Boulder, Colorado).

(6) Humble, S. (1982) *Voluntary Action in the 1980s : A Summary of the Findings of a National Survey*, The Volunteer Centre, UK

Further reading

The *Working with Volunteers* series of handbooks are all published by The Volunteer Centre UK, 29 Lower King's Road, Berkhamsted, Herts. HP4 2AB:

- *Recruitment and Selection* – Bob MacKenzie
- *Training* – Lisa Conway
- *Support* – Jill Pitkeathley.

Equal Opportunities and Volunteering – a guide to good practice is published by ADVANCE (Advice and Development for Volunteering and Neighbourhood Care in London, Brixton Enterprise Centre, 444 Brixton Road, London SW9 8EJ).

9

Learning from the Experience of Collective Teamwork[1]

Alan Stanton

This article by Alan Stanton draws on his extensive research with social services agencies trying to run collectively and collaboratively. It argues that applying the experience of such teams has been hindered by their characterization in the 1970s as prefigurative of a more equal and just society. As a result, they have often been judged less by their achievements than against an idealized model of direct democracy.

The development of social services agencies in the 1980s suggests a different picture. Successful collective working cannot solve but can balance the tensions inherent in workplace democracy; and in the process offer valuable experience of the practical problems of empowering the people these organizations seek to serve.

■ Introduction

Self-management at work means that staff are asked to become citizens of a small democracy. In saying this, what are some of the implications for their day to day practice? What conception of citizenship is implied, and are there lessons that can be transferred to other forums?

This article is drawn from research with some 20 organizations whose members try to run collectively and collaboratively. Since 1980 I have been meeting and writing about groups of workers in social services agencies ranging from law centres to advice agencies; social work offices to residential homes. Some are formally 'collectives' with equal pay and equal power, and perhaps rotation of work. Some are closet collectives, finding it easier to pass in the straight world of one-team-one-boss. Still others are collaborative teams who understand the dysfunctions of the hierarchies inside which they are lodged: problems like the individualistic parallel working that results; or in speaking truth to power.[2,3]

While such teams *are* different from the majority of conventional agencies, typically, their members are keen to play down the differences.

> 'They kept expecting this sort of thing to cause a riot and the riot's never happened. It's not news anymore. The main thing about that, it says how ordinary and mundane it is.'

This quotation comes from a social worker at Newcastle-upon-Tyne Family Service Unit, the sole self-managing Unit among the 22 Units within the national charity.[4] Elsewhere, a worker in a collective resource centre readily identified the similarities in her previous job – in commercial publishing.

> 'I think people are constantly struggling to work collectively on the lower levels or the middle. I was. With no theory or anything behind me. Everybody in the middle band was on fairly equal wages. We tried to be clear what was expected of people. There was a commitment to training ... regular meetings. The problem was that the management kept putting their oar in.'[3]

■ The future in the present?

Who then, expects collective teams to be special? Or even 'to cause a riot'? The obvious answer – 'management putting their oar in' – is not the only one. At FSU's national office I heard how all sorts of fantasies had circulated through the organisation about what self management at Newcastle might mean. 'Others were opposed because they thought it must be a bunch of sloppy workers ... Viet Cong flags flying or whatever ... People not doing the work.' Undoubtedly though, the biggest contribution to an image of collective working as exotic and special comes not from its opponents' fears, but from the overblown hopes of many of its supporters.

Since the late seventies, faced with the success of the Right, one response of activists and writers on the Left has been to locate and celebrate islands of struggle and resistance. In this spirit, warm endorsement has been given to projects aiming at participation and self-management. Common examples include: worker and housing co-operatives; collective self-help groups like women's aid; and of course, programmes like those of the Lucas Aerospace Stewards. Indeed, many socialists have seen in these initiatives a possible 'prefiguring' of future socialist forms.[5]

In the social policy field, a corresponding view stressed collective working and user involvement. Radical writing has proposed, 'working as collectively as possible, both in terms of the quality of the practice and to ensure political support',[6] and 'creating new social relations which challenge the traditional boundaries between client and worker'.[7] So, in health and welfare, schools and nurseries, teams were cast as the 'oppositional' standard bearers of 'Prefigurative Politics, the future in the present'.[5]

If current workers in collective teams are unlikely to use such rhetoric, the same wasn't always true in the seventies, when members played their part in raising expectations. For instance, in 1973, the first Community Law Centre (North Kensington in London) described its aim of 'Community Control of the information collected at the Centre'.[8] Centerprise, in Hackney, East London, runs a café, local writing and publishing project, bookshop, advice centre and other groups. In 1978 it wrote that:

> '. . . our co-operative working pattern is a political statement in itself, pre-figuring and demonstrating the possibility of forms of working life and social organisation that give hope for a future state of society.'[9]

One outcome of all those high hopes was hardly surprising. When teams were unable to live up to the image, there was a backlash. For example, Charles Landry and others' well known book, *What a Way to Run a Railroad* is uncompromisingly subtitled *An analysis of radical failure*. It makes a scathing attack on what the authors call the 'pathology' of collective 'non-organisations'.[10]

Elsewhere, collective teams have been seen as one more instance of the degeneration thesis derived from worker co-ops; the idea that forms of direct democracy must inevitably dissolve in the face of the realities of market and organizational pressures.[11]

In the United States, analysis of human service collectives – in fields such as medicine, law, and welfare – has painted a similar picture. Groups began with counter-cultural values, including a fierce egalitarianism – 'doing away with inequality'.[12] But they were then seen as compromising their principles and practice. For example, they modified job rotation and introduced specialism; or moved from community control through open meetings to policy decided by full time staff.

[. . .]

■ 'An exemplary project'

What stands out in this discussion is how rarely even sympathetic outsiders have approached collective working as an interesting experiment, with its own developing strengths and weaknesses. Instead of asking what can be learned from such teams – 'prefigurative' or otherwise, the tendency has been to measure them against an outsiders' model of how they ought to run – or even what they ought to stand for.

For, in one sense, teams have been 'taken up' by the Left,[13] and asked to provide an 'exemplary project'[14] that is to say, a demonstration of success. They've been challenged – and invited to challenge themselves – about whether they are a 'real' or 'proper' collective. Have workers strictly equal power? What about equal rewards, and are there harmonious and comradely social relations? Each of these difficult *aims* has been seen as a distinguishing *feature*. Yet when they are regularly and inevitably unrealised, it can be felt as failure.

> 'Within a collective there's this sort of ethos that the team is "wonderful" and everyone gets on fine. It's just that people have the image that conflict doesn't happen in a collective. That's in fact part of the pressure: that it shouldn't happen.' (*Community Worker*)[2]

There are many ironies in this situation. Not the least is when the chance of learning from the *process* of democratic workplace relations is sacrificed to a concern for *structure and form*. To put things another way, exploring how we might control our work, the product of our work, and find kinder and more respectful ways of working together[15] should not be displaced by a set of static ground-rules. Yet this is exactly what happens when either members or outsiders sanctimoniously talk about 'being a collective' as if adoption of the form itself resolved the tensions addressed.

Paradoxically, understanding this displacement is an important key to applying the experience of collective teams in other settings. For once we discard the notion that they should demonstrate success, we realise how the pattern described by [...] Landry and others suggests a distinct *stage* in the life of the democratic workplace. In brief, what commonly occurs is that teams intentionally moving away from or rejecting formal hierarchy, *reverse* what are experienced as the characteristic weaknesses and constraints of hierarchical working.

So a typical feature when beginning collective teamwork is laying stress on the removal of boundaries – both between one another as colleagues; and to users and others outside. Especially where staff have experienced private, individualised workspace, we can expect phrases like 'opening up to the community'. Teams have adopted an 'open door' to users.

However, such a reversal of closed hierarchical working has its own dysfunctions. It can mean that some users are first come, often served. Or that offices become bustly, noisy, and open-plan. This may initially encourage teaming-up. But the opposite can also happen. To avoid a huddle of people and desks in an 'open office' staff may build filing cabinet partitions, or work at home.

In a similar way, the attempt is made to dismantle barriers between different specialisms. Outsiders asking for the manager or a particular worker may be told, 'This is a collective. You can talk to me'. It can look and feel very much like Landry *et al.*'s 'non-organisation' [or that a team] without rules and ruler has become plain unruly.

> 'They were just very off-hand, and took no trouble at all to make me feel comfortable. Well, you'd be brought in; you'd be sat down in the reception room and just left to deal with whoever might be there. You know, clients and people from other projects and that kind of thing.'
> (*Assistant Director, National Family Service Units*)[3]

But what happens in maturing collective practice is that workers begin to address these new problems. They are clearer in their messages to outsiders about how to approach the team, and who is and is not responsible for which parts of the work. Among themselves, they renegotiate use of their collective space; acknowledging the necessity for new boundaries between different tasks and different users. There is a realisation of staff's need for *personal* space and quiet space.

The pattern is repeated if we look at the 'intimate' social relations, supposedly a mark of collective working. Usually this turns out to be another sign of an early, oppositional phase. If in some groups, 'We all lived together, worked together and f....d together ', such intensity is temporary. It often signals that members were young, unattached and in their first really demanding job.

Because if the aim *were* to create 'familial' social relations, collective working as a form of workplace organisation would indeed be exotic and marginal. In fact, the goal is far wider; a workplace community where we have to deal with 'bad' as well as good neighbours; and where hiring solely 'people like us' who we like, is a virtual guarantee of staleness.

The Chart (below) sets out these idea [Table 9.1 overleaf]. Column one lists some of the features of conventional hierarchy that teams aim to reverse. Column two indicates how this results in the early characteristics of collective teams. [. . .]

At the start of this article, I asked about the conception of citizenship implied by collective teamworking. Readers won't be surprised to recognise in this 'oppositional phase' a resemblance to the kind of all-consuming life-as-Left-politics criticised by feminist writers in the seventies. '. . . the meeting merged into and became life. Life thus became meetings!' It's as if participatory democracy meant nothing less than everyone[16] doing everything and spending forever discussing it with everybody else. 'Oh my God, it was terrible. You literally were in meetings half the week. It got so that if you didn't do it in a group it wasn't legitimate.'[3] Let me make it plain that, by labelling column three 'collective' I'm not presenting this as a kind of harmonious synthesis; a new blueprint for successful democratic working. The experience of collective teams is a continuing, not a completed process. But if there are no tried and trusted recipes for citizenship, what it does show are ways of confronting and balancing the *tensions* intrinsic in any initiative aimed at workplace democracy.

The tensions – specialism or generalism; close versus instrumental workplace relations; a desire for informality contrasted with a need for rules – are confrontable once we accept that they won't go away simply because there's no longer a boss. They can be balanced if we go on to understand, for instance, that power is not only a matter of 'over' or 'under', but that we can (and do) exercise power between one another as colleagues. In this respect, we have both the right and the obligation to demand their best work from our fellow workers – and to have that demand made of us.

Table 9.1

Hierarchy	Oppositional Phase	Collective
Communication		
Legitimate communication is deferential: according to status and position, up and down lines of accountability	Rejection of hierarchical channels. 'I'm one of the workers here. You can speak to me.'	Clear lateral rules of reference, e.g. 'X is dealing with this.'
Space		
Space is allocated according to rank. For example, managers have individual protected areas. Senior staff have the right to intrude into the workspace of subordinates.	Explicit dismantling of barriers. 'We all muck in together.' Suspicions that personal space will become private. Tendency to noise, muddle and overcrowding. Informal barriers rebuilt, e.g. with filing cabinets, and by staff working at home.	There is renegotiation of space as a common resource. For example, agreement about quiet rooms, and defined space for users. Different kinds of work have protected boundaries.
Power		
Managers must manage. Workers then enjoy the prestige of the victim, and can constantly blame 'the hierarchy'. Power exercised by subordinate staff is denied, and may take the form of gossip, office politics.	Unreal expectations of harmony. Notion that a need to discipline a colleague is a failure of collective working. The denial that power is exercised allows staff to avoid owning its informal use.	Acceptance of both group and individual power exercised openly. New procedures provide checks and balances. Criticism and support understood as inextricably linked.
Learning		
Training is regarded as a management function. Individual staff stress 'my professional development'.	Myth that everyone can do anything. Differences in ability and expertise are denied.	Individual and collective learning are both recognised as legitimate. Also that people learn from each other. There is respect for practitioners' knowledge – Who Knows? – rather than professional status – Who's Who.
Deciding		
Decisions are the prerogative of position. Formal process is top-down, with consultation as a privilege.	There's a tendency for everyone to decide everything together. Meeting time expands. Outsiders complain about 'a talking shop'.	Meetings streamlined. Extensive delegation, while authority rests with the group, which reviews its own and individuals' work.

■ Practitioners' knowledge

In the remainder of this article, I want to raise an area explored inside collective teams: the nature of practitioners' knowledge in contrast to professionalism. It's an issue with vital significance in other forums [which] aim at [empowering or] giving a voice to those who are now silenced or ignored.

For workers in service agencies, questions of expertise and specialism tend to take their most intractable form in debates about *professionalism*. As I said before, critics of the early states of collective teams were especially scornful of members' denial of skills and experience in the pursuit of a spurious equality. Well, most teams have since absorbed the commonsense lesson that if there is equality, it can only be rare and temporary. But this is hardly a 'failure' of collective working if it leads to members acknowledging their mutual responsibility for co-learning and teaching. Putting it another way, if I'm supposed to 'know it all' already, then I can hardly ask you to show me, and you'll also find it difficult to offer.

However, this only deals with pooling knowledge and skills among workers. What of the wider aim of sharing what we know with 'the community' or – more prosaically – an agency's users? Is what they know simply data to be turned into professionals' knowledge or are they also citizens who build their own 'popular knowledge'? In [Table 9.1] I've referred to 'practitioners' knowledge'. This idea is not original to collective teams,[17] yet it helpfully describes their practice, and suggests an approach to this problem. Let me explain.

I've said that one challenge for members of a collective team is to share what they know with each other; you take responsibility for others' learning and for your own. But that's only half of it. Because, inevitably, staff are at different stages in their learning. Some workers know more, and others learn faster. There are tangible differences in ability. So, just as important as sharing, is people *owning* their knowledge and skills – craft skills, if you like.

If this seems like smuggling professionalism back in again, let me insist that the aim is precisely the opposite. Clearly, we don't want experienced workers in a role like hospital consultant, with newcomers asked to assume the meekness of trainee nurses! But saying, for instance. 'Oh, anyone can do this', when they can't, is actually doubly mystifying. It's exercising skills while *not* owning them. The point is that to avoid overpowering colleagues and setting up a new hierarchy, practitioners need to find ways of uncoupling their craft skills from professional status. Those who know things, need ways of laying out what they know so that it becomes confrontable by their colleagues. 'We both know some things; neither of us knows everything. Working together we will both know more, and we will learn more about how to know.'[18] Users and other local people know things too, of course. And one strength of the early oppositional phase of many collective teams was that this was recognised and taken seriously. Their response was a series of experiments in 'community control' and involvement ranging from user management, to open community meetings which were supposed to decide the policy of particular agencies.

Unfortunately, the outcome was seldom encouraging. Large open meetings were especially disappointing because they could be 'packed' by a few determined people, or might lack continuity. And even if the same people turned up every time, there were few mechanisms for them to gain experience and grasp the effect on the day to day running of the overall policies they were supposedly making.

In a sense, the problem came from reversing 'what can users and local people possibly know about running an agency?' into an expectation that they would somehow know everything. Accepting that consultation was just another form of tokenism and placation,[19] groups would effectively put users on a pedestal as 'those who know what it's like round here', or in a particular disability group, or ethnic minority. But while users' experience and knowledge is vital as well as valid, what they know is also partial and incomplete.

The challenge is not just to respect and honour what fellow workers, users and other local people know. One valuable lesson from developing collective teams is their exploration of how these different kinds of knowledge can be put together. To foster *co-learning* requires the kinds of forums and a culture of open dialogue where practitioners and users can take risks; lay out their meanings, understandings and uncertainties. A safe place for people to say, 'I've got this problem and I don't know how to deal with it. I can't cope; give me some help here.'[4]

■ Conclusion

The last thing I want is to present current collective teamwork as an amended vision of the future. A soft-focus rose-tinted portrait belittles the energy and effort of their members. In any case, it hides what is most valuable about their experience – the fact that it constitutes a faltering, painful and frequently dull record of people who do gain greater control over their work-place, the product of their work and their relations with fellow workers.

Earlier, I asked about implications for other sorts of forums. We can begin to see a set of challenges, questions and alternative goals. Can a group of school governors become a learning community? Can one party or group on a local Council adopt new collaborative ways of organising and sharing power? We might guess, at least, part of the answer to these questions: that simply reversing what we have now is no solution, but the start of a process; that making such changes is difficult, messy, and subject to continued learning.

We might also conclude that *not* tackling this process of change serves to maintain and strengthen existing power and social relations. In other words, when formally oppositional groups on these bodies adopt the prevailing deferential and hierarchical culture and structure, they will undermine and inhibit their own aims of widening citizenship and enlarging people's control over their lives.

Notes

(1) Reprinted from 'Citizens of workplace democracies', *Critical Social Policy*, Autumn 1989, 26(9), No. 2. Harlow, Longman. The title of this extract is that of the editors.

(2) Stanton, A. (1983) *Collective Working in the Personal Social Services: A study with nine agencies*, MSc. Cranfield Institute of Technology.

(3) Stanton, A. (1987) *Collective Working and Empowerment: A study with Newcastle-upon-Tyne Family Service Unit*, PhD. Cranfield Institute of Technology.

(4) Stanton, A. (1989) *Invitation to Self Management*. London: Dab Hand Press.

(5) Davis, M. and Cook, M. (1981) *The Chartist*, No. 83, London.

(6) Corrigan, P. and Leonard, P. (1978) *Social Work Practice under Capitalism*. London: Macmillan.

(7) Mitchell, J., Mackenzie, D., Holloway, J. and Cockburn, C. (1980) *In and Against the State*. London: Pluto.

(8) Unsigned Article (1973) *Community law*, Community Action, March.

(9) Centerprise Annual Report 1978.

(10) Landry, C., Morley D., Southwood, R. and Wright, P. (1985) *What a Way to Run a Railroad*. London: Comedia.

(11) Mellor, M., Hannah, J. and Stirling, J. (1988) *Worker Co-operatives in Theory and Practice*. Milton Keynes: Open University Press.

(12) Case, J. and Taylor, R. (eds) (1979) *Co-ops, Communes and Collectives: Experiments in social change in the 1960s and 1970s*. New York: Pantheon.

(13) A similar phenomenon has occurred when individual worker co-ops have been 'taken up' by Left and feminist groups. For example, see Wacjman, J. (1983) *Women in Control*. Milton Keynes: Open University Press.

(14) Cooley, M. (1987) *Architect or Bee: The human price of technology*. London: Hogarth Press.

(15) Women's Self-Help Network (1984) *Why Operate Collectively?* Vancouver, British Columbia: Ptarmigan Press.

(16) Rowbotham, S., Segal, L. and Wainwright, H. (1979) *Beyond the Fragments*. Newcastle Socialist Centre.

(17) See, e.g. Schon, D. (1983) *The Reflective Practitioner; How professionals think in action*. London: Temple Smith.

(18) Maguire, P. (1987) *Doing Participatory Research: A feminist approach*. Amherst, University of Massachusetts.

(19) Arnstein, S. (1969) 'A ladder of citizen participation', *Journal of the American Institute of Planners*, July: p. 216.

PART FOUR

Organization and Effectiveness

10

Evaluating Innovatory Programmes:

An External Evaluator's View

Elliot Stern

This article is written from the viewpoint of a social scientist who often works as an external evaluator in the voluntary and community sector. The author therefore approaches evaluation from the outside, looking in at the dilemmas of managers and workers who face demands for evaluation. He draws on both his own and his colleagues' experience as members of a group within the Tavistock Institute which has done a wide range of evaluation work. The author addresses several questions that often concern project and programme managers: about why they need to evaluate their activities, about how to approach evaluation design, about the proper role of external consultants and evaluators and about the strengths and weaknesses of self-evaluation. Hopefully, practitioners in the voluntary and community sector will find it useful to hear how some of their questions are approached from an external evaluator's perspective.

■ Introduction: scope and definitions

Defining exactly what is meant by evaluation has become a minor academic industry in recent years. Advocates of different definitions vie with each other about the purposes, methods and outcomes of evaluation. Some favour experimental design whilst others see themselves as engaged in understanding (but not necessarily engaging with) change, and question the validity of so-called social experiments. Some evaluators, who are methods-led, argue about the respective merits of quantitative and qualitative data. There are advocates and opponents of self-evaluation – a topic considered later in this discussion. Experience of evaluation in many different settings tends to take the edge off these arguments. A pragmatic position is that few evaluations, if properly designed, are exactly the same, and what goes into an evaluation depends on circumstances. However, a broad definition is useful when beginning evaluation design.

It is particularly useful for independent evaluators to provide themselves and their clients with a definition that is explicit about orientation and values – which is what the following definition attempts to be:

> 'Evaluation is any activity that throughout the planning and delivery of innovative programmes enables those involved to learn and make judgements about the starting assumptions, implementation processes and outcomes of the innovation concerned.' *(Stern, 1988)*

This definition focuses attention on the *innovative* elements of programmes. It takes a broad view of the *timing of evaluation* – from the beginnings or feasibility stage through to implementation and outcomes. It is concerned with both the progress of innovation *and* making judgements, for example about success and failure. Finally, it makes explicit a value which is present in many action research and consultancy projects: that it is about enabling *those involved* to learn – and not just to assist the learning of external evaluators or senior managers or programme sponsors.

Selecting external evaluators can be difficult. Definitions, by revealing values, provide useful guidance. In our own work we recognize that evaluations are usually more successful when the values of those involved in an innovative scheme correspond with those responsible for an evaluation. Exploring the values of external evaluators at an early stage – by discussing their definitions, professional philosophies and working practices – may therefore be among the best ways for managers in the voluntary sector to make a selection. External evaluators who are concerned about the quality of their work and working relationships should also be prepared to enter into such discussions before accepting an evaluation assignment.

■ Evaluation and innovation

The significance of innovation within the voluntary and community sector is especially important at present. Caught between the hammer of the state and the anvil of pressing social need, voluntary organizations find their freedom of manoeuvre increasingly constrained. In order to maintain any kind of freedom, and to avoid simply becoming an agent for the delivery of state services, innovation becomes essential. This is a very different rationale for innovation from that of an earlier era – when the voluntary sector and community action pioneered the expansion of welfare services and future directions of social policy. The rationale of evaluation is also different today, but no less critical. When workers and managers (and even volunteers) within the voluntary and community sector ask 'Why should we bother with evaluation?' the beginnings of the answer should concern innovation. I would argue that evaluation is at the core of successful innovation and that innovation is essential for a vital voluntary sector with some capacity to influence its own destiny.

Evaluation is, understandably, a contentious topic for voluntary organizations. As a result, there is often little commitment to evaluative activities and the quality of the outputs of evaluation is often poor. 'Top-down' requests for information which is not perceived as relevant by practitioners get short shrift. Programme and project managers looking for funds are unsurprisingly more concerned to convince sponsors of their success than, self-critically, to examine their own assumptions and practice.

Yet there are two powerful arguments why evaluation should be taken more seriously by practitioners. First, many of the activities required in an evaluation are also part of project managers' and other key workers' responsibilities in their everyday work. In order to manage and plan, evaluation is also necessary. Being clear about objectives, deciding on a course of action, monitoring performance and feeding this back into future decisions is the work both of evaluation and of project or programme management. To that extent evaluation is an integral part of voluntary sector management activity and not, as is sometimes suggested, an additional burden. (The extent to which this is recognized and time is made available for it within most voluntary organizations is, of course, another matter.) The second reason why practitioners should take evaluations more seriously concerns 'stakeholders' in innovative programmes and projects. Stakeholders have a legitimate interest in projects and programmes which a balanced evaluation strategy can go some way towards satisfying. However, such a strategy that relates to most (if not all) of the interests of stakeholders is rare.

One of the reasons for this is the extent to which different evaluation agendas are recognized as legitimate. Too often there are attempts by one or another stakeholder to deny the legitimacy of the evaluation agenda of others. Managers and workers committed to innovative schemes may favour 'process' type evaluations. These will highlight implementation issues, the problems and achievements along the way. External sponsors (especially central government departments driven by Treasury-type imperatives) often care little for implementation. They are more likely to favour evidence of the success or failure of targets, often financial, rather than broader measures of effectiveness.

One reason for these divergent perspectives has already been suggested: it derives from a divergence of role and consequently of self-interest. Another reason is the absence of frameworks within which a balanced evaluation strategy can be designed. Most evaluations are put together in a haphazard way. For this reason one of the activities we undertake as independent evaluators is to equip practitioners with frameworks that allow them jointly to design evaluations with us.

■ Approaching evaluation design

The framework we have evolved and use in our work is not claimed to be a blueprint for evaluation. Rather it encourages practitioners (and fellow evaluators) to think through several key issues. The examples that follow are drawn from a more extensive set of questions. These examples are intended to illustrate the type and level of questions we think it important for project managers to be asked and to ask themselves when first contemplating the evaluation of some innovative activity. The first question, prefigured earlier, concerns stakeholders and their interests.

☐ **Who are the stakeholders in the evaluation and in what kinds of issues are they most interested?**

Although the answers are never the same there is a useful 'check-list' that can prompt a systematic response. Stakeholders usually fall into one of four categories:

- external sponsors who are most interested in achievements and outcomes in relation to targets
- projects themselves with a concern for effective management and implementation
- the users or consumers (the presumed beneficiaries of a scheme) who are interested in improvements in their circumstances
- a wider constituency (of both policy-makers and practitioners) which wants to learn the kind of lessons that can be 'transferred' or applied in other settings.

As often as not the debate between the interests of managers and external sponsors crowds out both 'users' or 'consumers' *and* the wider constituency. Yet a balanced strategy will at least consider all four classes of stakeholder.

The second question that needs to be addressed very early on in planning an evaluation concerns the central focus of the evaluation.

☐ **What are the key evaluation questions and when do different questions become salient?**

In part, the answer to this question is a reflection of stakeholders' interests. It also has to be informed by the nature of the project or programme itself. For example, we always argue that it is the *innovative* elements that should receive the most attention. In any scheme there are always some elements that are innovative and others that are not. Another way of identifying key evaluation questions is to focus on project or programme 'objectives' – even though, as is argued below, relying on these as benchmarks can be problematic. It is also important to put evaluation questions in sequence. Some questions – about starting assumptions, 'base-line' data and design – are usefully addressed early on. To a certain extent the sequence of evaluation questions follows the innovation cycle. As projects and programmes become established questions can be asked about early 'outputs' as well as about implementation processes. Of course, longer term 'outcomes' of an innovation can be addressed only when it is well advanced.

A useful device when planning an evaluation is to combine within a simple 'grid' the stakeholder interests described above and the stages in an evaluation just discussed. Table 10.1 shows a grid in a form that can be used by evaluators and practitioners at the design stage of evaluation.

Whilst a sequential approach helps organize evaluation questions over the different stages of a project or programme, it does not imply that all evaluation activities can be ignored until they become salient. For example, from the beginning of a scheme, before any progress has been made in achieving outputs or outcomes, information systems need to be designed that will eventually be able to record achievements or results. Utilization questions also need to be asked out of sequence which leads to the third question to ask at the design stage.

☐ **What will be the mechanisms for interpreting and utilizing the results of an evaluation?**

Everyone is familiar with the criticism of weighty evaluation reports that are never implemented or otherwise put to use. In our experience this problem has to be addressed from the very beginnings of an evaluation and can be, in several complementary ways. For example, stakeholders are usually identical or overlap with those who will, eventually, need to act on evaluation findings. A well-designed evaluation will include mechanisms for involving stakeholders in the process of

Table 10.1 Stakeholder interests and stages in innovation.

Stage in innovation cycle	Interests of stakeholders			
	Stakeholder 1	Stakeholder 2	Stakeholder 3	Stakeholder 4
Starting situation				
Project design				
Implementation				
Outputs				
Outcomes				

learning from an innovation – and will not wait until the end when reports are produced before this happens. Taking end-users along with the evaluation process also requires the creation of forums which allow interpretation and reflection. Building in 'review-days' and seminars is one way of approaching this. The evidence from many evaluations is that utilization only occurs if opportunities for interpretation and reflection are planned at the earliest stages of the evaluation process.

The fourth question that needs to be asked at the design stage concerns methods.

□   **What kinds of method are appropriate to an evaluation?**

One of the errors often made at the design stage of an evaluation is to *begin* with questions of means and methods. I have sat through many discussions – some of them in the voluntary sector – in which strong preferences are expressed for a particular method, say a questionnaire survey or using 'project diaries' or conducting case studies, before there is any clarity about evaluation questions. An 'iron rule' of evaluation design is that appropriate methods follow rather than precede the clarification of main evaluation questions. Equally important is the level of sophistication with which methods are conceived. Methods have to be chosen within their context and in many evaluation contexts quite modest systems and methods are adequate for the task. In some circumstances three case histories may help convince a stakeholder more thoroughly than any statistical table, and simple descriptive statistics will often be preferable to multi-variate analysis. The criterion 'what will convince the potential users of an evaluation' can usefully be applied when choosing from an array of methods.

Finally, an evaluation needs to be managed and ground rules for it have to be established early on, hence the fifth question.

□   **How will the evaluation be managed and who will take responsibility for managing evaluation activities?**

Any evaluation that extends beyond a one-off data-gathering exercise has to be managed. In order to give their co-operation to an evaluation, the staff of a voluntary organization have to be convinced of its worth. Who is going to take this on? If time has to be committed to evaluation activities (especially important where there is a significant self-evaluation element in the overall strategy), who is going to sanction the allocation of staff time? Devising appropriate guarantees about the confidentiality of information and clarifying who has access to reports and drafts of reports will concern both external evaluators (if they are involved) and those being evaluated. Many issues in the management of evaluation cannot be dealt with simply by agreeing ground rules from the beginning. However, some internal mechanism can be set up, for example a consultative group or a steering committee to take ongoing responsibility for managing the evaluation process.

■ External evaluation and self-evaluation: an unnecessary dichotomy

The fundamental design issue that has not been discussed so far concerns the familiar argument about the merits of externally conducted evaluations and self-evaluations.

Unless programme participants see that their evaluation questions are included in an overall evaluation strategy, their commitment is likely to be limited. As a result, the quality of information that they collect is likely to suffer. One strength of self-evaluation is that it increases the quality of information that is available as part of a broader evaluation strategy. (Uncommitted administrators collecting evaluation information which they do not value is not uncommon. Observing such processes at close hand feeds scepticism about the reliability of many evaluation measures such as performance indicators.) Another strength of self-evaluation is that it encourages programme administrators and managers to take an interest in the process of innovation and in utilizing the outputs of evaluation activities. However, on the basis of our portfolio of evaluation cases, we can identify several persistent problems with self-evaluation approaches. Two problems are particularly important.

- *Administrative and organizational limitations.* Most commonly there are time constraints on what programme participants can devote to self-evaluation activity. In order for self-evaluation to be effective, adequate time has to be made available as part of core staff time for evaluation activities. Another, more subtle, organizational problem is where the personal job security of programme or project personnel depends on the programme's success. Thus, staff who have a limited term contract, the renewal of which depends on the success of an innovative programme, are unlikely to be unbiased about the information they collect or the reports they produce.

- *Technical and resource constraints.* Programme participants are often limited in their evaluation-related skills. For example, setting up record systems for evaluation purposes is not the same as doing so for administrative purposes. Self-evaluators also need to establish a set of mechanisms which provide opportunities for reflection, to review and interpret data in order to draw appropriate conclusions. Many programme participants also lack the experience of such reflective forums, being more accustomed to decision-making or administrative mechanisms.

Given these problems, the external evaluator who is concerned to assure the quality of an overall evaluation needs first to consider in each case what is the appropriate division of labour between internal and external evaluations. Our approach has been to enlarge the scope of self-evaluation wherever possible, but this also requires an external resource input to provide support and training for internal evaluators.

In general, self-evaluation and external evaluation necessarily dovetail with each other. Most evaluations are 'composite' rather than pure cases.

■ The role of the external evaluator

The role of the external evaluator can take on many different configurations. For example, Figure 10.1(a) depicts the 'classic' independent evaluation commissioned by a sponsor such as a government department in order to meet demands for accountability.

In this figure the evaluation subject (S), for example an innovative programme, provides information to an external evaluator (E) who passes this information on to the commissioning agency (C). Even within this basic configuration there is scope for diversity. In Figure 10.1(b), for example, the evaluator also provides feedback to the subject of the evaluation. Furthermore, the information flow to the commissioning agent (represented by a dashed line) may be modified as an outcome of negotiations between evaluator and subject. For example, confidentiality guarantees may have been given by the evaluator to programme participants.

A second type of evaluation that we have been involved in as external evaluators is 'self-evaluation', although this can also take several different forms. Often these involve no external elements, as in Figure 10.2(a). However, our interest here is in the external role and the most common of these forms is managerial. Thus in Figure 10.2(b) the management sub-system (M) of the evaluation subject (S) commissions an external evaluator (E) to provide management with feedback. This raises a more general question that affects many evaluation assignments (and indeed many other applied or action research projects): that is, who is the client? Thus in many evaluations the evaluator needs to differentiate

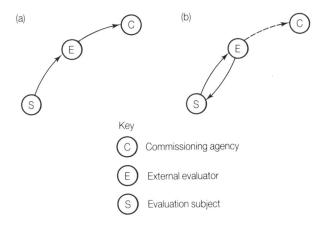

Key

(C) Commissioning agency

(E) External evaluator

(S) Evaluation subject

Figure 10.1 'Independent' commissioned evaluation.

between the various components of the evaluation subject which in a complex programme is rarely homogenous. In Figure 10.2(c), for example, the evaluation subject is extended to include the clientele of the programme, for example recipients of services (R), as well as programme staff and management.

The role of the external evaluator can also take different forms. Thus in Figure 10.2(b) the external evaluator (E) is directly involved in gathering and analysing information, indicated by the arrows. This is defined as self-evaluation because the subject (in this case, management) both commissions and receives reports from the evaluation. In Figure 10.2(c), however, the external evaluator (E) is not directly tied into the flows of information. Rather the link is through the evaluation subject (S), whose members or staff are trained and encouraged to undertake their own evaluation, that is to formulate questions, to gather information, to interpret data and use findings, etc.

A third class of evaluation involves multiple evaluation subjects, shown in Figure 10.3 as S_1, S_2 and S_3. This may be the case where several pilot projects are being run in different parts of the country. The external evaluator (E) may gather information from each evaluation subject, as in Figure 10.3(a). Alternatively, the unit of analysis may be sets of evaluation subjects. Thus Figure 10.3(b) represents a case of mutual evaluation where multiple evaluation subjects (S_1, S_2 and S_3) are involved in comparing and assessing each others' project outcomes. The external evaluation relates to the set of projects rather than to any one individually.

Few of the evaluations in which we have been involved are pure types. Nearly all involve a composite of the three configurations outlined above. Nor are the configurations represented in the figures comprehensive: many more variants are possible.

Figure 10.4 combines some of the different types and variants of evaluation already outlined. It is based on an actual case study of an evaluation undertaken by a Tavistock team in the voluntary sector in the UK. This included accountability-driven independent evaluation which led to regular reports prepared for a programme sponsor, albeit with confidentiality guarantees to safeguard subjects.

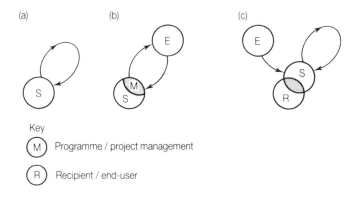

Key

(M) Programme / project management

(R) Recipient / end-user

Figure 10.2 Self-evaluation.

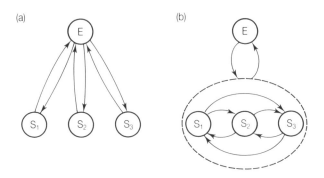

Figure 10.3 Multiple and mutual evaluation.

It also involved self-evaluation in two different forms – one in which the subjects (in this case local projects) specified the evaluation questions and received information from the external evaluation team and another in which the evaluation subjects, with assistance from external evaluators, designed and managed their own self-evaluation. The case study also involved co-operation between evaluation subjects who compared each others' practice and results in mutual evaluation groups. Finally, the evaluators did surveys of service recipients/end-users which were fed back to local projects and the commissioning agency.

■ Problems and dilemmas for external evaluators

External evaluators encounter problems that recur from one assignment to another. There are many sources of these problems: some are intrinsic to the role whilst others are rooted in preconceptions or expectations of sponsors, managers and other stakeholders. Few of the problems are amenable to easy solutions. More often than not, once recognized, they can only be 'managed'. However, we suggest that the 'problems' identified here are worth including on the agenda of both sponsors, managers and practitioners in the voluntary sector and other independent evaluators when they plan or review their evaluation activities.

☐   **Evaluation is often subject to tensions between its control and accountability functions on the one hand and organization learning functions on the other**

Most evaluations include elements of both these functions. Control may be part of external accountability to a public authority or it may be internal as when programme management seeks to manage, monitor and cumulatively steer a programme more effectively via evaluation activities. Organization learning at a

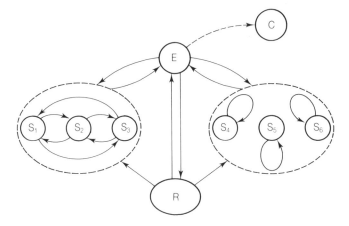

Figure 10.4 Composite evaluation.

minimum implies collective learning from mistakes and understanding why they occur. It depends on an 'open' organization culture, where participants feel sufficiently secure to expose their failings to scrutiny. Control functions tend to emphasize personal responsibility for mistakes and consequently encourage programme participants to put a positive gloss on their contribution and effectiveness. It therefore encourages a relatively 'closed' organization culture, unsupportive of organization learning. External evaluators often find it problematic to manage this tension and accommodate their own work to the contradictory demands of control and learning.

☐ **A lack of clarity about objectives makes the design of evaluations difficult**

A conventional design principle in evaluation work is to begin with project or programme objectives. These objectives then constitute a 'benchmark' against which subsequent success can be judged. As the earlier discussion about stakeholders makes clear, many innovative schemes – in the voluntary sector as elsewhere – bring together partners who have diverse objectives. Sometimes the objectives of the partners are to a degree incompatible although they have to have enough in common to come together for a particular innovative scheme. Very frequently objectives themselves evolve as an innovative project progresses. In our work we often find that objectives are not the stable benchmarks we had expected. It then becomes part of the evaluation itself to clarify objectives or at least understand why in the event clear objectives have not been built into the scheme. However, sponsors, managers and other participants involved in an innovation tend to regard lack of clarity about objectives or changing objectives as being a particularly sensitive subject. Evaluators are therefore likely to be advised to avoid what may be crucial to an understanding of project design, implementation and achievement.

☐   **The independence of the external evaluator is often threatened and difficult to sustain**

The most valued asset of an external evaluation is independence. However, this independence is vulnerable on several counts. First, there is the commitment of many of those who commission evaluations to particular outcomes. Thus programme managers or policy-makers who are committed to a particular policy direction apply pressures to ensure that certain kinds of results are emphasized and even that a limited range of questions is built into the terms of reference for an evaluation. Many evaluation contracts in the UK heavily restrict the publication of results and findings, which creates the possibility of other sources of bias at the dissemination stage. So-called independent evaluators are in fact dependent on their clients for contracts and for access to evaluation opportunities. There is therefore a tendency to self-censorship which must be guarded against.

☐   **Key groups are often excluded or little involved in evaluations**

Even in evaluations which recognize the importance of multiple stakeholders, there are two groups in particular that are often inadequately included. First, the supposed beneficiaries (clients, service recipients, end-users) of an innovative programme are rarely given a stake. They may be studied in order to see how far they are achieving evaluation criteria set by programme managers, but they tend to be unable to articulate their objectives, let alone shape evaluation criteria. A second group, often excluded for different reasons, is programme managers or senior decision-makers. They tend to see evaluations as focusing on others – junior project and programme staff or, more commonly, the end-users of services in their role as 'consumers'. A comprehensive evaluation that does not include programme management is incomplete. This group often shapes the programmes and projects in ways that, if analysed, go a long way towards explaining observed evaluation outcomes. Nonetheless it is difficult for external evaluators to convince those involved that how they shaped the implementation process should also be included in the ambit of the evaluation. Unless these managers are included, however, it is often impossible to tell whether problems are the results of 'policy failure' (that is, false assumptions about starting problems and realistic objectives) or 'programme failure' (that is, poor implementation irrespective of sound initial assumptions).

☐   **The time-scale for evaluations is often problematic – they are initiated either too late or too early for valid conclusions to be drawn**

Although it is becoming more common for evaluation to be thought of near the beginning of an innovation, it is still rare for it to shape programme or project design. For example, policy-makers sometimes try to superimpose an 'experimental' approach on evaluations, without having ensured that the necessary conditions for a true experiment exist from the outset. External evaluators are then faced with expectations that they will provide the kind of output that would only have been possible if they had been involved a year or more before. Even brief consultations at an early stage would make an enormous difference in these circumstances. At the other end of the time-scale, evaluations tend to end too early for preliminary results to be regarded as conclusive. Public authorities in the UK are often concerned with short-term results, governed as often as not by electoral cycles or even financial years. Thus, we know much about the first cohort of those helped by an innovative programme, but much less about subsequent cohorts passing through the same programme once it has become established. The sponsors of evaluations are usually oblivious to pleas for follow-up work and are often happy to draw long-term conclusions from preliminary results.

■ Conclusions

Although based on the experience of an external evaluator this article was an attempt to bring together 'rules of thumb' that also concern project and programme managers in the voluntary and community sector. By way of a conclusion I will underline three arguments that have run through this discussion.

The first argument concerns the part that evaluation plays in overall management and planning. Rather than seeing evaluation as an externally imposed burden, I have argued that it should be regarded as an integral part of good management. Evaluation, if properly conceived, makes an important contribution to enhancing effectiveness – especially if due thought is given to utilization and implementation. Given the current importance of innovation within the voluntary sector, evaluation takes on an even more crucial role. Evaluation, it has been argued, allows voluntary organizations to learn systematically from innovation and makes successful innovation more likely.

The second argument concerns the contributions of self-evaluation and external evaluations. In order to integrate evaluation into management, those involved with innovatory schemes have to set part of the evaluation agenda. Among the advantages of self-evaluation identified in the discussion are enhanced commitment to utilization and the likelihood of generating good quality evaluation data. However, there are also dangers in relying entirely on self-evaluation, particularly when it comes to problems of time and resources. There are also problems of independence and creativity if evaluations are undertaken on a 'DIY' basis. For all these reasons it is useful for practitioners in the voluntary sector to avoid dichotomies between self-evaluation and external evaluation. In each instance the division of labour should be assessed and a suitable 'composite' model designed.

The third argument concerns the way evaluation is designed. I have argued that haphazard decisions about evaluation design are common. Sometimes there is no explicit design process – sometimes the methodological tail wags the evaluation dog – and often utilization and implementation are entirely forgotten.

If there is one message that those involved in the voluntary sector whether as managers or as sponsors should take away from this discussion, it is the importance of consciously addressing issues of evaluation design. Only some of the key questions in evaluation design have been identified in the discussion. However, the main burden of the argument is to encourage practitioners in the voluntary and community sector to think through evaluation design as an internal management responsibility – irrespective of whether the outcome of their deliberations is an internal or an external evaluation activity.

Reference

Stern, E. (ed. 1988) *Developmental Evaluation*. London: The Tavistock Institute.

11

Stress in Voluntary and Non-profit Organizations

Vanja Orlans

This article covers a wide range of issues relevant to the diagnosis and management of stress within voluntary and non-profit organizations. It deals with the concept of 'stress', its origins and some of the difficulties which the term raises; the context of non-profit organizations where problems are likely to take a particular form; the kinds of issues you need to bear in mind when you undertake to intervene in these problems; and the question of responsibility for the management of stress and related difficulties – should it rest with individuals in the system or should employers take appropriate action to deal effectively with such problems?

■ Perspectives on stress

Stress and the questions surrounding this concept have attracted increasing interest among both academics and practitioners, even though there are often debates and disagreements about what exactly the term covers. The word 'stress' is unusual in the English language – it means two things, one 'good' (defined as 'challenge'), the other 'bad' (defined as 'distress'). Academics have generally been more concerned with the problems of 'distress', whereas organizational policy-makers, and to a large extent organizational members, have been more concerned (at least overtly) with 'challenge'. Interestingly, some recent research in Sweden combines these two ideas (see, for example, Frankenhaeuser, 1980), and has pointed to conditions under which individuals can expend considerable 'effort' without accompanying 'distress'. 'Effort without distress' was induced under conditions where individuals felt challenged but also that they were *in control* of the situation. 'Controllability' is therefore one factor which can give us a clue about whether situations may be regarded as either 'stressful' or 'challenging'.

It may nevertheless be easier to make such discriminations in the laboratory setting. Within many social settings, especially those which bring competitiveness and striving to the forefront, 'stress' in the negative sense carries a stigma – it is associated with failure to cope, weakness and vulnerability and can lead to real or imagined 'personal blame'. It is not surprising, therefore, that continuing efforts are made to deny its existence, or alternatively to re-cast even the negative aspects as 'challenge'.

There are several reasons why this state of affairs has come about. Firstly, we can point to a number of developments in our culture as a whole: the rise of science with its emphasis on logic and rationality and its down-playing of feelings; industrial and technological developments which have contributed to the break-up of close communities and promoted the 'cut and thrust' of the business culture.

Secondly, there is the part played by developments in the field of stress research itself. The eminent endocrinologist, Hans Selye, was instrumental in popularizing the term 'stress' in the 1940s and 1950s (see, for example, Selye, 1956). Although he is sometimes referred to as 'the father of stress' he did not invent the term. In fact, the word had previously been used within the scientific community in the earlier part of the 20th century and, according to the Oxford Dictionary, had been in use in lay settings as early as 1303! The important point, however, is the extent to which the term became widely popular within a medical and scientific framework which is traditionally orientated towards reducing phenomena to bounded problems which can be objectively measured and quantified.

Within this tradition, the dominant focus in stress research has been on *the individual* – on the experienced distress which might be physiological or psychological. Limiting the scope of investigations to the individual level, however, ignores the effects of social contact, the interaction between the individual and the culture at large and the role of social learning. There is also the possibility of a two-way process – that is, the individual affects the environment and vice versa.

More recent approaches to stress emphasize this two-way process and talk about the 'transactional' nature of the stress phenomenon (see, for example, Lazarus and Launier, 1978). Nevertheless, there has still been relatively little emphasis on levels other than the individual when it comes to conclusions about 'distress' – ownership is still assumed to rest with the individual.

An alternative perspective views the individual as inextricably linked with her/his environment, thus requiring that we focus on several different levels in our attempt both to analyse a problem and in implementing related solutions. For example, an individual might feel out of control and distressed but might work in an environment where such admissions are never made and would be taken as evidence of 'failure' on the part of the individual concerned. Individuals might prefer to leave such a system rather than be open about the extent of their distress.

In this example, we can see that the environment may be properly viewed as a central part of 'the problem', as it will affect both the extent to which such issues are actually identified and the way in which they are handled. Analysing such a problem would require that we pay attention to individual, group and organizational levels, focusing, for example, on the extent of individual distress, the extent to which work factors were relevant to this experience, how distress manifested itself at this level (for example, in terms of different conflicts), and the nature and influence of the prevailing climate within the organization as a whole.

From this perspective it is impossible to think in terms of a narrow 'cause and effect' model – problems are multi-causal and interconnected. Initial problems that are identified can often be regarded simply as the tip of the iceberg – as 'presenting problems' which need to be explored in more depth and should not necessarily be taken at face value.

It is worth saying a few words here about 'burnout'. This concept may be subsumed under the topic of stress and is often a particular focus for study within human service organizations, both voluntary and for-profit. Like 'stress', 'burnout' has also been the subject of much argument and debate.

Many years of servicing the needs of distressed individuals or groups under difficult conditions, with inadequate resources, low support and perhaps also a feeling that the task can never be achieved, can lead potentially to burnout of employees. Evidence cited as indicative of burnout in an individual includes diminishing commitment to the values and tasks of the organization and the clients or client groups, a distrustful and cynical attitude towards the organization itself, and a sense of profound tiredness.

Much has been written in recent years on the problems of burnout among human service professionals (see, for example, Cherniss, 1980). Very often, the major focus has been on the problems facing the burnt out *individuals*, rather than on the role played by job factors, managerial style and the problem of who is responsible. Clearly, not all individuals burn out – personal coping capacity is a relevant factor. Burnout, however, is also an organizational issue and needs to be tackled more extensively at this level.

One final point about theoretical and conceptual considerations. More recent approaches to stress highlight the individual as an active agent intent on making sense of her or his world and planning actions to achieve certain outcomes. Scientists are also active construers of their reality! What we end up with is a negotiated reality which reflects the needs of a range of individuals in any one system. This does not deny that in some situations certain people will have more power to define reality in their own particular way and insist that others go along with this definition! Nevertheless, the importance of this point is brought out when we consider the possibility of intervening in situations which are considered to be stressful or problematic. If individuals are involved rather than passive, an important area of involvement concerns their perceptions of problems experienced and their own views as to how such problems might best be solved or managed. These points are considered in more detail below when we consider some of the ways in which stress problems may be tackled within an organizational setting.

This brief review of the origins of the stress concept and the different perspectives on it which may colour the way such problems are approached has important practical implications. Implicit in the perception of stress as an *individual* phenomenon, for example, is the notion that the problem requires an *individual* solution. Likewise, it implies that responsibility for preventing or managing such problems lies with the individual.

In contrast, a conception of stress has been proposed which considers different levels – the individual, the group and the organization. It has been suggested that 'presenting problems' manifest themselves in a variety of ways at these different levels. Anyone trying to tackle stress problems within their own organization will find that this approach provides a more accurate and useful picture. In particular, it has the important implication that responsibility for problems lies at many levels and need not be be assigned to isolated individuals or groups.

■ Issues within the voluntary and non-profit sector

In considering those issues which are likely to give rise to stress problems within the non-profit sector, I shall draw mainly on my own experience working with trades unions to provide examples which make the points raised more concrete. The reader will, however, recognize the relevance of the examples cited to many other organizations in this sector. The main focus is on *organizational factors* within this context which predispose the emergence of stress problems at different levels.

□ The role of 'ideology'

'Ideology' is a central feature of most non-profit organizations. Of course, many for-profit organizations may also align themselves with a particular set of values. Organizations dominated by professionals such as nurses or top chefs might espouse fairly coherent sets of values concerned, for instance, with 'patient care' or with 'the quality of the meal', while also participating in a commercial enterprise. Furthermore, not all members of a particular non-profit or for-profit organization would necessarily identify with the ideologies in question.

Nevertheless, the emphasis here is on those organizations which require an *ideological commitment* of a kind which goes beyond the immediate work setting. In the case of trades unions, for example, virtually all full-time officers are committed to socialist and trades union ideals; they have usually spent many years as lay officials within other organizations before joining their union in a full-time capacity. In the face of difficult and stressful work problems, it is often the ideology which 'keeps them going', especially at earlier stages in their careers. 'Taking on the system' is exciting and challenging as well as stressful! What is important here, however, is the requirement for *commitment* of a certain kind by an organization's employees. This may indeed be a valid requirement, as well as an important motivator and key contributor to worker effectiveness. At the same time, it can mask managerial problems as well as being used as an excuse not to manage effectively. Commitment may not in itself be sufficient to enable employees to do their jobs effectively – they may also require certain kinds of training opportunities and adequate support structures. More seriously, difficulties which surface in the form of complaints by employees may be interpreted as showing a 'lack of commitment'!

The call for commitment can also be used to encourage employees to work longer hours than might be regarded as healthy, in terms of either their own physical health or the health of their relationships outside the work setting. In addition, commitment may be a source of competition among employees and may also be perceived (perhaps accurately) as relevant to promotion opportunities, particularly within the larger organizations in the non-profit sector.

☐   **The nature of the managerial role**

Managers of large non-profit organizations such as trades unions have frequently arrived at their positions through their long-term commitment to a set of ideals, as well as their personal ambitions 'to run things'. There is of course enormous variation across organizations in the non-profit and voluntary sector – many are very small and may have been managed from the start by a small group of committed individuals who run the organization on a 'group decision' basis. In the latter case, stress problems may arise which are directly related to the difficulties of group decision-making, especially where the organization concerned begins to expand and the procedures which worked originally among a group of individuals who knew each other well are no longer effective when newcomers arrive.

Size is also an important variable. In larger organizations more attention needs to be paid on a day-to-day basis to managerial functions. At the same time, administration in many non-profit organizations is under-valued – this is not what has traditionally fuelled the energy of participants and employees who want to be involved in 'more important' areas of work.

The case of trades unions presents a particularly interesting problem. They are by definition opposed to 'management'; 'managers' are often viewed as the very individuals (or groups) who give trades union members a difficult time. This is the group that is faced across the bargaining table in a 'win–lose' contest. Not surprisingly there is often a reluctance in trades union organizations to managing in any way which might begin to link such activities with 'the opposition'. There is frequently, therefore, a deep-seated ambivalence which, together with the reactive nature of the jobs of trades unionists, serves to promote and reinforce a 'crisis-management' style.

It is also true that, until recently, there has been very little appropriate management training available to enable individuals in the non-profit sector to learn some useful skills – assuming they might be willing to participate in such an opportunity! Managers within residential and day-care units, for example, have traditionally relied heavily on informal face-to-face communication rather than implementing efficient record-keeping that can be referred to as required or organizing more structured meetings to deal collectively with policy issues. Managers need both knowledge about the applicability of such procedures to their own setting and some training in ways to implement them effectively.

☐ The availability of support structures

Support structures may be either formal or informal, or a combination of both. The support function may be carried out by officially designated roles (for example, Welfare Officer) which are explicitly recognized by management or by colleagues and friends within a cohesive work group. Even in the smaller non-profit organizations, we could look, for example, at how much careful thought is given to the best way of initiating new employees into their organizational roles. In larger organizations we would expect to see a personnel section or department and possibly some formalized training. The existence of such departments, however, does not guarantee that such structures will operate in a supportive way towards employees. As in for-profit organizations, there is often tension between 'helping' and 'controlling' employees and it might be that the control function is more in evidence!

The conflicts which can arise between 'helping' and 'controlling' may also be linked with ambivalence on the part of staff towards 'managing' and 'management', as well as affecting the managerial role and style. For example, trades unions often exhibit a combination of bureaucratic and *laissez-faire* management. Some aspects of employee functioning are controlled by long-established procedures, scant attention being paid to others such as the induction of new officers where the 'sink or swim' rule invariably operates.

The training function, whether formal or informal, can play an important role in the development or management of stress problems. If employees need to write frequent reports as part of their jobs, and they are not told what is required and how to go about it, the scene is set for the development of a problem. This may be partly due to the coping strategies or opportunities of an individual employee but it is also an organizational issue, especially where the problems are more widespread.

☐ The unlimited requirement for services

In the non-profit sector, services are not 'sold' in the traditional sense; they are provided to meet the requirements of a value position – for example, the provision of day-care services for the elderly or counselling and advice to AIDS sufferers. In the case of trades unions, the membership is the key focus – the members must be adequately serviced and their needs must be met in a way which is likely to both help with presenting problems *and* engender a sense of continuing commitment to the union. Through this process, also, new members may be encouraged to join – what one officer described as 'some people's only insurance policy'.

This latter point is interesting as it points to the different ways of describing the 'organizational mission' – in the trades union example they are the difference between 'increasing the membership and looking after their needs' and 'selling insurance to people who by and large do not have access elsewhere to such a facility'. The mission statement selected has many implications for how problems are approached and handled. In the trades union case, there is often ambivalence or confusion about the 'mission', which relates to the embedded tensions and contradictions concerning commitment referred to earlier. The potential on the part of management for creating ambiguity and delivering mixed messages within the system is therefore considerable. (For-profit organizations are not necessarily any better off in this respect – frequently there are just as many tensions and contradictions in evidence!)

Within non-profit organizations there is the potential for what may be considered 'emotional blackmailing' over the work which will affect some individuals or groups more than others. Frequently workers are dealing with some form of distress – for example, if Mrs Jones fails to get her pay packet at the end of the week and calls out her trades union officer, she or he is under some pressure to deal with the case even if it means working at the weekend. Failure to come up with a solution may mean that Mrs Jones has no money for buying food or heating!

The demands in the non-profit sector frequently outstrip the resources available to deal with the problem. This is an inevitable feature of the underlying *raison d'être* of such organizations – not only are they formed to meet a much needed *deficit* in available services but also they depend for their existence on a strong set of values and commitment and possibly on 'donations' which may fall short of what is required to fund adequate resources. For these reasons, there may be genuine restrictions on the budget and a sense of not wanting to be seen to spend money on their own needs when others are suffering.

Other issues which are relevant to the question of demands versus resources concern the individual employee's capacity to cope on his or her own with this problem and the extent to which it is seen as a key managerial issue. There may, for example, be a case for some simple time-management training to encourage individuals to use their time effectively under difficult conditions. Assertiveness training may also be helpful for those individuals who have difficulty in saying 'no'.

The decision-makers in the organization, however, need to take some responsibility in setting up such facilities. This may run up against the problems outlined above of not wanting to be seen to 'spend money on ourselves'. Where managers refuse to take responsibility for providing adequate support, or where the problem is ignored, individuals may end up working ridiculously long hours leading, in the case of trades unions, to a situation where officers are fighting for a shorter working week for their members and meeting at the weekend or over several evenings to discuss the issue!

☐   **Autonomy and isolation**

The autonomous nature of many jobs in the non-profit sector relates to the degree of commitment required and the value base in general. In trades unions, for example, this autonomy is highly valued and is guarded jealously! So we have a situation where officers are spread out in small offices throughout the UK and, although there is a hierarchy in place (say two or three officers with a Regional Secretary as boss), each officer is in practice completely responsible on a day-to-day basis for his or her own 'patch'. Each organizes his or her own area of work and, when unavailable or off sick, the work generally piles up and awaits his or her return.

This is a double-edged sword. On the one hand officers are, in theory, free to organize their workload and decide on their own priorities – for example, on how much time will be needed for meetings, case presentations and negotiations, etc. and how much time will be required in the office for administration. Most officers enjoy their autonomy and freedom in this regard, as well as the opportunity on occasion to 'play God'. However, from another perspective their job is very reactive – members are constantly telephoning or writing with problems or potential cases, tribunal dates are notified, disputes may be brewing and Head Office may be sending out memos which contradict apparently agreed-upon policy.

A constant stream of demands requires a 'fire-fighting' response. In the middle of all this there are very few support structures available, making the line between autonomy and isolation a fine one for many officers. The structural arrangements add to these problems in that other staff are widely dispersed throughout the country, making extended contact with colleagues infrequent or impossible.

■ Taking effective action

Taking effective action on stress problems within the organizational setting is not a straightforward affair. It is not simply a case of identifying a 'real' problem and taking steps to implement a related solution. Instead, we become embroiled in the micro-politics of organizational life – stress is often a topic that the organization either *does not want* to deal with or towards which it feels highly ambivalent. As a consequence of this, *individuals* may be scapegoated – pointed to as incapable of doing their job, turning the stress issue into one of 'competence'. Equally, individuals could use stress as an excuse for *not* doing their job! Imposing solutions too quickly may not be a useful strategy, as it may not allow time for a fuller, more complex picture to emerge. This fuller picture may point to different or more wide-ranging interventions. The key issue to be addressed is how relevant practical strategies may be designed and implemented which meet the needs of the stressed individuals at a given time, those of individuals who might suffer at some future point and those of the organization as a whole. This is a demanding (and potentially stressful) agenda for the person who undertakes the task of attempting to deal with organizational stress. However, it is strongly recommended as a starting point, whilst recognizing that the goals outlined may not always be achievable in practice.

I emphasized earlier the importance of recognizing the extent to which conceptual issues are inextricably bound up with the planning and implementation of practical approaches for managing and preventing stress. In other words, if I view stress as an individual problem, I will be more likely to intervene at that level and possibly pay very little attention to wider factors. When dealing with stress problems in the community, it is often more difficult, although not impossible, to tackle the wider aspects of a particular issue (for example, housing, racial attacks). Within organizations, however, we have access to some of the broader context, at least as far as the work environment is concerned, so we do not have the same excuse. Organizations present us with a 'captive audience' which is usually contained within a structure with particular boundaries.

The importance of considering different levels – the individual, the group and the organization – when diagnosing problems and planning related interventions has also been emphasized. There is no one 'right' cause or one 'right' effect – instead, problems manifest themselves in different ways at different levels and require 'solutions' which are equally fluid and flexible. Adopting a rigid approach – for example, 'what we need here is a stress counsellor' – can lead to the implementation of what has been termed 'a solution looking for a problem'. It may well be that some stress counselling could provide relevant help to several individuals but it could also direct attention *away* from wider organizational factors which might, in the long run, be more important for the employee group as a whole. Also, employees who take part in a counselling programme, and whose problems are work-related, may become *more* dissatisfied as they experience being returned to the same old stressful environment where nothing much is changed to enable them to cope more effectively. Alternatively, they might become more willing to blame themselves for being unable to cope with *impossible* environmental difficulties.

In relation to these points, a useful distinction can be made between *managing* problems and *preventing* their recurrence at some point in the future. Ideally, both activities should proceed hand-in-hand but the time perspectives are often different, as are the related interventions. To return to our counselling example, such an approach might well be highly effective if combined with others which are designed to direct attention to wider problems. In this way, currently distressed individuals can receive some relevant help, while changes in how certain jobs are designed, for example, can help to ensure that stresses do not recur.

Previously I outlined several situational and organizational factors which are likely to influence the kinds of problems that arise and which are relevant to their solution. A crucial point about stress management is that adequate attention must be paid to the *particular* setting in which the intervention is to be made. This means that a 'package' of standard solutions is unlikely to be very helpful or lasting in its impact. Each setting has its own dynamics and motivations and part of the diagnostic problem is understanding these so that they can be harnessed in a productive and creative way towards the planning of successful interventions.

Trades unions, for example, are extremely 'macho' environments. People do not often admit to being stressed – in fact a physical illness, however serious, is frequently more acceptable. Officers often compete against each other for who has the most stress *and* who can deal with it 'like a man'! In this kind of environment, an in-depth understanding of these attitudes is required, together with much painstaking groundwork, in order slowly to change the awareness and the values concerning 'the problem of stress'.

In planning policies and changes to deal with emerging stress problems all the issues which we have covered so far need to be considered – for example, the ambivalence towards 'managing', the reluctance to 'do things for ourselves' and the shortage of adequate resources. On top of this there is the general stigma attached to being stressed in our culture and the subjective nature of the phenomenon. Understanding and managing particular stress problems is therefore a complex task. Notwithstanding these difficulties, it is useful to know about the different types of intervention which might be relevant to particular problems and I shall now review these briefly.

At the individual level, there is a range of interventions which might be considered, including the following.

- Medical screening – as a way of assessing physiological effects of stress-related coping (for example, alcohol consumption) and making individuals more aware of these effects.

- Lifestyle assessments – looking at such factors as diet and exercise patterns and raising individuals' awareness about them.

- Health education programmes – closely associated with life-style assessments but with a more focused, change-orientated approach (for example, stopping smoking campaigns).

- Relaxation training – includes both progressive relaxation and meditation and is a way both of re-training individual responses to stressful situations and of making individuals more relaxed in the assessment of such situations.

- Counselling, individual stress management and psychotherapy – these may include relaxation and assertiveness training but the main focus is on providing a confidential supportive relationship in which individuals can talk about their problems and assess and change some of their coping strategies.

At the group level, the following interventions can be included.

- Group counselling – an opportunity for individuals to share stressful experiences within a group setting in an environment which is confidential and supportive and which is facilitated by a trained counsellor.

- Self-help groups – similar to group counselling, but without the help of a facilitator.

- Training workshops – can deal with a range of stress-related issues by providing individuals with relevant skills; for example, the ability to manage their priorities and their own time more effectively.

- 'Job-design' interventions – strategies aimed at changing aspects of the job itself or the working environment; for example, how appointments are made or how responsibilities are allocated within specific settings.

Interventions at organization level are more wide-ranging and include the following.

- Employee assistance programmes – form a part of the official support structures for employees and are designed to provide confidential help on a range of emotional and practical issues; may offer to help the families of employees.
- Policy changes – changing overall policies in the direction of greater staff care or involvement.
- Cultural changes – the implementation of strategies to change cultural aspects of the problem – for example, how stress is viewed and the extent to which such problems may be openly discussed in the work setting. Organization level interventions are more complex and time-consuming and require a greater investment in both learning and resources. They are also more threatening to decision-makers in the organization as they are likely to challenge structures and processes which have been in place for some time. This is particularly true of the more established and larger organizations. A good review of the many different strategies which may be adopted to deal with stress problems in general is Quick and Quick (1984).

In practice, it makes most sense to focus not only on, say, individuals or groups but also to consider how any given plan might cross different levels of organizational functioning. For example, where counselling is highlighted as a potentially helpful resource for employees, it can usefully be linked with an evaluation scheme which is designed both to monitor the effectiveness of the counselling scheme itself *and* to ensure that organizational problems do not masquerade as individual difficulties. Such evaluation can be conducted in a way which does not violate individual confidentiality and which is viewed as more challenging than threatening to the system as a whole.

■ The question of responsibility

The question of who is responsible for dealing with stress problems in the organizational setting is an important one. The implicit assumption that such problems are the responsibility of the individual rather than the organization may be exacerbated by the British 'stiff upper lip' orientation which tends to promote the hiding of personal problems, especially within the work context.

Of importance also is the ethical argument that employers, whether in the non-profit or the for-profit sectors, have a duty to care adequately for the people they employ. In the non-profit sector we may come across the contradiction referred to earlier, where the organization espouses a 'caring' function but manages to implement it only in the 'client realm' – employees must cope as well as they can!

Yet the work domain is where many people spend the bulk of their time – often more than is available for leisure or family pursuits.

The view that organizations have a wide-ranging responsibility to their employees is reflected also in our Health and Safety legislation, although the 1974 Act places more emphasis on physical than on mental health. The requirements, however, are somewhat open-ended and vague and employers are expected to comply 'as far as is reasonably practicable'. Nevertheless, the ambiguities in the Act are open to challenge in the courts and there have been several cases of employees seeking compensation on mental health grounds. Also, the establishment of a single European market in 1992 may eventually lead to changes in the legislative environment regarding the role of 'psychosocial' factors in the work setting.

Changes in the legislative environment, however, are unlikely to deal effectively with all of the complexities of the responsibility question even though such changes might set the scene for more activities at the organization level. Many jobs in the non-profit sector, for example, are *inherently* stressful (for example, disaster relief), thereby potentially reducing the range of interventions which can usefully be made. In such a case, the primary focus would be on individual coping, although the organization as a whole could still play a valuable role in promoting a general awareness among employees of the problem of stress. More focused attention could also be paid to stress in the context of the organization's selection procedures and in providing adequate counselling for employees whose coping strategies prove ineffective.

The ideal would be to share responsibility for the effective diagnosis and management of stress within the work setting. Individuals themselves must 'take the risk' of talking openly about their stress problems in the knowledge that these problems are universally experienced and that many people will welcome such sharing. Management on the other hand needs to take seriously the existence of such problems and play its part in implementing relevant facilities and changes to work structures.

■ Conclusions

Dealing with the problems of stress poses a particular challenge to organizations in the non-profit sector. Apart from the general cultural difficulties associated with 'being stressed' and 'feeling unable to cope', non-profit organizations face a unique set of internal contradictions: their very commitment to caring values can inhibit them from putting these into practice with their own staff. In addition, taking the broad organizational perspective suggested in this article may be more difficult in a setting which traditionally pays less attention to 'managing' its staff proactively. Nevertheless, it may be that, once the problems are acknowledged, these organizational settings are well equipped with the necessary commitment and creativity to deal with the problem effectively.

References

Cherniss, C. (1980) *Professional Burnout in Human Service Organizations*. New York: Praeger.

Frankenhaeuser, M. (1980) 'Psychobiological aspects of life stress', in Levine, S. and Ursine, H. (Eds) *Coping and Health*,' pp. 203–23. New York: Plenum.

Health and Safety at Work Etc. Act (1974) London: HMSO.

Lazarus, R. S. and Launier, R. (1978) 'Stress-related transactions between person and environment', in Pervin, L. A. and Lewis, M. (Eds) *Perspectives in Interactional Psychology*, pp. 287–327. New York: Plenum Press.

Quick, J. C. and Quick, J. D. (1984) *Organizational Stress and Preventive Management*. New York: McGraw-Hill.

Selye, H. (1956) *The Stress of Life*. New York: McGraw-Hill.

12

The Role of Voluntary Management Committees

Margaret Harris

For professional managers in voluntary and non-profit organizations, voluntary management committees are an abiding source of confusion and ambiguity. They do not take on – nor should they – the conventional roles allotted to a board of directors in a company. But, as the following article graphically illustrates, managers and committee members invariably hold widely divergent views on what the management committee's role should be and how it ought to be implemented. In many respects, the voluntary management body – whether it is a board of trustees, national council, finance and general purposes committee or whatever – is the organizational joker in the pack. Its various formal and informal statuses and functions complicate arguments about policy, strategy and accountability; it is a common focus for endless wrangles and uncertainties over questions of power and authority in the organization. Moreover it can be a marvellous device for the interminable passing of managerial bucks – 'I shall have to take that to the management committee', says the director; 'We shall have to defer a decision, pending a full report from the chief executive' replies the management committee; 'What are we supposed to do?' say the staff and volunteers; 'Who's in charge of this organization?' says everyone.

This article suggests that these tensions and conflicts should not be seen as extraneous to the main structuring and management of voluntary and non-profit organizations. A single, all-purpose formula for resolving 'the problem' of voluntary management committees might be something of a chimera. What is called for is a framework which will enable different organizations to come to their own conclusions about the best way of defining and implementing the ever-ambiguous role of the voluntary management committee.

■ Introduction

Even the smallest and most informal of voluntary agencies usually has some kind of written guideline about the role of its governing body or *management committee*[1]. Yet, in practice, formal statements of functions and responsibilities do not seem to be sufficient. The *implementation* of the voluntary management committee role can be fraught with difficulties.

In the course of research done at the Centre for Voluntary Organization, professional and paid staff have described management committee members as 'grossly over-committed' or as 'interfering' so directly in day-to-day matters that they were prevented from using their specialist skills and 'getting on with the job'. Professional staff also complain of having 'no support' from their management committees or of committee members who 'won't take responsibility' and who 'have no understanding of what is involved in running the agency'. In extreme cases, I have been told of management committees which are so 'detached' from the work of their agencies and so 'uncommitted' that, if the paid staff were to leave, 'the organization would just die'.

Members of management committees may find their role problematic too. Some describe themselves as 'pushed out' by the specialist competence and professional knowledge of staff and powerless to make any contribution to policy, decision-making or services. Others sense that paid workers regard the management committee as a structure which has been 'imposed' on them or that staff would prefer them to confine their activities to 'background support and encouragement'. Yet other committee members worry because they do not have sufficient free time to do operational work for their agencies.

Management committees operating at the local level of a national or regional agency may be frustrated by the 'controls' placed on their activities and decision-making. They are told they are 'autonomous' but find that, in practice, they can only make decisions within the confines of policies set by 'headquarters'. They may be anxious about projects, standards and regulations 'parachuted' on to local management committees by the national organization.

In contrast with management committee members who feel they should be doing more, some adopt a minimalist approach to their responsibilities. They are angered, for example, by suggestions from their staff that there might be more to their role than occasional attendance at committee meetings and social gatherings.

In addition to these expressions of problems by individual members of committees and staff, there are numerous examples of generalized ill-feeling between management committees and staff. Often these reflect uncertainties about 'who appoints whom', 'who controls whom' and 'who does what'.

Research at the Centre for Voluntary Organization reflects the findings of other writers. The Handy Committee Report (1981), for example, pointed to difficulties in defining the roles of chief officers and management committees. And a Gallup survey of directors of charities (Gerard, 1983) found 'an interacting set of component problems' expressed about 'the structure, role and effectiveness of management committees' and about 'the consequent implications for management and staff structure, style and responsibilities'. Platt and his colleagues (1985), who studied the role of voluntary committees of housing associations, found they were frequently 'a charade' – only 'talking shops' which did not 'exercise any control'.

Why is it that, however clear the formal statements of an agency, issues and problems arise around *implementing* the management committee role? The search for answers to this question, and solutions to the problems, is an important task for the voluntary sector. In law a voluntary agency *is* its governing body. A management committee represents those who want to further the special objectives of a voluntary agency and it is accountable for everything done in the agency's name. The very survival of voluntary agencies depends on the work done by governing bodies.

In this article I will examine the work of local voluntary committees and suggest some organizational explanations for the problems that arise. I will draw primarily on my own research (Harris, 1985, 1987, 1989), supplemented by data from other studies in the United Kingdom. Material derived from North America will also be cited where appropriate. First, I will outline the findings of a case study of local management committees in one national voluntary agency – the National Association of Citizens' Advice Bureaux (NACAB)[2]. This material throws light on how management committees work and how members of committees perceive their role and their relationships with agency staff.

■ Case study – National Association of Citizens' Advice Bureaux

□ Functions allocated to management committees

Local Citizens' Advice Bureaux (CAB) rely primarily on local sources of funding and are constitutionally autonomous. However, membership of the National Association (NACAB), which entitles CAB to support services and to use the CAB name, requires local bureaux to conform with several rules which are intended to maintain consistency in the quality of advice services throughout the country.

At the time of the study, official statements circulating within the CAB service allocated the following functions to management committees of local CAB.

- Securing resources – applying for grants, administering them so as to ensure accountability and securing premises and equipment.
- Legal responsibilities – as charity trustees and as employers.
- Representation – bringing in knowledge from the local community and representing the interests of CAB to the community.
- Policy-making – on local issues and as a part of the national organizational structure in which local management committees elect regional bodies which in turn elect national ones.

- Monitoring – ensuring that the quality of service met requirements for membership of NACAB.
- Staffing – selecting and appointing staff (paid and voluntary) and general responsibility for bureau staff.

Bureau managers,[3] management committee members, volunteer advice workers and NACAB staff were interviewed. This revealed that formal statements provided only a partial picture of the management committee role in the CAB service. In practice, there was a range of perceptions not only about what management committees were doing but also about what they should be doing.

□ Employment and staffing functions

Although management committees were the legal employers of the paid bureau staff, they were regarded by staff interviewees as 'casual' in their attitude to such matters as conditions of service, pay increments and written contracts of employment. The regional and national staff interviewed felt that the employer role of management committees was 'very inadequately' executed and that this was 'their most obvious failing'. Management committees were seen as lacking the personnel expertise and the understanding of CAB work necessary to make decisions on selection of staff and to evaluate staff performance.

Interviews with managers and management committee members confirmed that staffing matters were the *de facto* responsibility of bureau managers, management committee involvement in selection, assessment, development and training being no more than a formality. Thus, in one bureau which was faced with possible closure through lack of local authority funding, paid staff were left 'in a rather difficult situation of having nobody to negotiate with' about their future employment.

It was not clear whether managers carried out staffing functions because their management committees could not or would not do so or, as one interviewee suggested, because managers took on the responsibility and management committees then 'deferred' to them. Whatever the reason, it seemed that a self-reinforcing pattern was established in which management committees did not develop skills or experience in personnel matters because managers did the job for them. Managers, in turn, did not want to entrust delicate staffing matters to management committees which were inexperienced in personnel work.

Management committees seemed to be detached from staffing matters in part because of the high value they placed on voluntarism. The corollary was reluctance to acknowledge the existence of employer/employee relationships, even in those cases where bureau staff were in fact being paid. For example, the chairperson of a bureau which had several volunteer workers and a paid manager and deputy manager said he 'did not see the management committee as employers'. This was not an abdication of responsibility so much as a reflection of his view that the two paid staff were 'honorary volunteers'; they were to be treated on 'a friendly basis' and given the 'gratitude' due to volunteers.

Despite their distance from employment and staffing work, management committee members took their legal obligations as employers very seriously. It seemed that they needed to have the formal status of 'employer', in order to feel that they had a worthwhile job, but that they mostly expected the staff to do any practical tasks involved in implementing employer functions.

☐   **Policy-making and planning**

In addition to their involvement in national policy-making through elections to regional and national committees, management committees were officially expected to set policy at the bureau level. They were also supposed to be well-grounded in the principles and aims of the CAB service so that they could offer 'informed support' to bureau staff. In practice, as with staffing and employment functions, bureau staff did the majority of policy-making and priority-setting tasks.

Indeed, committee members did not usually view policy-making as something that they *should* be involved in, even in a nominal way. One chairperson, for example, thought that a management committee could never develop the expertise 'to make decisions on priorities'. Other committee interviewees thought that policy was 'a job for NACAB' (the national headquarters). They had an impression of 'tight control' from 'a central machine', management committees having 'more mundane functions'. One committee member said, 'policy is determined by NACAB'. Another thought that it was not even necessary for management committees to understand the policy laid down by NACAB, this being the function of the bureau manager.

This approach may be ascribed to realism. Management committee interviewees felt that, as volunteers themselves, they did not have the necessary time to consider broad issues. They thought the bureau staff had the time, the expertise and the understanding of the national structure; they should therefore take the initiative in matters such as commenting on national CAB circulars, establishing priorities and suggesting new areas of work.

There were indications, however, that the attitude of committees towards policy-making was a reflection of the same circular pattern noted above for the employer role of committees. The managers interviewed often felt that management committees were unable or unwilling to understand what general advice work entails or the local implications of national policy. They therefore tended to take a dominant role themselves in policy and planning decisions, leaving management committees in ignorance of bureau work. However effective this approach may have been in terms of 'getting things done', it seemed to reinforce the committee members' views that the staff and NACAB were getting on with the job of policy-making and that they did not need to involve themselves.

☐ **Obtaining resources**

None of the management committee interviewees saw dealing with finance and funding as any more than a formality for committee members. The honorary treasurer, a post which officially carries prime responsibility for a bureau's financial affairs, was described by bureau staff as a 'front man' and a 'figure-head'. Grant applications were, in practice, prepared by managers. Long-term budgetary planning and negotiation with funders was done, if at all, by managers and NACAB staff.

Two bureaux had recently been threatened with closure because of lack of resources. The financial crises had encouraged the respective management committees to become more concerned about the fate of their bureaux. Nevertheless, the bulk of the lobbying had been prepared and done by bureau and regional staff, albeit 'in the name of the management committee'. For the staff interviewed, the value of the management committees during the crises had been in how they had provided a 'buffer' between bureau staff and elected members of local authorities, averting direct confrontations between funders and service providers.

Several reasons for the lack of committee involvement in fund-raising emerged from the interviews, including unwillingness to 'get involved with local politics' and lack of understanding about the precarious nature of voluntary-sector funding. It was also suggested that managers sometimes 'withheld' from committees the information they would need to play a full role in resource acquisition.

But the explanation favoured by most staff interviewees was that management committee members did not really 'identify' with the fate of bureaux. They saw themselves more as 'observers' of CAB than as 'members' or 'owners'. Staff commented that committee members 'tend not to feel that they are CAB people' and that 'the osmosis from being a representative of an organization to becoming a CAB person just never happens'.

☐ **Monitoring**

The management committee interviewees were generally appreciative and admiring of the work done by bureau staff. References were repeatedly made to their 'professionalism' and 'commitment'. Interviewees described their 'absolute faith' in their managers, which meant that they only had to concern themselves with 'very mundane' decisions. Some committee members seemed to be overawed by the competence of paid and volunteer staff and were surprised by questions about monitoring or evaluating the quality of the service provided. None of the management committee interviewees saw a role for themselves in monitoring, except perhaps in 'keeping an eye' on the bureau manager.

Committee members' unconditional confidence in the ability of staff to provide an acceptable standard of service was confirmed by the staff. They thought that management committees appreciated that 'the buck stops with them' but that they also had 'complete confidence that it will all be all right.' One manager was resentful about this. She described herself as 'dumped on' by her management committee members; they regarded her as a 'friendly minion'.

What was the basis for the management committees' confidence in bureau staff? It seemed that committee members were largely ignorant of the difficult problems that can and do arise in general advice work and in responding to local needs. This, in turn, was because bureau staff tended to deal with them within the bureau, or by consulting national or regional staff, rather than by involving their committee members.

The question remains whether managers were deliberately 'withholding information', as one NACAB officer suggested, 'to keep the management committee out of the day-to-day running of the bureau' or whether, as other interviewees suggested, they were reluctant, as with staffing matters and policy-making, to entrust sensitive and complex issues to inexperienced and busy people. In either case, the effect on management committees was to reinforce their remoteness from the reality of CAB work and to encourage their idealized view of the bureau staff's abilities.

☐ Supporting the staff

Although the staff interviewed felt that management committees were remote from the work and purposes of the bureaux and that they did not fulfil many of the functions formally allocated to them, their general attitude towards their committees was one of appreciation and tolerance. In several interviews, management committee members were described as 'supportive' and 'caring' – a reference to their sympathy for the stresses experienced by staff in their work and the tendency to agree to staff initiatives and suggestions.

Generally, both management committees and local bureau staff were content with the existing relationships and balance of power. Regional and national staff, however, were concerned. One of them found it unacceptable that committees were rendered 'ineffective' by managers 'deliberately restricting communication'. Another talked of the implications for the regional and national governing structures of 'impotent' local management committees; because lower levels provided the membership of higher level committees, the effect was 'to allow staff views to dominate all the way through the organization'.

■ Discussion: themes and explanations

So far I have suggested that the implementation of the management committee role can be problematic. And I have described a case study which illustrates the range of opinions about the work of local management committees which can exist within one national voluntary agency. In this section, I will distinguish the themes that emerge from the case study. I will also look beyond the CAB example, indicating how the findings link with other research studies and how they help to explain problems of role implementation described at the start of this article.

☐ Different perceptions of the management committee role

The CAB case study indicates a gap between official agency statements about management committee functions on the one hand and the perceptions and working assumptions formulated by committee members and staff on the other hand. Thus, although management committees were officially supposed to 'apply for grants' for their bureaux, in practice neither staff nor committee members really expected committees to be involved in the grant application process, except in a nominal way.

This kind of gap between prescription and practice, or 'manifest' and 'assumed' statements, is not unusual within organizations (Rowbottom, 1977). Its existence has been noted by commentators on the North American voluntary sector (Fink, 1989; Kramer, 1985) and it suggests a possible explanation for the expressions of confusion and frustration described at the start of this article. Some people might base their expectations of management committee performance on a literal interpretation of official statements, expecting committee members who are officially 'financially responsible', for example, to be actively involved in fund-raising or assuming that, as 'legal employers', management committees will behave like bosses in business. At the same time, however, others within the agency might have quite different expectations of management committee work, perhaps unaware that their own assumptions are not universally shared.

The CAB case study further suggests that a gap can exist not only between official statements and working assumptions, but also between both of these on the one hand and normative statements on the other hand; what is considered appropriate, desirable or 'requisite' (Rowbottom, 1977). For example, CAB national and regional staff felt that management committees should be involved, literally, in the management of staff, although this reflected neither official statements nor working practice. And management committee members thought that it should be part of their role to give emotional support to bureau staff and participate in operational work, although these functions were not prescribed for them officially.

The discovery of such gaps between formal statements, working assumptions and perceptions of what is requisite suggests a possible explanation for problems that arise in voluntary agencies about the management committee role, especially conflicts about the duties of committee members and staff. Many voluntary agencies place a high value on flexibility, innovation, personal commitment and informality (Brenton, 1985; Kramer, 1981). In keeping with these values, their formal statements about roles leave space for a range of interpretations. However, as the case study indicates, that space can also result in a range of different expectations of a role being held within the same agency. The different expectations can surface as misunderstandings, conflicts and 'personality clashes', unless the diversity of perceptions can be brought in to open discussion (Harris, 1985: Holloway and Otto, 1985).

□ **Role interdependence**

The CAB example illustrates how management committees may approach different functional areas of their role, such as staffing, fund-raising and policy-making. It appeared that how committees carried out functions and the degree to which they did them at all were often a reflection of the expectations and assumptions of staff. Conversely, staff expectations seemed to be heavily influenced by past experiences with, and assumptions about, the abilities and preferences of their management committees.

This finding is in line with both British and North American writers who have drawn attention to how the implementation of governing body and staff roles are linked in voluntary agencies. For example, Furedi (1979) describes the relationship between staff and management committees as 'a delicate balance of support and control, consultation and decision-making'. And Conrad and Glenn (1983) write of a 'dynamic tension' between boards and staff that 'rests on mutual trust and need'. Herman and Tulipana (1985), drawing on a study of seven local nonprofit organizations in the United States, suggest that such agencies are subject to 'dominant coalitions' comprising both staff and board members.

Building on this literature and the CAB case study, a second explanation for the problems surrounding management committees emerges. Many of the expressions of discontent and confusion appeared to come from an assumption that the management committee role is *sui generis*, that is, susceptible to analysis or implementation in isolation from other organizational roles. However, we can now surmise that, with the exception of legal obligations (Edgington and Bates, 1984; McLaughlin, 1986), the management committee role in local voluntary agencies is more appropriately conceptualized as *interlinked and interdependent* (Kramer, 1985; Middleton, 1987) with other organizational roles. Moreover, the case study suggests that the degree of interdependence varies according to the organizational function under consideration.

This concept of the special, interdependent character of the governing body role in the voluntary sector has implications not only for management committee members but also for voluntary agency staff and for trainers who help committees to put their role into operation. The approaches that are likely to prove most useful are those that do not treat staff and management committee roles in isolation but rather that proceed from the perspective of the voluntary agency as an operational whole; a totality of the tasks and functions performed by the various groups that together constitute the organization. The management committee role can then be considered *in relation to* other roles. Analysis can be directed towards understanding how tasks and functions are *shared* between paid staff, volunteers, local management committees and regional and national bodies (Harris, 1985; Leduc and Block, 1985).

☐   **Cycles of expectations**

If the role of management committees in local voluntary agencies is conceptualized as interdependent with those of staff, the most significant of those roles with which the management committee is interlinked is the senior member of the paid staff[3]. In the CAB case study, the key position of bureau managers was mentioned by most interviewees. Managers themselves were well aware of their powerful position, especially as the management committee's main source of information. They recognized that '... information is power. If you withhold information, you withhold power' (Holloway and Otto, 1985).

In fact, the CAB case study illustrates the complex process by which managers can use their pivotal position within the communication system of a voluntary agency, deliberately or unintentionally, to obtain and maintain control. A self-fulfilling cycle of expectations can develop, as illustrated in Figure 12.1

Starting at position (A), managers may not 'share' professional and administrative information, decisions and problems with their management committees. This might be because they want to retain power for themselves or because of a genuine desire to shield busy people from unnecessary work. Or it may be based on their own perceptions of 'manifest' and 'requisite' roles of managers and management committees as described earlier.

Whatever the motivation of managers, the effect is that management committees feel distant from the practicalities of running the agency and from its guiding purposes (B). Nor do they gain experience in handling major problems and decisions. Their remoteness (evidenced, for example, by their asking 'naïve' questions at committee meetings or their failure to make any contribution at all)

Figure 12.1 Cycles of expectations.

reinforces managers' opinion that management committees do not understand the purposes of the agency and cannot be entrusted with important issues and decisions (A).

This self-reinforcing cycle of expectations may sit within a larger cycle. Because the nature of the agency's work and the practical problems of managing it are not understood by the management committees (B), they tend to be in awe of staff professionalism and competence (C). The possibility of challenging the staff or evaluating the service they provide is not seriously considered (D). This, in turn, means that managers have no incentive, and are not obliged, to share information and problems with their committees (A). The circle is closed.

In the CAB case study, this model could be considered an organizational 'success', insofar as open conflict was avoided and both management committees and staff expressed satisfaction with their existing relationships. They had established '. . . a shared set of role expectations with which they [were] relatively comfortable' (McLaughlin, 1986). This was despite them both being aware that management committees were not performing many of the functions allocated to them in formal statements. As in an earlier study of local Councils of Voluntary Service by Leat and her colleagues (1981), there appeared to be 'an informal, customary understanding' between staff and management committees that '. . . the latter [would] not assume the powers of direction implied in their title'.

In collaborative research projects with voluntary agencies we have found that, although the details of the dynamic process may vary, the cycle of expectations is a pattern widely recognized by both committee members and staff. Acknowledgement of its existence in agencies has provided a useful starting point for problem-solving discussions. Using the descriptive model as a basis, questions can be raised, for example, about how the cycles are established, how they are sustained, the extent to which they are requisite or should be broken, and the accountability implications.

☐ **Agency culture and organizational structure**

So far in this section, I have suggested three broad organizational explanations for the practical problems surrounding the management committee role – varied perceptions of what the role entails; the interdependent nature of the role; and self-fulfilling cycles of expectations between management committees and staff. The CAB case study suggests a further explanation – that the distinctive cultural and organizational features of local voluntary agencies are particularly conducive to the development of confusion and conflicting expectations about the role of management committees.

For example, an ethic of voluntarism may prevail in local voluntary agencies which induces a high degree of trust in staff, irrespective of whether or not they are in fact volunteers. Committee members may feel that controlling or monitoring staff would be inappropriate – unwarranted 'interference' or a mark of 'ingratitude' rather than a legitimate activity of an employer. Conversely, the ethic of voluntarism may influence staff views about what it is appropriate to ask of management committee members. They may be unwilling to 'bother' committee members who work in a voluntary capacity.

The reluctance of management committee members to confront or control staff may reflect another aspect of agency culture – a tendency to draw behaviour guidelines from the world of informal relationships rather than from the formal world of bureaucratic organizations that employ staff. As Billis (1989) has argued, voluntary agencies may be poised in an 'ambiguous zone' between the worlds, in which the 'rules of the game' of both worlds apply. The reluctance observed in local CAB to accept the organizational implications of employing and managing staff, with an emphasis instead on 'smooth personal relationships', is consistent with this conceptualization.

The case study suggests that not only organizational culture but also aspects of an agency's *organizational structure* may be conducive to the development of implementation problems. For example, the remoteness of management committees from the work of local CAB seemed to be facilitated by the existence of active national and regional offices and committees. Local management committees were aware that bureau staff had, and frequently used, this alternative source of support and advice. There was an obvious 'safety net' if they themselves failed.

The practice of appointing representatives of other local agencies to management committees could be another organizational factor contributing to their 'remoteness'. From the local agency's viewpoint, the purpose of the arrangement, which is frequently prescribed in its constitution (Harris, 1989; Mellor, 1985), is to cement useful local contacts and to ensure liaison with community groups and those working in related fields. The representative members themselves are expected to keep the agency informed about the local community and to keep the local community informed about the agency.

In practice, representatives may find their 'community link' function difficult to combine with a close identification with the interests of the agency. Thus, Leat and her colleagues in their study of Councils of Voluntary Service (1981) found that '. . . many committee members interviewed evidently interpreted their role on the executive as primarily to serve the organizations from which they were elected by keeping them informed of CVS activities.' Similarly, McLaughlin (1986) argues that a high proportion of representatives can seriously hamper strategic planning by governing bodies because representatives are likely to experience conflict between that function and their own interests. So it seems that a constitutional provision which is intended to improve 'community representativeness' of management committees may have an unintended, organizational consequence – management committee members whose prime loyalty lies elsewhere.

Another potential source of difficulties for management committees is the key 'gatekeeper' position of managers or 'directors' within the organizational structure. McLaughlin (1986) describes the distinctive 'hourglass configuration' of many voluntary organizations in which there is a 'bottle-neck' between the executive director and the executive committee. In a similar vein, Kramer (1985) notes how directors 'because of their location in the communications structure of the agency, have access to and control over information which can then be shared selectively with board members and staff.'

This pivotal position of managers can have important organizational consequences as shown in Figure 12.1. If a management committee, for whatever reason, does not assert itself, it is then not difficult for the senior staff officer to perpetuate that situation and 'dominate' the committee indefinitely (Gouldner, 1969). Without information and experience, management committee members can be indefinitely locked in to a self-perpetuating cycle of powerlessness. They may be resentful and uneasy but quite unable to initiate any change; unless they are willing to risk full confrontation with staff. But, as I suggested above, there may be other cultural factors which make 'keeping the peace' the preferred choice.

■ Conclusion

Building on a case study and other research literature, I have suggested some explanations for the difficulties encountered in implementing the role of voluntary management committees. I have pointed out the wide range of perceptions within agencies about management committee work; the interdependent nature of the management committee role; the self-reinforcing cycles established between management committees and managers; the culture of voluntary agencies and their distinctive organizational features.

These explanations have been tested in the UK voluntary sector and they appear to provide useful 'tools' for practitioners who want to start tackling practical problems. But many questions remain for further study and analysis. To what extent, for example, do the explanations outlined in this article apply to governing bodies which operate at the regional and national level of voluntary agencies? What are the implications for the implementation of the management committee role of permitting paid and voluntary staff to be active participants in committee meetings? And what is the impact on management committees of the expectations of statutory authorities and other actors in their environment?

Although there is still much to be learned, work to date has already provided an important lesson. Despite the impression given by some constitutions and handbooks, the role of local management committees in the voluntary sector is not amenable to definitive prescriptions or rules. In the real world of voluntary agencies the governing body role is open to a range of interpretations. The search for clear and permanent boundaries to the role may be a chimera.

Notes

(1) I am using the term 'management committee' to refer to the governing bodies of local voluntary agencies. Other terms in common use include 'council', 'executive committee' and 'board'.

(2) The material does not necessarily reflect the current situation in the CAB service. Since the study was done, the service has been subject to a review of its organizational structure and new regulations have been introduced which are intended to strengthen the involvement of local management committees in several spheres. A national working party has also been set up to examine the role of management committees.

(3) The senior paid member of staff in a local CAB is called 'the manager'. The equivalent post in other voluntary agencies may be referred to as 'the director', 'the co-ordinator' or 'the chief executive'.

References

Billis, D. (1989) *A Theory of the Voluntary Sector: Implications for Policy and Practice.* Working Paper 5. London: Centre for Voluntary Organization, LSE.

Brenton, M. (1985) *The Voluntary Sector in British Social Services.* London: Longman.

Conrad, W. and Glenn, W. (1983) *The Effective Voluntary Board of Directors.* Ohio: Swallow Press.

Edgington, J. and Bates, S. (1984) *Legal Structures for Voluntary Organisations.* London: Bedford Square Press.

Fink, J. (1989) 'Community agency boards of directors: viability and vestigiality, substance and symbol', in Herman, R. and Van Til, J. (eds) *Nonprofit Boards of Directors: Analyses and Applications,* pp. 89–117. New Jersey: Transaction.

Gouldner, A. (1969) 'The secrets of organizations', in Kramer, R. and Specht, H. (eds) *Readings in Community Organization Practice.* Englewood Cliffs, NJ: Prentice Hall.

Furedi, V. (1979) *Working with Your Management Committee.* Leicester: National Youth Bureau.

Gerard, D. (1983) *Charities in Britain: Conservatism or Change?* London: Bedford Square Press.

Handy, C. (1981) *Improving Effectiveness in Voluntary Organisations.* London: Bedford Square Press.

Harris, M. (1985) 'Let's try another route', *MDU Bulletin,* 5, pp. 15–16.

Harris, M. (1987) *Management Committees: Roles and Tasks.* Working Paper 4. London: Centre for Voluntary Organization, LSE.

Harris, M. (1989) *Management Committees in Practice: A Study in Local Voluntary Leadership.* Working Paper 7. London: Centre for Voluntary Organization, LSE.

Herman, R. and Tulipana, P. (1985) 'Board–staff relations and perceived effectiveness in nonprofit organizations'. *Journal of Voluntary Action Research* 14, 4, pp. 48–59.

Holloway, C. and Otto, S. (1985) *Getting Organized: A Handbook for Non-Statutory Organizations*. London: Bedford Square Press.

Kramer, R. (1981) *Voluntary Agencies in the Welfare State*. California: University of California Press.

Kramer, R. (1985) 'Towards a contingency model of board–executive relations in nonprofit organizations', *Administration in Social Work* 9, 3, pp. 15–33.

Leat, D., Smolka, G. and Unell, J. (1981) *Voluntary and Statutory Collaboration: Rhetoric or Reality*. London: Bedford Square Press.

Leduc, R. and Block, S. (1985) 'Conjoint directorship: clarifying management roles between the board of directors and executive director', *Journal of Voluntary Action Research* 14, 4, pp. 67–76.

McLaughlin, C. (1986) *The Management of Nonprofit Organizations*. New York: Wiley.

Mellor, H. (1985) *The Role of Voluntary Organizations in Social Welfare*. London: Croom Helm.

Middleton, M. (1987) 'Nonprofit boards of directors: beyond the governance function', in Powell, W. (ed.) *The Nonprofit Sector: A Research Handbook*. New Haven: Yale University Press.

Platt, S., Powell, J., Piepe, R., Paterson, B. and Smyth, J. (1985) *Control or Charade*. Portsmouth: Portsmouth Polytechnic.

Rowbottom, R. (1977) *Social Analysis*. London: Heinemann.

13

Organizational Structures in the Voluntary Sector:
A Theoretical Overview[1]

David C. Wilson

Those responsible for voluntary and non-profit enterprises often have conflicting reactions to the notion of organizational structure. On the one hand, there is an urgent need to do something about the fact that things never seem to settle down; to get some resolution of the constant round of internal meetings, working groups and departmental reorganizations, all of which aim, once and for all, to make the organization more effective as a whole and improve internal and external communications. On the other hand, there is a deep-seated unease about becoming too bureaucratic, about locking the organization into a wholly inappropriate shape which will stifle the very flexibility and sensitivity to which it aspires. Structure is seen to imply hierarchy and rigidity – values which run contrary to those on which most voluntary and non-profit organizations base their self-image and their practice.

David Wilson has extensively researched the structure of many of the larger and more complex voluntary organizations. The following article is a brief summary of his findings to date. He is not concerned to identify an ideal framework which voluntary organizations ought to adopt in order to achieve the most coherent and effective ways of ordering their complex affairs. His overall argument is that an approach to structure based on the ideas of the contingency school of organizational analysis will enable managers to avoid the twin dangers of 'the tyranny of structurelessness' and the 'sclerosis of bureaucracy'. One can, nevertheless, identify such key determinants of structure in voluntary organizations as size, technology, operating environment, culture and history and strategy. Moreover, one can also point to several sorts of structure commonly encountered amongst large organizations. Wilson has dubbed these the *functional-bureaucratic*, the *divisional*, the *federal* and the *matrix* or *project-based*. It will be interesting for readers to explore the applicability of Wilson's approach to structure – which derives primarily from work on national, service-providing charities – to voluntary and non-profit organizations in the non-charitable arena and in more localized advocacy and campaigning contexts.

■ Organizational structure: differentiation and integration

Probably the most immediate and accessible way to describe an organization is to outline its structure. Knowledge of its structure is indispensable as a first step to understanding the processes which occur within it. When asked to describe their organization, individuals will frequently sketch out an organization chart to show how their organization 'works'.

The organization chart gives some tangible evidence of who reports to whom, how many levels of hierarchy there are and how the whole organization is assembled together. It shows the formal authority and communications structure of the organization. It says little, of course, about the informal processes which occur within an organization. Nevertheless, an understanding of organizational structure is fundamental, for structure can influence several key areas.

The essential problem of organizational structure is that, if it is not sensible for everyone to be involved in everything, how is the work to be divided up? How will the various activities be kept in step with one another? Activity groupings can be created along many different lines such as geographic area, type of client, professional skills, administrative function, a self-contained project or piece of work, and so on. However, each grouping will develop its own 'local' perspective concerning what it feels the organization should be doing. This means that maintaining coherence between the different parts of an organization – between head office and branches, between fund-raisers and service-providers, between experimental projects and core activities – can be difficult and time-consuming. The local perspective which develops from working in different parts of the organization also forms a strong part of the organization's political system and it takes more than appeals for 'good communication' to avoid conflict, inconsistencies, oversights or duplication of effort. Organizational mechanisms, such as role descriptions, procedures, policy statements and systems, need to be developed.

The question of organizational structure therefore revolves around choosing appropriate forms of *differentiation* and *integration*.[2] Appropriate structures will depend on a range of contingent circumstances, such as the size of the organization, the technology it uses and whether it is in a stable or an unpredictable environment. In other words, because these *contingencies* impact on the patterns of communication, the need for specialist skills, the vulnerability of the organization and so on, they affect the advantages and disadvantages associated with different structures (forms of differentiation and integration). These contingencies are considered in more detail next.

■ Contingencies affecting the structures of voluntary and non-profit organizations

☐ Size

Whilst voluntary organizations remain small, there is little need for extensive differentiation and little consequent need for complex or sophisticated integration devices. As organizations grow, the need to differentiate and to set up integration procedures becomes a greater priority. The organization is no longer under the control of one person or group. Also the number of functional areas requiring specialist attention may have expanded (for example, fund-raising, maintaining contact with field personnel, communicating with trustees, etc.).

☐ Technology

The kind of technology (or technologies) used by an organization will also affect the possibilities for integration and differentiation (Woodward, 1965; Perrow, 1967). In larger charities, such as Oxfam or RNLI, integration by computer networks has become relatively commonplace. The number of different units which go into providing sea rescue or third-world overseas aid may be very large indeed, resulting in the need for a relatively high degree of horizontal differentiation. To change levels of both integration and differentiation would bring with it implications for the technology of service delivery.

☐ Operating environment

The nature of the operating environment will also have a contingent effect on the extent of differentiation and integration. In general, the greater the complexity of the operating environment of the voluntary organization, the greater the need for a highly differentiated organizational structure. Where an organization faces many different demands from its immediate environment, it is appropriate to adopt a differentiated structure with specialist sub-units to cope with those demands.

Simple environments (where the tasks are relatively well specified and do not require many specialisms to work together) demand a less differentiated structure. Differences in the level of predictability in operations will also demand different structural designs. Where the operating environment is certain (changes are relatively predictable), a bureaucratic structure is most appropriate. In uncertain and unpredictable environments, a more decentralized, 'organic', 'adhocratic' structure is required.[3]

The Citizens' Advice Bureaux (CAB) is a good example of an organization which is being pressured by increasing complexity in its operating environment to introduce more specialisms in its structure. The previously general information and advisory services which CAB provides now require increasing use of specialists in areas such as debt counselling, welfare regulations and legal advice. Operating contingencies are demanding the adoption of a more differentiated structure.

☐ Age and history of the voluntary organization

Organizational structure is also related to where the organization is in its 'life cycle' (Kimberley and Miles, 1980). Like individuals, organizations are born, mature and die. At the foundation stage, organizational structure is likely to reflect the preferences of the founders. The organization is their complete focus of attention; they do most jobs and set the climate and the culture (Wilson and Rosenfeld, 1990, pp. 319–320). During maturity, the organization needs strategic and managerial direction and it is now that the structure begins to take shape as functions, departments and tasks are defined. There is also a need for control to be built in to the structure. There is an obvious correlation with size in the life cycle perspective because most organizations also grow as they age.

☐ Strategy

Ever since Chandler's (1963) contention that strategy and structure were related, researchers have been at pains to modify, qualify and generally extend this large field of enquiry (see, for example, Channon, 1973). Despite their different approaches and their analytical perspectives, all generally agree that, given a strategy of growth, the structural form of an organization will in due course match the strategy it is pursuing. For example, many organizations in the third-world overseas-aid sector which have grown rapidly over the last few years fit the pattern of becoming divisional structures (one corporate headquarters and multiple divisions operating in different locations and often providing different services).

☐ Dependence

An organization's dependence on other organizations for funding and for continued survival also has an impact on its structure (Pugh *et al.*, 1969). The more an organization depends on a single other organization, the more likely it is to have a structure that ensures centralized decision-making. For example, those voluntary organizations which grew rapidly on the basis of the Manpower Services Commission (MSC) Community Programme became highly dependent on the MSC. In the process, their structures were completely transformed from relative adhocracies towards centralized bureaucracies, largely because of the imbalance in power relationships between the MSC and the contracting organizations (Addy and Scott, 1988).

■ Structure in voluntary organizations

□ **The current state of knowledge**

There has been very little systematic study of organizational structure in the British voluntary sector.[4] In North America, there are more studies although care should be taken in making direct comparisons between North American non-profit organizations and British voluntary organizations. Tsouderos (1955) and Chapin and Tsouderos (1956) examined the levels of formalization and bureaucratization in 10 North American voluntary organizations. Using time-series analysis, they argued that there appeared to be a tendency for newly established and initially informally structured voluntary organizations to progress towards the institutionalization of their structures to become formal bureaucracies. Other authors have also alluded to this bureaucratization process (Moyer, 1983; Scott, 1981; Brooke, 1984).

Yet if formalization *is* a 'natural' progression for charities as they develop, there are some fundamental implications for their management. We know, for example, that bureaucratic organizations are slow to adapt to change, rarely innovate, are inflexible and often display several other inbuilt dysfunctions. They can also promote the creation of the 'bureaucratic personality' in all levels of staff (Merton, 1940; Allinson, 1990). Largely through the process of (over) socialization, individuals in bureaucratic structures develop repertoires of responses to varying situations. These responses become valued by both the individual and the organization as being effective and efficient. The bureaucratic personality, however, applies such repertoires to all future situations, regardless of whether they represent substantial change from current practice. As Merton (1940) notes:

'. . . actions based upon training and skills which have been successfully applied in the past may result in inappropriate responses under changed conditions.'

If charities develop this institutional hardening of their arteries, they are likely to lose much of their operating flexibility and strategic adaptability, two of their most prized and arguably distinguishing features. In a study of International Advocacy Associations, Young (1990) argues that continued success and strategic flexibility stem from the adoption of a decentralized structure. This concurs with the findings of Gerlach and Hine (1970), who studied the Black Power movement and the Pentecostal movement. However, they also found that organizational growth and longevity put enormous pressures on managers to centralize and to bureaucratize their organizational structures.

The question of appropriate structures for organizations in the multi-million pound industries of the voluntary sector is, therefore, fundamental. The success of some organizations and the demise of others may be due to the structure they adopt. In Chandler's (1963) terms, those organizations which have appropriately matched strategy and structure are likely to grow, thrive and survive.

Peters and Waterman (1982) and Kanter (1983) argue that 'excellence' in organizational performance is at least partially achieved through adopting particular structures. They give evidence that some of the most successful firms in North America share a structure which allows both flexibility and autonomy to managers and employees but which is also well defined enough to ensure efficient delimitation of rules and administrative procedures. Such organizations are a combination of both 'loose' and 'tight' structures. They have the flexibility of decentralization and the control and discipline of centralization.

Research in Britain indicates that voluntary organizations are rarely characterized by the above structure (Brooke, 1984; Saxon-Harrold, 1986; Butler and Wilson, 1990). Data indicate that there are four dominant structures adopted by the majority of voluntary organizations. Each structure may of course have its 'local' variations. The four dominant structures are *functional, divisional, federal* and *matrix* or *project-based*.

■ Functional structures

In a purely *functional structure* tasks are differentiated into separate departments or sections on the basis of the function performed. These are arranged in some sort of hierarchy with information and communication flowing from the various sub-units to the managerial and executive apex. It is a bureaucracy in the strict rather than the colloquial sense of the term. Organizations such as the Royal Commonwealth Society for the Blind (RCSB) and the Royal National Lifeboat Institution (RNLI) are examples of this type of structure (see Figures 13.1 and 13.2).

Functional structure can also be reflected as a hierarchy of committees often superimposed on the functional sub-divisions. Figure 13.3 overleaf shows a simplified committee structure for the RNLI which neatly corresponds to the subdivisions shown in Figure 13.2.

Both these organizations have a long history. The RCSB and the RNLI have been established for over 40 years and 166 years respectively. The reasons for adopting a functional structure is not solely a reflection of the heavy hand of history. In the RCSB a decision was made, after the appointment of a new Director, to:

> '. . . develop a more precise and formalized structure. Specific posts added have been for fund-raising, to develop administrative procedures, public relations and advertising. Formal procedures recently adopted have been a written policy description and written research reports. Centralization has also been increased.' (*Butler and Wilson, 1990, p. 88*)

The functional structure is the result of a formal managerial decision – an example of the exercise of 'strategic choice' (Child, 1972). Like the RCSB, the RNLI is a large organization (employing about 630 full-time staff). The effects of organizational size on increased bureaucratization will inevitably play a part in

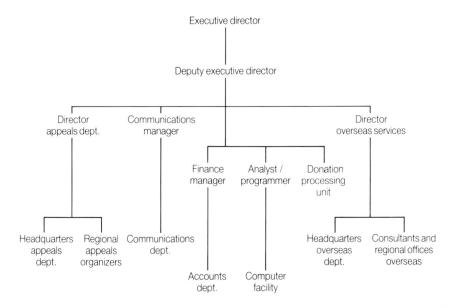

Figure 13.1 Royal Commonwealth Society for the Blind: a functional organizational structure.

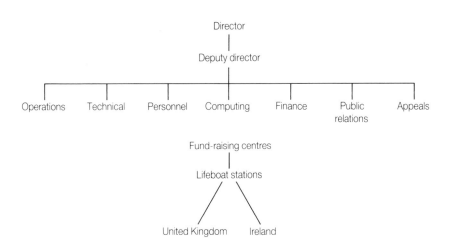

Figure 13.2 Royal National Lifeboat Institution: a functional organizational structure.

Figure 13.3 Royal National Lifeboat Institution: a committee structure. *Note:* Committees shown in parentheses are sub-committees which report to the main committees indicated.

both organizations, but for the RNLI the primary effect is likely to be its unique position as sole provider of sea rescue services.

Since competition for funds and for service provision are reduced to a minimum, the RNLI can concentrate on efficiency as a primary strategy mediated through a formal and functional structure. It is worth noting that both organizations have built in to their structures sub-units which specialize in handling technological changes. These represent the flexible wing of each organization. However, the operating context of relative stability, planned change, long organizational history, large size and a managerial desire for efficiency and effectiveness has resulted in the adoption of a functional structure.

■ Divisional structures

Divisional structures allow distinct divisions of the organization to operate relatively independently of particular geographic areas or types of client. Each division or branch has many of the functions needed for its operation, so is not unlike a small organization. However, divisional structures are still co-ordinated and controlled by a head office from where the remaining service functions are provided. For example, Save the Children Fund (SCF) has divisions for home-based activities and the provision of services overseas, each headed by a divisional director and assistant directors. The home-based division has several regional branches that are further broken down into groups in towns and cities. These groups have a fund-raising role but, as SCF operates in the UK as well as overseas, they can also act as operational units. The overseas division of SCF covers operations in Africa, Asia, the Americas and the Pacific regions. In addition, head office has several functional departments. The heads of these departments report directly to the Chief Executive (see Figure 13.4).

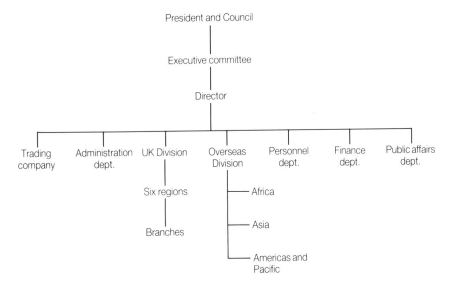

Figure 13.4 Save the Children Fund: a divisional organizational structure.
Note: This structure was modified towards the end of 1990. Hence this figure should not be taken as depicting the current form of the organization.

SCF is a large professional charity. It accords with Chandler's (1963) view that strategy and structure are closely related.

■ Federal structures

Head office plays a less directive role in the co-ordination of federal structures. Take, for instance, the Workers' Educational Association (WEA; see Figure 13.5).

Although formally part of the same national organization and governed by the same constitution, principles and policies, each WEA district (that is, region) has, until very recently, been wholly autonomous in both its policy and operations and in the ways in which it combines the elements of local branch voluntarism and the professionalism of full-time and part-time staff. Increasing external resource pressures are now forcing the WEA to consider adopting a more unified and centralized structure.

Hoekendijk (1990) has also identified how, in many federal forms of voluntary organization, structure is mostly designed around a common ideal, a vision or an overriding ideological principle. There can be local centres of voluntary activity throughout a country, yet there is often no central co-ordination structure. Consistency and control (as well as an essentially representative political process of policy-making) are achieved throughout the structure by shared, common beliefs, some of which are summarized in Table 13.1.

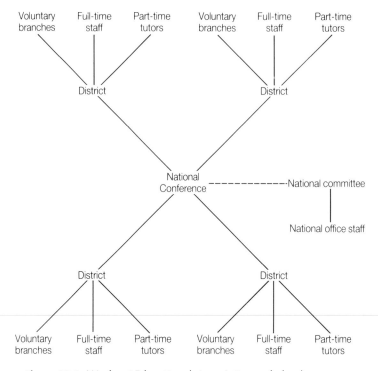

Figure 13.5 Workers' Educational Association: a federal structure.

Table 13.1 Structuring principles in federal structures.

Belief/common aim	Typical examples
(1) Criticism of existing provision of services by statutory and voluntary organizations	Youth/family services, alternative shops, legal centres
(2) Organized friendship networks aimed at providing a specific service	Houses for battered women, immigrant groups, help lines, literacy projects
(3) The strength of the individual through common experience	Self-help groups, social minority groups, many 'anonymous' groups
(4) Democracy: a fair deal for all	Interest groups, associations for the old, children, patients, divorcees, etc.
(5) Achieving change through political action	Neighbourhood groups for more parks, playgrounds and houses, abolition of nuclear plants, etc.

As Chandler (1963) notes, divisional and federal structures differ considerably from purely functional structures. Divisionalization facilitates growth and flexibility. Since divisions operate relatively autonomously, resources and energies can be channelled into those parts of the organization where they are needed the most. This can occur without affecting the other branch or branches of the organization. In general, they are planned structures, rather than just the product of organizational history and continued growth. Conflicts can occur, however, where headquarters not only assumes a co-ordinating role but also wants to retain policy control. In more federal structures any fragmentation of ideology can result in the loss of cohesion across the local units and splinter groups can often emerge, formed around a competing ideology.

In divisional and federal structures, tension can arise betweeen the operating divisions 'in the field' and central headquarters. Operating divisions and branches assume that they have the appropriate knowledge to implement and modify policy decisions as local conditions require, whilst headquarters insists on its rather more distanced policies being followed. Conflict can also occur between different divisions (or branches) of the organization, particularly where resources are scarce and demand from the divisions exceeds supply. In the case of medical charities, Deans (1989) describes the tension between offering a welfare service to relieve medical conditions and doing research to find out the cause of maladies, such as cancer, AIDS or coronary diseases. The scarce resources, often exacerbated by funding from outside agencies, highlight this conflict because funders tend to pick only one of the two organizational objectives.

■ Matrix or project-based structures

In theory, the matrix structure would seem to be ideal for the operations of many charities because it is organized around specific projects rather than a fixed hierarchy or divisionalization. This structure is extremely flexible and adaptable in the face of change. Project teams, groups and special working parties are formed to handle a particular project (for example, fund-raising in 'new' areas or developing existing services) and they can be abandoned or retained as circumstances dictate. Any formal hierarchy is put on one side during project membership and a project leader may be from any level in the hierarchy.

Control in a matrix organization is more difficult than in most other structures. Essentially, each member of a project or team will have *two* managers – the project manager and the retained control of functional or top management who oversee all projects. This alone can create ambiguity, each person in the team having two bosses, but, coupled with any scarcity in resources which might emerge, matrix organizations are potentially fraught with conflict as competition between projects is fostered and some teams feel badly treated or unfairly discriminated against whilst others appear to receive preferential treatment.

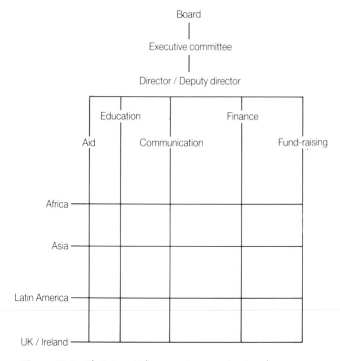

Figure 13.6 Christian Aid: a matrix organizational structure.

Butler and Wilson (1990) found that only one organization had attempted to adopt a full matrix structure (Christian Aid; Figure 13.6), although others, such as Oxfam, were actively considering, or had seriously considered in the recent past, adopting a matrix or a matrix-like structure.

Christian Aid formally adopted its matrix structure in April 1986 after having a functional-bureaucratic structure. Members of the organization found the matrix 'challenging, dynamic and refreshing'. It certainly opened up the potential for more strategic flexibility. Some of the problems encountered with it were the need for increased liaison between the various project groups and the organization as a whole becoming more difficult to manage, especially in the area of strategic decision-making. Currently, Christian Aid is refining the matrix structure to avert some of the process problems that such structures can cause.

Many voluntary organizations operate a semi-matrix structure by operating with two lines of authority. As Brooke (1984) notes, many organizations have a dual structure in which regional offices are accountable both to headquarters and to local membership committees. However, it is unusual for charities then to move wholly to the matrix structure. There tend to be pressures both from the internal organization and the external environment which push voluntary organizations towards bureaucratic structures. Equally, other pressures favour structures which reflect greater local autonomy, for example:

☐ **Pressures to decentralize**

- lack of expertise at head office
- unity of outlook and common purpose across the organization
- need to stimulate local activity
- need to campaign to a greater extent
- absence of urgent controversy

☐ **Pressures to centralize**

- constitution more than 50 years old (devolution is sometimes not posed as an alternative in older constitutions)
- maintaining charitable status
- safeguarding vital knowledge
- alleged irresponsibility or lack of expertise in offices or local branches
- views of donors and registering authorities
- danger of dissent and thus alienation of donors and potential donors
- expense of contacting members
- time, effort and other expenditure in maintaining liaison and co-ordination between offices

(*Adapted from Brooke, 1984*)

■ Summary

Studies of organization strategy and structure reveal that while structure virtually always follows strategy, managers are limited in their choice of structures. Child (1972) called this area of discretion 'strategic choice'. It means that managers can choose a particular configuration of structure forms, such as planning systems, level of computerized support, level of decentralization, spans of control and degree of formalization, to suit particular operating and environmental conditions.

For voluntary organizations, this choice can range from the bureaucratic to the divisional to the federal or a combination of these in a matrix structure. Each structural type brings with it particular constraints and opportunities, in particular for staff motivation, managerial control and retaining organizational flexibility in the face of change.

There is, therefore, no one best structure for voluntary organizations. A strategy of growth usually involves some measure of decentralization. However, structure also depends on the social, political and economic context in which the organization operates. Bureaucratic structures work well in contexts which are relatively predictable and have not too much change or competition. They are not built for flexibility and dynamic change. Those changes which do occur are often dealt with by small organizational sub-units, leaving the rest of the organization relatively untouched. Divisional structures are usually the result of planned growth and adaptation to operating circumstances (for example in the third world sector or an alliance of pressure groups). Maintaining strategic coherence across units and managing conflict are major problems in federal structures. Conflict includes that between operating units in the field and headquarters (for example in a third-world overseas-aid organization) or that between different constituent organizations in a federal structure. An ideological or political split is difficult to manage in these structures since they are often designed explicitly to exclude any form of centralized control (or headquarters) which could act as final arbiter in such cases.

The importance of organizational structure cannot be over-emphasized. It should be some comfort to those working in the voluntary sector, however, to know that questions of appropriate organizational design have puzzled theorists and practitioners alike for many years. There are no easy answers from either public or commercial organizational experience. More cases, research and experience from the voluntary sector are desperately needed to begin building a substantial knowledge base.

Notes

(1) This article is based largely on empirical work in voluntary organizations in Britain in the late 1980s (see Wilson, 1984; Wilson and Butler, 1985; Butler and Wilson, 1990).

(2) These terms were central to the thinking of Lawrence and Lorsch (1967). The issue has not always been presented like this. Early in the 20th century, researchers tried to define principles of organizational structure which would be effective in all circumstances. The Classical School focused on job design and administrative efficiency (Taylor, 1911; Gilbreth, 1908; Urwick, 1943). The Human Relations School argued that organizations should be structured around the needs of individuals. If these needs were 'blocked' through the adoption of a particular structure, the structure should be changed (Mayo, 1949; Roethlisberger and Dickson, 1939). For both schools, however, proof of a link between particular structures and effective performance remained elusive.

Subsequently, the Contingency theorists argued that there is no one best way of structuring an organization (for example Lupton, 1971).

(3) These findings are based on empirical work by Burns and Stalker (1961) in Britain and Lawrence and Lorsch (1967) in North America. They identified the following.

(a) *Mechanistic Structures* (Bureaucracies): typically with many tasks broken down into functional specializations, clear and formal definitions of duties and responsibilities, a precise hierarchy and levels of formal authority, information flowing up the organization chart and decisions filtering down. The continued development and survival of these organizations rests on the assumption that sets of rules and procedures outlast the life-span of individual human beings. Thus, each well-defined role in the mechanistic structure can be filled with several different individuals.

(b) *Organic Structures* (Adhocracies): tasks are not so precisely defined, relatively little functional specialization, flexible definitions of duties and responsibilities and information and decisions flowing across and up and down the organization. The continued development and survival of these organizations lies in the continual development of ideas and innovations rather than in the formality of the structure itself. The term 'adhocracy' comes from Mintzberg (1983).

(4) Isolated examples are Billis (1990); Butler and Wilson (1990); Cornforth and Hooker (1990). There is also much literature on the structure and the functioning of communes and collective organizations (see, for example, Kanter, 1972, 1979; Rothschild-Whitt, 1979). The structure of worker co-operatives and kibbutzim has also been fairly extensively covered (Bradley and Gelb, 1982 on the Mondragon co-operative in Spain; and Eccles, 1981, Leviathan, 1984 and Wilson and Rosenfeld, 1987 on co-operative forms of organization). These studies are a good point of departure, but they are really too general to be applied to the specific contexts of British voluntary organizations.

References

Addy, T. and Scott, D. (1988) *Fatal Impacts? The MSC and Voluntary Action*. Manchester Business School.

Allinson, C. (1990) 'Personality and bureaucracy', in Wilson, D. C. and Rosenfeld, R. H. (eds) *Managing Organizations: Text, Readings and Cases*. London: McGraw-Hill.

Billis, D. (1990) 'Planned change in voluntary and government social service agencies', *Proceedings of the 1990 Conference of the Association of Voluntary Action Scholars*. Centre for Voluntary Organization, London School of Economics.

Bradley, K. and Gelb, A. (1982) 'The replication and sustainability of the Mondragon Experiment', *British Journal of Industrial Relations*, 10, 1, pp. 20–23.

Brooke, M. Z. (1984) *Centralization and Autonomy: A Study in Organizational Behaviour*. London: Holt, Rinehart and Winston.

Burns, T. and Stalker, G. M. (1961) *The Management of Innovation*. London: Tavistock.

Butler, R. J. and Wilson, D. C. (1990) *Managing Voluntary and Nonprofit Organizations: Strategy and Structure*. London: Routledge.

Chandler, A. D. (1963) *Strategy and Structure: Chapters in the History of the American Industrial Enterprise*. Cambridge, Mass: MIT Press.

Channon, D. (1973) *The Strategy and Structure of British Industry*. Cambridge, Mass: Harvard University Press.

Chapin, F. S. and Tsouderos, J. E. (1956) 'The formalization process in voluntary associations', *Social Forces*, Vol. 34, pp. 342–344.

Child, J. (1972) 'Organizational structure, environment and performance: the role of strategic choice', *Sociology*, 6, 1, pp. 1–22.

Cornforth, C. and Hooker, C. (1990) 'Conceptions of management in voluntary and nonprofit organizations: values, structure and management style', *Proceedings of the 1990 Conference of the Association of Voluntary Action Scholars*. Centre for Voluntary Organization, London School of Economics.

Deans, T. (1989) 'Organizing medical research: the role of charities and the state' in Ware, A. (ed.) *Charities and Government*. Manchester University Press.

Eccles, T. (1981) *Under New Management*. London: Pan Books.

Galbraith, J. R. (1973) *Designing Complex Organizations*. Reading, Mass.: Addison-Wesley.

Gerlach, L. P. and Hine, L. (1970) *People, Power, Change: Movements of Social Transformation*. Indianapolis: Bobbs-Merrill.

Gilbreth, F. B. (1908) *Field System*. New York and Chicago: Myron C. Clark.

Hoekendijk, L. (1990) 'Cultural roots of voluntary action in different countries', *Proceedings of the 1990 Conference of the Association of Voluntary Action Scholars*. Centre for Voluntary Organization, London School of Economics.

Kanter, R. M. (1972) *Commitment and Community: Communes and Utopias in Sociological Perspective*. Cambridge, Mass.: Harvard University Press.

Kanter, R. M. (1979) 'The measurement of organizational effectiveness, productivity, performance and success: issues and dilemmas in service and non-profit organizations', *Program on Non-profit Organizations*, Working paper no. 8, Yale University.

Kanter, R. M. (1983) *The Change Masters: Corporate Entrepreneurs at Work*. London: Allen and Unwin.

Kimberly, J. R., Miles, R. H. and Associates (1980) *The Organizational Life Cycle*. San Francisco: Jossey-Bass.

Lawrence, P. R. and Lorsch, J. W. (1967) *Organization and Environment*. Cambridge, Mass.: Harvard University Press.

Leviathan, V. (1984) 'The kibbutz as a situation for cross-cultural research', *Organization Studies*, 5, 1, pp. 67–75.

Lupton, T. (1971) *Management and the Social Sciences*. Harmondsworth: Penguin.

Mayo, E. (1949) *Hawthorne and the Western Electric Company: The Social Problems of an Industrial Civilization* London: Routledge.

Merton, R. K. (1940) 'Bureaucratic structure and personality', *Social Forces*, 18, pp. 464–474.

Mintzberg, H. (1983) *Structures in Fives: Designing Effective Organizations*. London: Prentice Hall.

Moyer, M. (ed.) (1983) *Managing Voluntary Organizations: Proceedings of a Conference Held at York University, Toronto*. Toronto: Faculty of Administrative Studies.

Perrow, C. (1967) *Organizational Analysis: A Sociological View*. London: Tavistock.

Peters, T. and Waterman, R. (1982) *In Search of Excellence: Lessons from America's Best Run Companies*. New York: Harper and Row.

Pugh, D. S., Hickson, D. J., Hinings, C. R. and Turner, C. (1969) 'The context of organizational structure', *Administrative Science Quarterly*, 14, pp. 378–398.

Roethlisberger, F. J. and Dickson, W. J. (1939) *Management and the Worker*. Cambridge, Mass.: Harvard University Press.

Rothschild-Whitt, J. (1979) 'The collectivist organization: an alternative to rational bureaucratic models', *American Sociological Review*, 44, pp. 509–527.

Saxon-Harrold, S. K. E. (1986) *Strategy in Voluntary Organizations*, unpublished PhD. thesis. University of Bradford.

Scott, D. (1981) *Don't Mourn for Me – Organize: The Social and Political Uses of Voluntary Organizations*. London: Allen and Unwin.

Taylor, F. W. (1911) *Principles of Scientific Management*. New York: Harper.

Tsouderos, J. E. (1955) 'Organizational change in terms of a series of selected variables', *American Journal of Sociology*, 20, pp. 206–210.

Urwick, L. (1943) *The Elements of Administration*. New York: Harper.

Wilson, D. C. (1984) 'Charity law and the politics of regulation in the voluntary sector', *King's Counsel*, 34, pp. 36–42.

Wilson, D. C. and Butler, R. J. (1985) 'Corporatism in the British voluntary sector', in Streeck, W. and Schmitter, P. C. (eds) *Private Governments as Agents of Public Policy*. London: Sage.

Wilson, D. C. And Rosenfeld, R. H. (1987) 'Cultures and co-operatives', paper presented at the *International Conference on Organizational and Behavioural Perspectives for Social Development*, Ahmedabad, India.

Wilson, D. C. and Rosenfeld, R. H. (1990) *Managing Organizations: Text, Readings and Cases*. London: McGraw-Hill.

Woodward, J. (1965) *Industrial Organization: Theory and Practice*. London: Oxford University Press.

Young, D. (1990) 'Organizing principles for international advocacy associations', *Proceedings of the 1990 Conference of the Association of Voluntary Action Scholars*. Centre for Voluntary Organization, London School of Economics.

PART FIVE

Strategy and External Relations

14

Co-operation and Competition in the Voluntary Sector:
The Strategic Challenges of the 1990s and Beyond

David C. Wilson

How far can voluntary organizations model themselves on commercial enterprises? With all its ideological, political and strategic implications, that question has been at the heart of many of the 1980s debates about the management of voluntary organizations. Drawing on his own research into a group of large charities, Wilson examines, in some depth, the impact of adopting commercial and competitive strategies on voluntary organizations. The analysis highlights several problems associated with 'niche strategies' – for commercial as well as voluntary organizations. Wilson's critique of such strategies leads him to explore the potential for joint ventures and collaboration. By implication, Wilson is raising far-reaching questions about some of the dominant management assumptions shaping the voluntary sector's thinking about the 1990s.

■ Introduction

Only relatively recently has attention been paid to the strategic profiles of organizations in the voluntary sector. Theoretical and empirical work is rare. On the other hand commercial organizations have long been scrutinized by researchers and theorists, to the extent that many elements of strategy and organizational success have become almost inextricably linked. However, important trends have emerged over the last decade concerning the relationships between voluntary organizations and the state, the strategies pursued by voluntary organizations and the likely role of voluntary activity in the 1990s.

This article argues that, as far as strategic responses to environmental challenges and changes are concerned, close parallels can be drawn between the voluntary sector and commercial organizations. It is proposed that the 1990s present a broadly similar range of changes and challenges to both voluntary and commercial organizations. It concludes by arguing that knowledge gained from both sectors does not seem to support the adoption of competitive strategies by voluntary organizations, and suggests the adoption of co-operative strategies as an alternative way of supporting growth and sustained success.

■ Changes in strategy for voluntary organizations: the last decade

Since 1978, when the Wolfenden report was published, changes in the strategies of voluntary organizations can be mapped out as a set of relatively consistent themes and progressions. The predominant changes have been from pluralism in the 1970s and early 1980s to competition in the late 1980s and early 1990s[1].

The systematic mapping of strategy begins with the pioneering work of the Wolfenden Committee. The Wolfenden report adopted a theoretical approach to strategy (pluralism) and was a milestone which allows us to assess the development and philosophies of later research. The context for Wolfenden was primarily one of securing strategic advantage through organizational flexibility. Voluntary organizations were characterized by their ability to respond rapidly to needs and to mobilize the entire organization around events which were unpredictable and rapidly changing. This was their strategic advantage over more bureaucratic and less flexible organizations such as state agencies. In the Wolfenden era, the dominant 'competition' for the voluntary sector came from state agencies.

The socio-political context of this flexibility has been characterized by Gladstone (1982) as 'gradualist welfare pluralism'. This views the state and the voluntary sector as partners. Whilst the state often funded specific voluntary organizations for the provision of specific services which it was itself unable or unwilling to provide, the notion that state and voluntary organizations should work hand-in-hand was dominant under the banner of welfare pluralism. The strategy of voluntary organizations in this context appears clear, with the benefit of hindsight.

Achieving *independence* from state funding became high on the strategic agenda. Where total independence could not be achieved, state monies which had explicit strings attached were to be avoided if possible. Voluntary organizations had to try to achieve *autonomy* over the level and nature of the state funding they received. In this way, they could retain autonomy from a set of political stakeholders (state agencies), which would ensure that, in theory at least, they remained independent of any governmental piper who wanted to call the tune.

Leat *et al.* (1981), for example, describe how voluntary organizations are constrained strategically largely through their financial dependence on central or local government agencies. Voluntary organizations in receipt of government monies enjoy commensurately less autonomy over the level and type of services they offer. Wortman (1983) argues that strategic planning and goal-setting by Canadian voluntary organizations are constrained by the influence of governmental funding bodies. Scott (1982) produces Australian data to show that, where the state has the power to increase, withdraw or reduce funding, acceptance of funds incurs the penalty of a subtle 'constraining influence' on organizational actions.

In the UK, the history of the Royal National Lifeboat Institution (RNLI) illustrates the overriding concern with state dependence. Founded in 1824, the RNLI remained financially independent of state funding until the 1850s, when it had a brief period of being partially financed by the state. This led to accusations of increased bureaucracy, a greater level of interference from government officials at lifeboat stations and an increase in the volume of formal paperwork. The RNLI reverted to financial independence, supported wholly by voluntary contributions. It has resisted several attempts to nationalize the service (see Butler and Wilson, 1990, pp. 134–5).

Research data indicate that dependence on state funding has the following consequences.

(1) It reduces the range and scope of decisions a voluntary organization can take. State agencies often have an influential voice over strategies, even to the extent of specifying projects to be funded by state monies. Voluntary organizations which are almost wholly state-funded have virtually no say in policy or strategic direction.

(2) The link between the state and the voluntary sector is portrayed as a kind of see-saw whereby increased provision of social welfare services by statutory bodies will reduce the level of voluntary provision. Similarly, reduction in state provision results in an increased scope and scale of activities in voluntary organizations.

(3) Certain kinds of service provision are viewed by the state as acceptable for the voluntary sector to provide (such as care for the mentally handicapped) and others are viewed as rather less acceptable (such as pressure groups or lobbying bodies). State funding levels reflect this. In the extreme, voluntary organizations which provide services disfavoured by the state have little chance of obtaining state finance should they want it.

The pluralist view was a powerful influence over how we could examine strategy and how any constraints or opportunities were to be explained. It was centred on the financial and regulatory relationships between the state and the voluntary sector. But the world was changing. The context in which most voluntary organizations found themselves in the 1980s had changed markedly from one of pluralism. These changes reflected wider developments which were beginning to take place under the Conservative government of Margaret Thatcher. In particular, the attempts by the government to overcome any kind of dependency culture put paid to welfare pluralism, placed the task of management firmly at the sector level and forced a culture of individualism, competitive aggression and competition between all kinds of organization. The voluntary sector was expected to stand on its own feet. It should be 'properly' managed in line with what was considered best practice from the successful commercial firms and it should look towards private sources of funding rather than depend on state aid. The era of competitive strategies in the voluntary sector had arrived. The enterprise culture was predominant[2].

■ Competitive strategies in voluntary organizations

Keat and Abercrombie (1990) neatly summarize this changing context. The creation of an enterprise culture (as opposed to a pluralist culture) led to some identifiable central characteristics. These are summarized in the following list.

□ **Economic characteristics**

- Continual process of privatization
- De-regulation of industries (especially financial services)
- Reorganization of publicly funded bodies
- Reduction of the culture of dependency

□ **Socio-cultural characteristics**

- The commercial view of the organization becomes the dominant role model.
- The vocabulary of all organizations becomes predominantly that of commercial practice (for example market niche, product differentiation, sustainable competitive advantage).
- A noticeable trend towards the homogenization of organization models. All organizations are encouraged to adopt commercial modes of operation.
- The idea of running even one's own personal life as if it were a business becomes highlighted.

  (*Adapted from Keat and Abercrombie, 1990*)

During the changing period of the 1980s, Butler and Wilson (1990) undertook a major longitudinal study of the strategies of 31 charities. They found many of the elements outlined in the above list to be consistent with features of organizational strategies in the voluntary sector. The study revealed five broad types of strategy pursued by voluntary organizations, ranging from outright competition (for both funds and clients) to those organizations which merely reacted to events as and when they occurred – they had no identifiable strategy at all. Table 14.1 summarizes the five strategy types.

The important thing to note about these five types of strategy is that, for the first time since the Wolfenden Report, it was possible to show that voluntary organizations were pursuing strategies which did not fit easily into the pluralist analysis. There is not much here about state dependence (although many authors in the academic journals still continued to argue the pluralist case). The dominant theme is rather one of competition. This can be competition for funding, for service provision or for both. The philosophy is that voluntary organizations can be managed along the emerging lines of commercial 'best practice'.

The data indicated that managers of voluntary organizations viewed their organization as a single competitive entity, battling to cope with the demands of the enterprise culture and locked into competitive struggles with their peer charities over funding, service provision and corporate image. Competition would somehow lead to distinctive competence (that is the organization is perceived to be the best at what it does by other charities and by givers). If necessary, the organization must be changed to accommodate the goal of competition. Butler and Wilson found that this involves substantial changes to organizational structures (for example Christian Aid), to the employment of professional managers from the commercial sector (for example the RNIB) or to the establishment of overtly commercial/competitive practices such as management by objectives or 'right first time' quality programmes (for example the World Wide Fund for Nature).

Table 14.1   Five strategies pursued by voluntary organizations.

Strategy	Example organizations (all registered charities)
Extending/innovating (high competition)	Oxfam, War on Want, British Red Cross
Co-operation mainly for funds (compete in service provision)	Royal Commonwealth Society for the Blind, Sense, British Leprosy Relief Association
Co-operation mainly for service provision (compete for funding)	Action Aid, Royal National Institute for the Blind, Catholic Agency for Overseas Development
Acquisition (service level relatively constant; emphasis is on competitively acquiring more funds)	Royal National Lifeboat Institution, British Wireless for the Blind
Reaction (no identifiable or consistent set of strategies)	St Dunstan's Methodist Relief and Development Fund, Scottish Institute for the War Blinded

(*Adapted from Butler and Wilson, 1990*)

With the exception of the final cluster, reactor strategies (comprising only) three of the 31 organizations studied), the common themes of strategy in the enterprise culture appear to be:

(1) managing the image of the organization
(2) managing the change process towards a future desired state of increased competition and distinctive competence
(3) managing organizational culture and structure so that they support the goal of increased competition.

The pressures on voluntary sector managers to make their organizations more competitive, more distinctive, more effective and more efficient are almost universal. All the above three areas displayed evidence of consistency. Image was to be professional (as defined by the best commercial practice); the change processes were aimed at securing organizational learning, often characterized by hiring senior management from outside the voluntary sector; culture and structure were reorganized to achieve decentralization and project management and to secure lasting organizational flexibility. From the perspective of organizational strategy, this broadly represents the pursuit of niche strategies, to secure distinctive competence within a particular area, or areas, of service provision (Miles and Snow, 1978). The aim is for managers of voluntary organizations to try and achieve a 'market niche' in which their organization is perceived as a consistently good performer compared to others in the same field of activity. In commercial parlance, the aim is to become a 'brand leader' in the provision of services.

Securing professionalism in management was apparently ubiquitous. Organizations were either already hiring managers from commercial practice (Oxfam, National Institute for the Blind) or thinking of doing so in the near future. An alternative route was to develop professionalism in-house by introducing management development courses or similar training. In terms of organizational structure, achieving decentralized project management was seen as the most pressing need, especially in organizations with a long history of centralization and bureaucratization. In short, voluntary organizations are being managed through change processes aimed at 'creating a culture of enterprise' throughout the sector (NCVO, 1990).

■ Are competitive / niche strategies the way forward?

□ Niche strategies

It seems almost heretical to raise doubts over niche strategies in the 1990s. Much time and effort was spent by all types of organization in the late 1980s in trying to become the 'best' provider of specific goods and services. Such practices, often subsumed under the broad banner of organizational change, were also normatively encouraged by the government. Terms such as the 'enterprise culture' were spread throughout the popular press, whilst the academic, the popular and the 'good practice' literature of organization theory and related disciplines became saturated with the concept of 'excellence' (see, for example, Peters and Waterman, 1982).

From the perspective of organizations in the voluntary sector, the urgency to embrace excellence and distinctive competence is pressing both from increasing competition within the sector (that is between organizations providing similar services) and from encouraging noises from outside the sector (in particular from central government). The notion of self-help, rather than caring for others, has gathered considerable momentum over the last decade.

One important result of these changes has been the increasing tendency to view the commercial (corporate) sector as an alternative source of funds for voluntary organizations. The level of corporate giving by commercial organizations is increasing. Stuck for some years at around £58 million, current levels of corporate giving are now (1990) approximately £91.5 million. Yet this is relatively little in comparison with the sector's overall income. Corporate support for the voluntary sector is also unevenly spread. It would be an unwise manager who attempted to pursue a niche strategy aimed primarily at securing increased commercial income.

In rank order of magnitude of funding, commercial organizations support voluntary activity in the areas of education, health, secondments (where an employee of a commercial organization works for a time in a voluntary organization) and the arts generally (although this is relatively a very small category of funding). Substantial funding from commercial monies will rarely be achieved outside these areas. Furthermore, Saxon-Harrold (1987) indicates that corporate givers are concerned that standard accounting practices are adopted throughout the voluntary sector so that the relative effectiveness of charities can be assessed using accounting criteria. As Wilson (1989) notes:

'Standardisation of accounting practices across the voluntary sector is likely to be extremely difficult to achieve. Decisions will have to be made concerning what is, and what is not, accountable, what is quantifiable and how current organizational performance is to be assessed ... even if such accounting algorithms can be achieved, they are likely to reflect the ideologies and biases of commercially based accounting practice ... the economics of such calculations are invariably going to appeal to neoclassical concepts of economic wealth and welfare and virtually ignore other aspects of value.'

Since pure commodity production is outside the scope of most voluntary organizations, assessing them on measures designed to show marginal profits on productive output is meaningless (Tinker, 1985, p. 169). Yet current governmental favour towards tripartite funding with commercial organizations is forcing voluntary organizations to produce standardized accounts to convince commercial givers of their merit and organizational efficacy.

☐   Problems in following a niche strategy

Competitive strategies aimed at securing a distinctive niche have doubtless worked for many commercial organizations. Indeed, one of Peters and Waterman's (1982) eight maxims for successful performance is 'stick to the knitting'. Find your market niche, stick to it and you will probably do well. Many commentators claim this to have been the result of a rational, planned strategy of excellence and sustainable quality. It is open to question whether managers in commercial organizations really knew so clearly what they were doing in such unambiguous and ideological language. Empirical evidence shows that most strategic decision-making in commercial organizations is a case of 'muddling through', either because information is incomplete or because political games are being played by those most affected (see Hickson *et al.*, 1986). The danger of recipes such as Peters and Waterman's (and much of the good practice literature) lies in their unreflective and uncritical nature. These recipes are assumed to be applicable to any organization. In the voluntary sector, such recipes for excellence raise three major issues: dependency, achieving a niche strategy and the possibilities of collaboration.

(1) Reducing dependency The most common reduction of dependency recommended is to decrease the levels of state income and dependence and to adopt a more stand-alone strategy for voluntary sector funding. In particular, commercial firms are seen as alternative funding sources. As outlined above, this is unlikely to work. The overall income from corporate donors is very small indeed and corporate sponsorship is selective towards particular areas of voluntary activity. The pressures from corporate donors are for the voluntary sector recipients to show that they are enterprising and competitive in their outlook. This raises an ideological question as well as the more obvious economic issue. Many voluntary organizations are designed specifically to work with and for the *un*enterprising. Their central task precludes the adoption of commercial practices and techniques. How, then, are they to secure funding from commercial sources?

(2) Achieving a niche strategy Of course, some voluntary organizations can adopt a more competitive stance than others. They will find alternative sources of funding relatively easy to secure. But the adoption of a niche strategy brings with it some very worrying corollaries for voluntary sector organizations such as should they be there in the first place? There is a substantial body of empirical research on commercial organizations which shows that niche strategies rarely work as a stand-alone practice. They require other fundamental organizational changes.

 Miller and Friesen (1984) found that piecemeal adaptation to changes in the environment appear to lead to strategic failure. First, the adoption of niche strategies alone is unlikely to bring success (even in the commercial sector). Second, successful niche strategies (that is where the organization survives and grows) appear to require relatively functional and/or hierarchical structures to support them. The only exception to this is in the pursuit of an incremental strategy, but even here the support of an elaborate or formal committee structure appears necessary.

These structural changes are fundamental for most voluntary organizations and are, in some cases, ideologically contrary to their flexible, autonomous and decentralized ethos. They are major changes which are difficult to achieve and are a heavy price to pay for the achievement of a strategy which might not succeed anyway. Evidence from the voluntary sector indicates that many organizations are doing well without importing commercial good practice recipes (Butler and Wilson, 1990). The RNLI is virtually the sole provider of its services. There have been changes in technology (faster lifeboats) and the scope of service provision because the increased popularity of sailing as a leisure activity (sailboarding and pleasure boating) has meant that there are more casualties who get themselves into trouble more quickly. The RNLI has been successful by any criteria of organizational performance. Yet it is probably because of its unique provision of services that it has sustained its success through adopting an *incremental* strategy, supported by a relatively centralized structure of standing and special committees. When individuals give to a charity which saves life at sea they inevitably give to the RNLI. Its operating context precludes the adoption of a niche strategy.

The very different sectors of third world aid or the visually handicapped reveal a different position. Here the giver has a choice about which organization to support – Oxfam or Save the Children, the Royal National Institute for the Blind or Guide Dogs for the Blind? As already noted, organizations in these sectors have attempted to pursue niche strategies either through the recruitment of 'professional' managers from commercial organizations (RNIB), through structural reorganization (Christian Aid) or by installing strategic planning mechanisms such as management by objectives (Worldwide Fund for Nature). Each organization has encountered difficulties in this process, in particular with achieving changes in structure and the orientation of staff.

A further problem will be the increased level of competition thus created between voluntary organizations in the same service sectors. There will inevitably be some areas of service provision which are not met in the long term, since those organizations which fail to compete will go out of business as charities or as non-profit organizations. Given the rising levels of income to the voluntary sector overall, it is questionable whether or not such overt competition is necessarily a good thing for individual organizations. Maybe joint ventures between organizations in the same line of service provision would be beneficial (to both givers and receivers as well as to the organizations themselves).

(3) Competitive strategies overlook the possibilities of collaboration It is a truism that managers in the voluntary sector have embraced many principles gained from commercial organizational practice. However, they appear to have done so selectively, leading to an overall strategy of competition. There is substantial evidence to show that joint ventures between organizations can bring with them immense benefits ranging across the more effective use of resources and talents, greater ease

of structural change and a firm basis for sustaining and supporting strategic change (Harrigan, 1985).

Joint ventures are alliances or agreements between different organizations to work together to attain some mutually desired strategic goal. They do not necessarily mean the demise of either of the partnership organizations as a separate entity, although in the extreme a full joint venture could bring with it the need to set up a new organization which embraced the activities of the joint venture.

Many organizations have engaged in joint ventures because the increasing pressures of the competitive environment have meant that they can no longer invest in the skills and assets necessary to maintain competition with rivals. It is easy to see how this might apply to voluntary organizations operating in a particular service sector, such as third world aid or the visually handicapped.

Joint ventures exist in the voluntary sector already, but between very different partners. Government agencies, private building firms and community-based charities are one such alliance in the area of urban renewal and inner city development. The problems with this kind of alliance is that the basis for the long-term success of the joint venture is undermined by the different interests of the agencies concerned. Each organization in the joint venture has very different motives for joining the venture in the first place, and has very different preferred outcomes from collaborative efforts.

Other forms of joint venture (through collaboration) are equally widespread throughout the voluntary sector. This is particularly true of well-resourced, well-established charities, such as Save the Children or the Worldwide Fund for Nature, working through smaller community-based organizations. However, a joint venture between peer voluntary organizations in the same sector of activity would be a different proposition altogether. They would share a common set of interests, and it is almost inevitable that economies of scale could be realized by many joint ventures in terms of lower operating costs, increased levels of service provision and, of course, increased political potency in lobbying government agencies and the like. The argument here is not for the creation of 'super-charities'. That would be a backward step resulting in the same problem as that outlined before, where gaps in service provision would inevitably appear as charities pulled out of areas of activity which received less financial support. The argument is rather for a rethink of where the voluntary sector and its constituent organizations are going and what the future might hold if competitive strategies are pursued over the next five or ten years.

■ Summary

This article has argued against the adoption of competitive, niche strategies between individual voluntary organizations as a way forward into the 1990s. Based on empirical evidence from the voluntary sector and from commercial practice, it is proposed that strategic alliances between voluntary organizations which operate in the same or similar service sectors could be a more productive way forward.

Pleas for development in the voluntary sector generally, ranging from management development and training needs to the more efficient and effective provision of services (NCVO, 1990), are unlikely to occur if the net result is overt competition between voluntary organizations. Perhaps it is time to draw breath and critically appraise the implications of competition, and at least consider the advantages of alliance, co-operation and joint activities, factors which were, after all, at the heart of the origins of many established organizations in the voluntary sector. It is important not to lose sight of this in the rush towards competition, effectiveness and efficiency.

Notes

(1) To help map strategy in the voluntary sector, some intellectual 'borrowing' is employed. Models of strategy drawn from research on commercial organizations are used to characterize the strategies of voluntary organizations. The works of Thompson (1967), Miles and Snow (1978), Miller and Friesen (1984) and Butler and Wilson (1990) form the theoretical underpinnings of the current argument.

(2) The transition from pluralism to competition within the enterprise culture was not as abrupt as this passage may imply. Under the Conservative government, initial changes were towards a more 'corporatist' structure for the voluntary sector (as well as for other business sectors). This was an attempt to restructure the state/voluntary sector linkages by developing intermediary bodies (such as NCVO). These umbrella bodies were to represent constituent organizations and to mediate policy on behalf of the government. Corporatism was short-lived. Wilson and Butler (1985) reported that, despite the new structure, state agencies still had direct influence over the policies and decision-making of many voluntary organizations. By 1986, the corporatist structure was history. The era of the enterprise culture had taken its place.

References

Butler, R. J. and Wilson, D. C. (1990) *Managing Voluntary and Non-Profit Organizations: Strategy and Structure*. London: Routledge.

Gladstone, F. (1982) *Charity Law and Social Justice*. London: Bedford Square Press.

Harrigan, K. R. (1985) *Strategies for Joint Ventures*. Lexington, Mass.: D. C. Heath, Lexington Books.

Hickson, D. J., Butler, R. J., Cray, D., Mallory, G. and Wilson, D. C. (1986) *Top Decisions: Strategic Decision Making in Organizations*. Oxford: Blackwell and San Francisco: Jossey-Bass.

Keat, R. and Abercrombie, N. (eds) (1990) *Enterprise Culture*. London: Routledge.

Leat, D., Smolka, G. and Unell, J. (1981) *Voluntary and Statutory Collaboration: Rhetoric or Reality?* London: Bedford Square Press.

Miles, R. E. and Snow, C. C. (1978) *Organizational Strategy, Structure and Process*. New York: McGraw-Hill.

Miller, D. and Friesen, P. H. (1984) *Organizations: A Quantum View*. Englewood Cliffs, New Jersey: Prentice-Hall.

NCVO (1990) 'Effectiveness and the voluntary sector', *Report of a Working Party*, Chaired by Lord Nathan, April, London.

Peters, T. and Waterman, R. (1982) *In Search of Excellence: Lessons from America's Best Run Companies*. New York: Harper and Row.

Saxon-Harrold, S. K. E. (1987) 'Trends in the top two hundred company donations to charity', *Charity Trends*. London, Charities Aid Foundation.

Scott, D. (1982) *Don't Mourn for Me – Organize: The Social and Political Uses of Voluntary Organizations*. London: Allen and Unwin.

Thompson, J. D. (1967) *Organizations in Action*. New York: McGraw-Hill.

Tinker, T. (1985) *Paper Prophets: A Social Critique of Accounting*. London: Holt, Rinehart and Winston.

Wilson, D. C. (1989) 'New trends in the funding of charities: the tripartite system of funding', in Ware, A. (ed.) *Charities and Government*. Manchester University Press.

Wilson, D. C. and Butler, R. J. (1985) 'Corporatism in the British voluntary sector', in Streeck, W. and Schmitter, P. C. (eds) *Private Governments as Agents of Public Policy*. London: Sage.

Wolfenden, J. (1978) *The Future of Voluntary Organisations: Report of the Wolfenden Committee*. London: Croom-Helm.

Wortman, M. (1983) 'Strategic planning in voluntary enterprises', in Moyer, M. (ed.) *Managing Voluntary Organizations*. Toronto: York University.

Young, D. (1988) 'Private enterprise for the public good', paper presented to the *London School of Economics Industrial Policy Seminar*, 2 March.

15

Voluntary Organizations, Contracting and the Welfare State[1]

Ralph Kramer

Ever since 1601, when the Statute of Charitable Uses was placed on the statute book immediately after the 'Poor Law' Act, the changing role of a large part of the voluntary sector has been inextricably bound up with the changing role and development of the Welfare State. For almost three hundred years, the two sectors have, in one form or another, been partners in a sort of non-stop political, economic, organizational and ideological quadrille. In the early 1990s, one of the major anxieties for voluntary organizations has been whether or not a new melody – 'The Contract Culture' – and some new steps – 'Contracting for Services' – threatens not only to change the dance but also the character of the dancers.

This article by Ralph Kramer, a doyen amongst American researchers into voluntary organizations, puts both the problems and the possibilities of contracting for the provision of services into a wider perspective. By comparing what is happening in the UK with wider trends and transformations in the Welfare Capitalisms of Western Europe and North America, Kramer argues that there is a need to disentangle the ideological from the pragmatic aspects of contract relationships between voluntary and statutory agencies. (He also wryly observes that not so long ago voluntary organizations were worried about a declining role; now there is equal unease because they are faced with an expanding role!)

UK readers may find that his analysis does not always square easily with their own assessment of the organizational politics of welfare in the early 1990s. For instance, his arguments about the linkages between, and popularity of, privatization and voluntarism may seem a bit odd to managers and activists in UK voluntary organizations. It is worth persevering. As well as suggesting ways in which managers can get a practical purchase on the ambiguities and problems of cross-sector contract relationships, the article strikes a note of balance and caution about an issue which may not necessarily prove to be as cataclysmic as it is sometimes suggested or feared. Once we have got used to it, 'Contract Culture' may only be the latest variation of the well-known tune for the same old Welfare State-Voluntary Sector quadrille.

■ General trends

Since the mid-seventies there has been an astonishing upsurge of public interest in North America and Western Europe in the role of voluntary organizations, particularly as an alternative to government in the provision of public services. [...] There are two related trends which may help explain this [...] interest, both of which are a response to the 'crisis of the Welfare State' in Europe and North America. The first is ideological; as part of the effort to halt the expansion of the Welfare State, there has been a rediscovery of the special virtues of voluntarism by both the Right and the Left. Because it is so rare, one might be suspicious of such a consensus! Voluntary organizations have come to be viewed [by some] as a bulwark against further governmental intervention, or at least as an alternative, if not a substitute for it. [...] Others look upon the [voluntary] sector nostalgically, as a means of recovering a lost sense of community by promoting volunteerism, self-help and other forms of citizen participation. Hence, there is [...] support for privatization, partnerships and welfare pluralism in the UK, and for empowerment and co-production in the USA. [...]

[...] The second [trend] stems from [a] convergence of three [streams of] policy in North America and Western Europe, all of which are conducive to the greater utilization of non-governmental organizations to implement public policy. They are: governmental decentralization, deinstitutionalization or dehospitalization, and the more selective targeting of services to specific [...] groups. Thus, even though the Welfare State may be perceived as being 'dismantled', 'in retreat' or 'at an impasse' – at least its growth has slowed – an entity called 'the Contract State' has rapidly emerged as voluntary organizations have been used to deliver public services in the fields of health, education, personal social services, housing, the environment and community development. Through its grants, subsidies and fee-for-service payments, the State has everywhere become a partner, a patron or a purchaser of service for voluntary organizations [...]. In fact, [wherever] there is a substantial voluntary sector, [it] is dependent on governmental support to a greater or lesser degree (James, 1989). In the USA, for example, governmental funds have become a more important source of revenue in the non-profit sector than all private giving combined (Salamon, 1987). Similarly, in the UK, despite the slowing down and cut-backs in public expenditure since 1975, statutory fees and grants have been the fastest growing source of voluntary sector income, almost doubling in amount and as a percentage of total income in the last 15 years (Knapp and Saxon-Harrold, 1989).

The increased interdependence of government and the voluntary sector is recognized in the popular concept of a mixed economy [of welfare], a pervasive and complex mingling of public and private funds and functions, producing quangos and para-governmental organizations (Hood and Schuppert, 1988), with the consequent blurring of the traditional boundaries between the State, the market and what is, I believe, mistakenly called the 'independent' or third sector. [...] In the USA, local government and non-profit organizations both compete actively for foundation grants and for Federal funds. [...] Cost differences among voluntary agencies providing residential care [can be] greater than the differences between them and those of the Local Authorities (Knapp *et al.*, 1987). As a result, one can at least question the validity of the concept of a 'sector' and wonder whether it refers to a distinctive and coherent group of organizations; whether the prohibition against Board members appropriating for their personal use any excess of income over expenditure is a sufficient basis for generalizing about a class of organizations. It has been observed that the sector metaphor obscures the external convergence of these organizations and, on the other hand, masks the internal diversity within each of the sectors (Langton, 1987).

[...]

Welfare States vary greatly in their dependence on non-governmental organizations. The Netherlands, where voluntary organizations are the primary service delivery system, stands at one end of a continuum – the government allocates seventy percent of the GNP, but directly controls only ten percent. Sweden, where practically no non-governmental organizations are used – although some are subsidized for the purposes of advocacy – stands at the other end. Closer to The Netherlands is West Germany where well over half of the social services are subsidized by government but provided by voluntary organizations, some of which are similar to conglomerates or cartels. Other countries with similar patterns are Italy, Belgium and Austria. Britain and Switzerland are closer to Sweden because of the dominance of their statutory systems, while France and Canada stand between them and the USA.

In these countries, there is a growing interdependence between the voluntary organizations and the departments of central and local government. They are involved in fiscal, planning, co-ordinating, regulatory, legal, as well as political relationships. At the same time, there is enormous variation in these inter-organizational relationships, few of which are standardized or even formalized. Generally, they are of greater importance to the voluntary agencies than to government for whom expenditures to voluntary organizations rarely exceeds three percent of their budgets. Usually there is coexistence and accommodation between them, with infrequent collaboration or partnerships, but relatively little competition or conflict. Contrary to the conventional wisdom, there seem to be few successful attempts of the State to control, regulate, monitor, evaluate or to press for greater accountability. Some exceptions are found in the USA and in The Netherlands. In the latter, motivated by both fiscal austerity and ideological reasons, four major trends have emerged. After a struggle over fifteen years, the central government has succeeded in transferring the responsibility for the funding of most voluntary organizations to the provincial and municipal governments; restructuring and reducing the number of national organizations in the personal social services from 95 to 35; providing for greater consumer advocacy; and continuing the policy of shifting expenditures for the mentally handicapped from subsidies and grants to inclusion in social insurance.

Despite the variations in their reliance on voluntary organizations, all Welfare States in the advanced industrial countries have encountered similar problems in their personal social services; the spiralling of costs, problems of over- or under-use, fragmentation of services and difficulties of access, planning and co-ordination (Kahn and Kamerman, 1980). At the same time, curiously, the standards of quality – insofar as we have data other than expenditures – do not seem to be markedly different between The Netherlands, Sweden, West Germany or Switzerland. This suggests that legal 'ownership' of an organization may not be as important as organizational factors such as size, structure, degree of formalization and type of staff. *How* may be more important than *who* delivers a service.

■ [Contracting, quasi-markets and organizational change]

Although the blurring of the boundaries between the public and the private is widely acknowledged (Bozeman, 1987) there are still no generally accepted concepts, models or theories to describe and explain this process of interpenetration of the State by the market and the voluntary sector (Streek and Schmitter, 1985). Instead, there are numerous metaphors such as the 'new political economy', 'welfare pluralism'; 'third-party government', 'non-profit federalism' and the 'franchise State' in the USA; 'indirect public administration' in Finland, West Germany and Denmark, or the 'social economy' in France. The most recent addition to this collection is the 'Shadow State' – the title of a new book by Jennifer Wolch about the voluntary sector in the USA and the UK [...] (Geiger and Wolch, 1986). Her concept of the 'Shadow State' refers to those voluntary organizations receiving governmental funds which are by definition outside the political system, but still subject to some State control.

It is this condition that has aroused considerable fears; namely that dependence on government will [...] undermine the autonomy and distinctive qualities of pioneering, flexibility and advocacy associated with voluntary organizations. It has been asked: What is 'voluntary' about an organization that depends largely on statutory funds to deliver public services? If providing established public services becomes the dominant role for many voluntary organizations, who will develop new needed services, represent unpopular or controversial interests, dissenting views, and press for changes in policy and practice? There are additional worries about increased bureaucratization and professionalization; the crowding out of small, local and minority organizations by the large national agencies; increased competition and scarcity of funds (NCVO, 1989). These questions, which trouble many in the voluntary sector in the UK, are also being asked in other countries where there is a re-evaluation of the role of government, the market, and the non-profit or voluntary sector in the financing and provision of public services. There seems to be more concern and activity in Britain than one finds in the USA where we gradually drifted in the late 1960s into vendorism and grantsmanship (Kramer, 1987). Perhaps one of the reasons for the greater concern in the UK is the accumulation of fairly radical changes in public policy, resulting in considerable turbulence and uncertainty. This seems to be a transitional or interim period, signifying the end of one era and the prelude to another.

There has been an unprecedented and rapid succession of governmental reports and legislative initiatives since 1985 involving major shifts in tax and incomes policy, in housing, education, health, in the financing of local government, and in the delivery of the personal social services, particularly relating to community care. These changes represent a significant break in a tradition of incrementalism and social reform, and reverse expenditure trends of more than two decades (Glennerster *et al.*, 1989). They reflect an ideology based upon a revival of nineteenth century Liberalism in which reliance on market competition and individual responsibility is to replace the role of the State. Other related nineteenth century beliefs which have resurfaced are: the residual philosophy of social welfare and its kin, the principle of subsidiarity; invidious stereotypes regarding the virtues of voluntary organizations and vices of government; and traditional arguments about the dangers of government funding of voluntary organizations (Warner, 1894; Kramer, 1981).

Essentially, there is a lack of confidence in the ability of government, particularly local government, to directly provide cost-efficient services; rather, it [should become] an enabler of voluntary and private provision [and] perhaps a monitor and regulator [of that provision]. Just as there is an 'enterprise culture' stemming from the privatization of state-owned enterprises, so there is a 'contract culture' based upon the belief that contracts are a more efficient and effective form of funding services than grant-aid. As Griffiths put it, 'Local Authorities should be purchasers of care services and not monolithic providers' (HMSO, 1988). The proposed changes [...] (HMSO, 1989) [come] into effect in 1991. They give sweeping new powers to local authorities to support the voluntary and private sector [...]. Contracts, as we have learned in the USA, are distinguished by tighter, more explicit and rigorous criteria for funding. Contracting requires greater specificity of objectives and a credible capacity to achieve particular service outcomes in a cost-effective and accountable way (Kuttner and Martin, 1987). The uncertain environment in which this occurs will probably be more competitive, perhaps with a more active role for consumers, but certainly with pressures on local government to function more as a funder and contract manager. Although the White Paper (HMSO, 1989, Section 3.4.14) endorses core grants and support for advocacy, campaigning, education and development work – and also wants to avoid the crowding out of small organizations – such worthy purposes would probably have a lower priority when funds are increasingly scarce. Consequently, there may well be a reduction in general purpose, 'arms-length' or core grants for general administration, [in favour of] more project-orientated funding.

Throughout the 1990s, voluntary agencies are likely to be viewed by Government [increasingly] as a substitute service provider or public agent; a preferred alternative, rather than, as in the Wolfenden Report (1978) a decade ago, as a supplement or complement to statutory provision. This reverses the historical pattern whereby voluntary services were eventually taken over and provided by government [...]. It was not so long ago that the major concern of the voluntary sector was about its declining role because statutory agencies had taken over more and more in the preceding decades. Now, in contrast, there is great unease because it faces an expanding role.

Yet one should be cautious in generalizing about 'the future of voluntary agencies' as a class because of the enormous diversity among them. They vary greatly in age, size, complexity, purposes, scope of concern – national or local – degree of professionalization and bureaucratization, the type of management committee, the extent of service provision and advocacy, consumer participation, the nature of their clientele and constituencies. Indeed, these variables probably influence their performance much more than their [common] legal status as registered charities. This means that different types of voluntary agencies will have different futures as they react in their own way to the contract culture which may emerge. For example, rate-capping, and the financial incentives for local authorities to divest themselves of residential facilities, may be regarded as an opportunity to be seized by large national organizations, but as a dangerous threat to the survival of small, community-based organizations whose grant-aids may be eliminated, or who may be unable or unwilling to compete for contracts because they cannot meet the requirements for greater specificity, accountability and compliance with regulations. Then, too, local authorities also vary greatly, and depending on their history and politics, they may not be interested in 'partnerships' with voluntary agencies; they may be reluctant to invest resources in their development, if, as is often true in many communities, the voluntary agencies are too small, weak and generally lack the capacity to serve as contractees. Under these circumstances, local authorities may set up their own surrogates in the form of non-profit trusts, limited companies or contract instead with the private sector. However voluntary organizations look upon contracting, it does change their relationship to local government: from supplicant–patron, to supplier–purchaser; from asking for support or generosity, to negotiating deals.

Yet much of this speculation about the effects of governmental funding is, unfortunately, based mainly on anecdotes and impressions. Little is actually known because there is a paucity of empirical research on this topic, despite its importance [. . .]. There are still a host of methodological problems that make it exceedingly difficult to disentangle the consequences of government funds on [such] organizational changes [as] an increase in bureaucratization [and] professionalization or [a reduction] of advocacy and campaigning (Leat *et al.*, 1986). In addition to the inherent problems of analysing the effects of a multiplicity of funding sources, any change in the structure and performance of an organization is the result of the interaction of numerous internal and external factors.

There are in modern societies many different sources of pressures on organizations to become more formalized and professional. Incidentally, there is often an assumption that increases in size, formalization or the use of professional managers are to be deplored in voluntary organizations. It may be, however, that such changes are conducive, if not necessary, to producing higher quality services, greater accountability, efficiency and effectiveness. In one of the few recent empirical studies in England (Leat *et al.*, 1986) it was found that, paradoxically, local voluntary organizations receiving high statutory grants were able to raise more, not less, money from the general public, and that they involved more volunteers than those receiving less or no statutory funds. While the costs of such aid were reported as some uncertainty and loss of independence, these were seen as relative to the costs of funding from other sources. Also, the reduced autonomy reported was compensated by the informal, relaxed and minimal accountability required.

This finding is similar to those of several other independent studies in other countries where some of the disadvantages of governmental funding were more than off-set by the opportunity to extend and/or improve services for a larger clientele (Kramer, 1987). Many agencies believed that they had more influence on public policies because they were on the inside, not outside and that their service programs did not pre-empt their advocacy.

There are many reasons why governmental funds are not necessarily corrupting, co-opting or controlling, and why organizational autonomy may be less affected than is widely believed. Agencies [may] have multiple sources of funds and [may not be] dependent on a single governmental source; dependence is usually inversely related to the number of income sources. The relationship between funder and provider is usually one of interdependence because the governmental agency needs the services of the voluntary agency as much as the latter requires income. For government, the costs of more intrusive monitoring or control are generally too great, both fiscally and politically. Typically, government lacks the incentive and capacity to be a more effective controller of its grants, subsidies and contracts (Gutch and Young, 1988). The fragmentation of services among a large number of providers and the difficulties of evaluation are further obstacles. Consequently, more often than not, insufficient accountability is more likely to be found than lack of autonomy.

This is not to minimize the risks and uncertainties, the problems and dilemmas of contracting about which a great deal has been written (Demone and Gibelman, 1989). Much depends on how one views contracting, i.e. the extent to which it is conceived, in ideological terms, as part of the debate on privatization, or whether it is regarded more as a pragmatic expedient. In any case, the metaphor of a 'quasi-market' is more useful and appropriate than the usual concept of a 'partnership' which tends to obscure the power relationships involved.

This quasi-market is structured by four sets of conditions.

(1) The *demand* for contracting as manifested in legislative mandates, governmental pressures, preferences, precedents, and / or pragmatic considerations such as the existence of a non-governmental organization with appropriate and sufficient capacity for service delivery at a reasonable price. In many instances, government finds itself dealing with few sellers of a service [...].

(2) The *supply* of potential non-profit and for-profit providers, whose number, type, capacity and readiness is a function of the extent of competition in the market. Many voluntary agencies find they have few buyers for their services apart from government [...].

(3) The *character of the service product*: the extent to which it is tangible, measurable, scarce, costly and complex. For example, it makes a difference whether the service purchased involves meals, medical or nursing care, day treatment, residential care, education or training, community development or counselling. These services vary greatly in the degree to which performance criteria and outcomes can be specified and monitored.

(4) Finally, *the socio-political context* including the history of governmental–voluntary relations in the community, the organizational character of the relevant providers and their political influence, the quality and type of executive leadership, the special interests of local politicians and administrators, etc. Social service markets, like others, are influenced not only by supply and demand, but also by informal networks, individual and group preferences and the distribution of power (Kramer and Grossman, 1987).

It is also overlooked that aside from its effects on voluntary organizations, contracting has other consequences for the governmental agency, the service delivery system, and for consumers, although we have very little data to draw on. It is clear that if the local authority is to become more of a supervisor and regulator of contracts, such a change in its role would require retraining and / or appointment of qualified staff to carry out these functions. For the social service industry as a whole, decentralization and privatization may produce more flexibility in adminstration, but it can also bring about an increase in what some describe as 'fragmentation', but which others regard as pluralism. Another likely consequence is that equity and entitlements would be considerably lessened by the use of a large number of non-governmental service providers (Kahn and Kamerman, 1980).

As for the consumers, we really do not know; there is virtually no information on what difference it makes to users of [a] service if it is under one auspice or another. There are some [early] efforts to monitor existing contracts and obtain opinion data, although one suspects that the findings will be equivocal, and not readily transferable from one type of service setting to another.

In any case, it is apparent that most voluntary and statutory agencies will have to adapt to some major changes in their environment. There is considerable variation among voluntary agencies in their ability to recognize and to deal effectively with such changes. Some are more opportunistic or expedient than others. Some make plans and can anticipate and prepare for change; others are less able to adapt. [...] I have been impressed in the course of my [...] research in England with the capacity of some of the largest, oldest and most traditional charities to be revitalized, after overcoming long-standing and serious financial management problems. In almost half of the sample of twenty national organizations serving the physically and mentally handicapped, new Directors were appointed, mostly from outside the organization, but with high-level managerial skills acquired mainly in the field of social welfare. Most of them initiated a planning process involving the Management Committee and staff, in which goals and objectives were clarified and priorities established, many for the first time. This also included restructuring and streamlining organization, decentralizing, instituting more efficient managerial, personnel and fiscal practices and, at the same time, greater consumer participation.

What role did government play in all of this? While it is difficult to determine, there was little evidence to suggest that the increased bureaucratization and professionalization of these voluntary organizations stemmed from their growing income from governmental fees and grants over the decade. Nor did this greater reliance on statutory funding seem to constrain advocacy, consumer participation or voluntarism – all of which expanded considerably during this time. Also, there was apparently no significant increase in monitoring, evaluation or regulation on the part of the government, or other such activities presumed to reduce the autonomy of voluntary organizations.

The experience of some of these agencies may be instructive. They found it helpful to ask themselves a series of critical questions regarding what they want to be and what they can do best.

With respect to contracting, such questions as the following have been useful:

- Why do we want to contract and take over services formerly delivered by government?
- To what extent do the interests and priorities of the local authority conform to ours?
- Do we have the resources to deliver these required services and to deal with possible deficits?
- What effect will contracting have on other parts of our programme?
- To what extent would it deflect us from advocacy and campaigning?
- Are we prepared to specify service objectives, programme operations and costs, and to be accountable for their outcomes by accepting some monitoring and other forms of regulation?
- To what extent do we have the appropriate staff to develop quality assurance and performance standards, better information and management systems?

- Are we able to restructure ourselves to participate in the negotiation of contracts?
- Finally, what are the implications for our various constituencies; Board, staff, volunteers, contributors and consumers?

■ [Conclusions]

All this suggests that the next phase of the Welfare State will be characterized by a much great use of voluntary, non-profit organizations as service providers (Salamon, 1989). This seems to be quite functional, permitting the continuation of many Welfare State programs and benefits which most people want, but not necessarily provided directly or only by a governmental agency. Thus, by separating funding from production, people can have their cake and eat it. Using voluntary agencies as service providers offers reluctant Welfare States like the USA and others an acceptable way of dealing with the decline in the legitimacy ascribed to government, and the lack of confidence in its capacity to provide economic, equitable and effective public services. [...] So, until there is a new, competing and more compelling rationale for the Welfare State for the 1990s, this may have to suffice. [...] The fate of the voluntary sector will continue to be inextricably linked to the future of the Welfare State.

Note

(1) This article is an a bridged version of a lecture delivered by the author at the Centre for Voluntary Organization, London School of Economics, on 29 November 1989. The text of the full lecture is published as Working Paper No. 8 by CVO.

References

Bozeman, B. (1987) *All Organizations are Public*. San Francisco, California: Jossey-Bass Inc.

Demone, H. and Gibelman, M. (1989) *Services for Sale: Purchase of Service Contracting for Health and Human Services*. New Brunswick, New Jersey: Rutgers University Press.

Geiger, R. K. and Wolch, J. (1986) 'A Shadow State? Voluntarism in Metropolitan Los Angeles'. *Environment and Planning D: Society and Space*, 4, pp. 351–366.

Glennerster, H., Power, A. and Travers, T. (1989) *A New Era for Social Policy: New Enlightenment or New Leviathan?* Welfare State Programme Discussion Paper Number 39. London: STI–CERD, LSE.

Gutch, R. and Young, K. (1988) *Partners or Rivals? Developing the Relationship between Voluntary Organizations and Local Government*. London: NCVO.

HMSO (1988) *Community Care: Agenda for Action, A Report to the Secretary of State for Social Services* by Sir Roy Griffiths. London: HMSO.

HMSO (1989) *Caring for People*. Cmd. 694. London: HMSO.

Hood, C. and Schuppert, G. F. (eds) (1988) *Delivering Public Services in Western Europe: Sharing Western European Experiences of Para-government Organisation*. London: Sage Publications.

James, E. (ed.) (1989) *The Nonprofit Sector in International Perspective*. Oxford: Oxford University Press.

Kahn, A. J. and Kamerman, S. B. (1980) *Social Services in International Perspective*. New Brunswick, New Jersey: Transaction Press.

Knapp, M., Robertson, E. and Thomason, C. (1987) *Public Money, Voluntary Action: Whose Welfare?* PSSRU Discussion Paper 514. Canterbury: University of Kent.

Knapp, M. and Saxon-Harrold, S. (1989) *The British Voluntary Sector*. PSSRU Discussion Paper 645. Canterbury: University of Kent.

Kramer, R. M. (1981) *Voluntary Agencies in the Welfare State* Berkeley, California: University of California Press.

Kramer, R. M. (1987) 'Voluntary agencies and the personal social services', in Powell, W. W. (ed.) *The Non-Profit Sector: A Research Handbook*, pp. 240–257. New Haven, Connecticut: Yale University Press.

Kramer, R. M. and Grossman, B. (1987) 'Contracting for social services: process management and resources dependence'. *Social Service Review* 61:1 (March), pp. 32–53.

Kuttner, P. and Martin, L. (1987) *Purchase of Service Contracting*. Beverly Hills, California: Sage Publications.

Langton, S. (1987) 'Envoi: developing non-profit theory'. *Journal of Voluntary Action Research* 16:1 and 2, January–June.

Leat, D., Tester, S. and Unell, J. (1986) *A Price Worth Paying? A Study of the Effects of Governmental Grant Aid to Voluntary Organisations*. London: Policy Studies Institute.

National Council of Voluntary Organisations (1989) *The Contract Culture. The Challenge for Voluntary Organisations*. London: NCVO.

Salamon, L. M. (1987) 'The voluntary sector and the future of the welfare state'. *Non-Profit and Voluntary Sector Quarterly* Vol. 18, No. 1, Spring, pp. 11–24.

Salamon, L. M. (1989) 'Partners in public service: towards a theory of government–non-profit relations', in Powell, W. W. (ed.) *The Non-profit Sector: A Research Handbook*. New Haven, Connecticut: Yale University Press.

Streeck, W. and Schmitter, P. (1985) 'Community, market, state – and associations', in *Private Interest Government: Beyond Market and the State*. London: Sage Publications.

Warner, A. (1894) *American Charities: A Study in Philanthropy*. New York: Crowell.

Wolfenden Committee Report (1978) *The Future of Voluntary Organisations*. London: Croom Helm.

16

Creating Common Cause:
Issues in the Management of Inter-agency Relationships for Voluntary Organizations

Julian Batsleer
and
Steve Randall

This article looks at issues similar to those discussed by Wilson in the earlier article on Strategic Challenges. Batsleer and Randall, however, adopt a very different focus in their examination of four strategic choices facing voluntary organizations in the 1990s. They examine the conflicting political implications of those choices and link inter-agency relationships to debates about the future unity and identity of the voluntary sector. In deciding its priorities, strategies and the related management styles and options, the interests of an individual voluntary organization are inextricably bound up with its wider perception of the voluntary sector as a whole. Within their broad overview of different strategies, they pay particular attention to both traditional and newer ways in which voluntary organizations can form alliances and coalitions with one another and, through the processes of collaboration and joint-working, build organizational bases for solidarity and common cause.

■ Introduction

'New Times, New Challenges' is how NCVO describes the situation confronting voluntary organizations in the 1990s (Taylor, 1989). As a slogan, it does not really capture the profound sense of ambiguity with which most voluntary organizations face the last decade of the millenium.

In the classic arenas of charity, social welfare and community development, voluntary organizations have become embroiled, not as innocent bystanders but as key participants, in the reshaping of the Welfare State (McCarthy, 1989). Moves towards the privatization of welfare services and the importation of the 'Enterprise Culture' into social and public administration have forced them on to a fiercely contested political terrain. Commercial activity raises similar dilemmas. What are the implications for radical environmental groups of their flourishing trading activities — especially at a time when being 'green' and promoting an image of care and concern for the environment is a major marketing ploy of large corporations? Fund-raising and promotion conducted on the basis of a system – market competition – which has been the source of much environmental destruction is a source of widespread tensions for such organizations. There are two main aspects to these various confusions.

The first concerns what we will call *sectoral identity*. Phrases such as 'rich diversity', 'local flexibility' and 'a plurality of response' can no longer mask deep-seated conflicts between organizations within the traditional voluntary sector. Philanthropic volunteering and voluntary class and community self-activity spring from opposing political traditions; the values and practice of service often run contrary to those of advocacy, campaigning or self-determination. It is by no means clear whether there is a common identity or similarity of purpose among organizations which consider themselves part of the voluntary sector.[1] Equally the 'New Times' have blurred the classic distinctions between the voluntary, statutory and private sectors.

The second source of confusion is associated with questions of autonomy, collaboration and accountability. The dominant imperatives of organizational management in an increasingly competitive environment sit uneasily alongside a commitment to make common cause with other agencies. The fragmentation of established values and institutional arrangements has undermined accepted ways of balancing the perennial tensions between autonomy and self-determination on the one hand and accountability to wider social movements and constituencies on the other.

Again, these tensions and confusions are expressed in contradictory ways. Charity law, for instance, very powerfully protects the independence of individual organizations, despite common sense assumptions of a broad unity of social purpose amongst voluntary organizations. Alternatively, for belief-based organizations, such as churches or single-issue campaigns, it is by no means straightforward to jettison core commitments and methods of working in favour of more pragmatic, liberal or ecumenical forms of co-operation.

We will use these two general issues as the basis for our examination of inter-agency relationships. We must stress that we are not looking for yet another set of essential characteristics of voluntary organizations. Quite the opposite, in fact. We will be examining four contrasting approaches to the management of inter-agency relationships. The options we discuss are based on conflicting assumptions about sectoral identity and organizational autonomy. They are rooted in very different social and political analyses of the 'New Times' and the responses voluntary organizations might make.

In deciding its policy and strategy towards other agencies, any voluntary organization has to consider two underlying questions. The first is to what extent does it see itself as part of a sector which, however diffuse, can be distinguished from other sectors, public and private? Irrespective of the mechanics of inter-agency relationships, how strongly does the classic categorization of state, market and voluntary underpin its approach to external relations? The second question is does it believe that, in order to achieve its aims and wider social goals, it is obliged to collaborate and enter into alliances, coalitions and joint working relationships with other agencies? Or does it believe that those aims and goals are attainable through the exercise of its own autonomous self-determination? Clearly such questions are rarely posed so starkly or abstractly. Together, however, they can be represented as in Figure 16.1.

Using this matrix we can identify four basic approaches to inter-agency relationships from recent literature and debates. They represent four distinct ways in which voluntary organizations can manage their external relations. We have called them:

- New Pluralism   (quadrant 1)
- State-orientated Radicalism   (quadrant 2)
- 'Entrepreneurialism'   (quadrant 3)
- Movement-building   (quadrant 4)

We will briefly examine the underlying assumptions and characteristic management strategies and processes of each of these options, and discuss their respective problems and possibilities.

■ New Pluralism

□ Assumptions

This is a 'mixed economy of welfare' option. It sees the 'New Times' as an opportunity to extend already existing relationships between voluntary and statutory agencies into new forms of partnership. Its main focus is the organization and provision of welfare services.

New Pluralism's major theoretical and political underpinning is the Welfare Pluralism of the early 1980s (Gladstone, 1979; Hadley and Hatch 1981). Notwithstanding its critique of statutory provision and its call for more flexible and sensitive responses to social and community needs, Welfare Pluralism was premised on a clear, sectoral distinction between statutory and voluntary. The emergence of 'the enabling state' has not, for the New Pluralists, fundamentally altered the validity of that distinction or its importance for the conduct of inter-agency relationships. Given that private provision is of limited significance in the post-war welfare state, the partnerships now being developed between 'enabling' (or

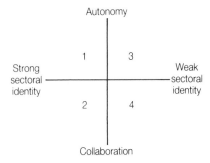

Figure 16.1 Organizational orientations.

regulatory) authorities and non-statutory service-providing agencies are a framework on which the historic relationship between voluntary organizations and the state can blossom and flourish (Gutch and Young, 1988).

In practice, since the late 1980s, attention has focused mainly on the contractual relationships between individual voluntary agencies and statutory bodies. Much less attention has been given to collaboration between voluntary organizations, beyond acknowledging a need for umbrella bodies. The management of partnership, joint ventures and co-operation is defined in terms of the statutory–voluntary relationship. The extent to which public institutions are being privatized is not really addressed.

☐ **Strategies and processes**

From this standpoint, a voluntary organization will need a pragmatic clarity to prevent it from violating its core values and principles whilst it enters into more tightly defined relationships with other, usually statutory, agencies. There are several ways of achieving such clarity and balance.

It is no longer feasible, for instance, to see the general grant-aid relationship as the only model for inter-agency work. NCVO's Community Care Project (NCVO, 1989) has identified six ways of managing joint work (see Figure 16.2 overleaf).

Each of the six approaches is accompanied by distinctive processes for funding, accountability, evaluation and project management, all of which need to be weighed up when deciding what sorts of partnership to develop.

Work on the management of contracts for service provision has identified professionalization, distortion of aims and centralization as some of the risks of this option. Contract relationships will require more responsive information systems and decision-making processes, specialization and disaggregation, market research, financial plans, sharper management accounting and more training. Organizational changes of this order will constantly need to be checked against such 'good practice' criteria as user involvement, local accountability, equal opportunities and safeguarding the interests of volunteers (MacFarlane, 1990).

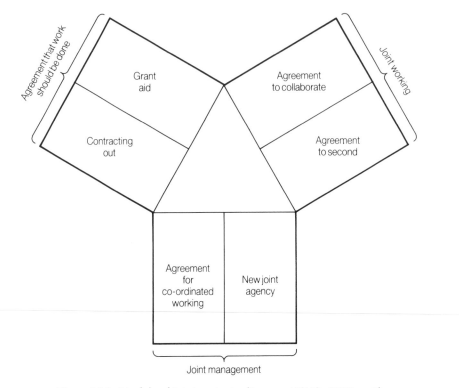

Figure 16.2 Models of joint projects. (Source: NCVO, 1989, p. 5)

☐ **Discussion**

New Pluralism undoubtedly represents the dominant approach to inter-agency relationships within the British voluntary sector in the early 1990s. It basically proposes 'business as usual'. A changing social and political environment has not, in any fundamental way, re-defined the roles, purposes and identities of voluntary organizations.

What characterizes its management strategies and processes is the quint-essentially pluralist aspiration for partnership frameworks which will nourish the garden of autonomy and diversity but keep at bay the jungle of competition. It has brought to the forefront of management thinking, at least in the area of service provision, ways for individual voluntary organizations to manage external demands with greater clarity. It is worth noting that the inter-agency structures and processes of this option can be generalized. The models of joint project management, for instance, could be used for collaboration with other voluntary and commercial agencies as well as with statutory authorities; tools developed to manage contracts are applicable to other forms of inter-agency co-operation.

New Pluralism is particularly suited to the work of larger organizations which already have close working relationships with statutory bodies. For instance, charities providing accommodation for the elderly or homeless or services for those suffering from alcohol abuse already have complex financial and administrative links with local authorities, health authorites, probation services, etc. New Pluralism enables them to locate and develop their work with greater clarity and control.

The basic weakness of New Pluralism lies in its assumptions. It only holds true, for instance, if service provision is deemed to be the purpose of voluntary organization. It cannot readily accommodate such processes as advocacy and campaigning. Nor does the focus on the management of partnership take full account of inequalities of power in cross-sector relationships. New Pluralism does not help sort out the dilemmas of state-driven attempts to re-structure entire areas of social policy such as education. The legally imposed 'pluralism' of the local management of schools and colleges, for instance, does not fit with this option's assumptions about organizational autonomy and self-determination.

New Pluralism also fails to consider how voluntary organizations might respond to demands and constraints emanating from the private and commercial sectors, particularly at a time when they are in the ascendant. The harmonious, mixed social economy of welfare advocated by the New Pluralists is at odds with the wider political economy of welfare arising from the processes of privatization and re-structuring of the state. We will return to this in our discussion of the next option.

■ State-orientated Radicalism

□ Assumptions

This option for managing inter-agency relationships has its roots in the various critiques of Welfare Pluralism (Scott and Wilding, 1985, 1986). What it shares with New Pluralism is an assumption that the state, market and voluntary sectors are clearly differentiated. Both give a primacy to the voluntary–statutory relationship. They differ in their accounts of how that relationship is enacted and the role they ascribe to voluntary organizations.

State-orientated Radicalism argues that the primary role of voluntary organizations since 1945 has been to operate in the interstices of the welfare state and to explore those 'needs-spaces' which a clumsy, rule-bound institution cannot adequately address. Having identified new or hitherto neglected needs in the community, the voluntary sector serves as advocate – encouraging, when appropriate, its take-up by the relevant statutory authority. It has an innovative and pioneering function, doubling as a kind of unofficial research and development body for the local state. In a relationship of 'creative tension' with the statutory sector, voluntary organizations are principally concerned with how services are to be provided, rather than taking primary responsibility for their ultimate delivery. That is deemed, given an overriding commitment to universal public provision, to be the responsibility of the statutory authorities. (There is a more libertarian version of this position which maintains that mutual aid, participation and user control require at least some services to be kept outside the ambit of a controlling, authoritarian state machine.)

This analysis has several consequences. It locates voluntary organizations unequivocally in the public domain and not as a third sector somewhere between public and private. To achieve their purposes, however, it is important for voluntary organizations to retain a *relative* autonomy from the statutory sector and an independent social and political agenda. As part of a wider social movement, voluntary organizations should collaborate with one another – although it is recognized that voluntary status does not, of itself, create a common cause between, say, national, service-providing charities and local campaigns and community groups. Unlike New Pluralism, State-orientated Radicalism entails a more explicit opposition to the privatization of public institutions. It also recognizes that there are limits to what voluntary organizations, individually and collectively, should properly seek to achieve. Their role is essentially intermediary between the self-determination of social and political groups and movements on the one hand and the resource and policy mechanisms of public institutions on the other.

☐   **Strategies and processes**

Echoing the 'in and against the state' (Cockburn, 1980) strategies of the 1970s, inter-agency relationships conducted on this basis give rise to a mixture of collaborative and adversarial structures and processes. They attempt to reflect a sense of movement or common purpose and to reinforce and complement the actual working relationships between staff and volunteers from different agencies. They include processes such as the following.

- *Affiliations* – the formal procedures of affiliation create structures for reciprocal representation in the policy and decision-making processes of voluntary organizations. In the literature of management committees this is often seen as a source of conflicting loyalties (see the article by Margaret Harris). From the perspective of discrete organizations, this may well be the case. As a way of facilitating the negotiation of areas of common interest between organizations, affiliations are by no means so detrimental.
- *Consortia, Coalitions and Federations* as structures for advancing new issues and areas of common concern. Their strength often lies in their separation from established channels of communication within and between agencies. (We will examine coalition strategies more fully later.)
- *Single Issue Alliances and Campaigns* which, at both national and local

levels, try to create a unity of purpose by enabling organizations to define for themselves the extent and the form of their involvement.

- *Networking* as a way of pursuing inter-agency development outside the framework of formal, organizational relationships. What is the source of the strengths, weaknesses and perennial ambiguities of networking? On the one hand it embodies the virtues of flexibility, sensitivity to needs, interpersonal support, sharing of knowledge and resources. On the other hand, networks can be notoriously opaque, the source of in-crowds and out-crowds, unaccountable, whimsical and self-justificatory. One woman's network is another man's 'old school tie brigade'.

There is a dual aspect to all these processes. Arrangements to facilitate flexible working between voluntary organizations are also a basis for defending their identity against the encroachments of statutory and commercial agencies. The preservation of sectoral identity is central to this option. A tendency to give *process* priority over *outcome* means that there is a reluctance to enter into cross-sector contracts to deliver welfare or other services. Preference remains for the negotiation of 'arms-length' agreements over the allocation of resources. Accountability to the community and constituency is the overriding criterion by which inter-agency relationships are judged. At the end of the day, in this option, all forms of inter-agency relationship are managed as mechanisms for enhancing what are seen as the voluntary sector's central roles of advocacy and the mobilization of self-activity.

These sorts of strategies are often found at the grass-roots, community development end of the voluntary sector. They inform the work of those councils for voluntary service, for instance, which see their role as supporting and strengthening the work of local voluntary self-activity; issue-based groupings – anti-racist consortia, disabled worker alliances, forums on volunteering, etc. – are characteristic outcomes. Notions of user participation and empowerment and the development of distinctive good practice amongst voluntary organizations are key motifs in any service-providing agencies which manage their external relationships on this basis.

☐   Discussion

There is a sense in which this is also a 'business as usual' option. What the 'New Times' call for is a continuation of the same sorts of contestation to generate the same sorts of diversity and sensitivity within a public domain which has to be defended (MacGregor, 1990). This poses a crucial problem, however, for a strategy which has historically been built out of a critique of the public sector. To what extent does it coincide with other critiques of state provision and other moves to realign the institutional framework of social policy and welfare?

Hall (1989) has neatly identified the dilemma. Have 'the enterprise culture' and 'the enabling authority' opened up the possibility for the realization of the radicals' traditional dreams of diversity and self-determination? Or have they effectively closed off further progress of a historic political project which has been inextricably rooted in a commitment to universal public provision and a particular form of democratic legitimacy? Is it really feasible for voluntary organizations to build common cause on the basis of the slogan: 'Forward to Greater Autonomy! Defend the Public Sector!'? What is the viability of embarking on a strategy which could be summed up as 'In and Against the Contract Culture'?

In different ways, both options fail to acknowledge the increasingly dominant role of the private and commercial sector. It is worth noting Salamon's (1989) analysis of the statutory–voluntary relationship in the USA. He contends that the penetration of market mechanisms into the operation of all agencies in the public domain has effectively rendered redundant the classic paradigms of rivalry and partnership between the statutory and voluntary sectors. The statutory–voluntary axis is unlikely to remain the central organizing principle of social welfare in the 1990s. Of much greater consequence, across both sectors, is the switch from principles of public planning and democratic accountability to integration into the private, market economy. Recasting client relationships as customer relationships inevitably changes organizational cultures and identities and sets new terms of reference for the ways in which voluntary organizations manage their relationships with one another and with statutory agencies.

Our next two options, therefore, will explore – with the help of material drawn from the experience of the American non-profit organizations – approaches to inter-agency relationships that derive from the fracturing and dissolution of traditional sectoral identities.

■ Entrepreneurialism

□ Assumptions

This will be seen by many as the 'Pandora's box' option for managing inter-agency relationships. Without a sense of sectoral identity to guarantee at least some degree of coherence and unity of social purpose, will William Horder's experience of mental health work in Indiana become the norm?

> 'The not-for-profit sector, drawing its funds from contract services, fees and local fund-raising is bewilderingly varied ... [T]here were dozens of agencies of this kind; a nightmare for clients trying to find help but, for those in the know, offering a wide range of choice and independence. Standards were variable and, because of the volatile behaviour of media and public opinion, a service offered this year may have disappeared by next year leaving no trace. There was no co-ordination of this network of services and no responsibility for planning future needs.'
> (*quoted in Gutch and Young, 1988, p. 78*)

Clearly the weak sectoral identification and strong sense of organizational independence which shape Entrepreneurialism can result in voluntary organizations adopting fiercely competitive strategies in their external relations. It is worth making at least a theoretical distinction, however, between two versions of this option.

One derives from a commitment to organizational self-determination. Brody (1982) has pointed out that collaboration is not always the most desirable way to advance the concerns and interests of community organizations. Collaboration can entail goal displacement, dilution of purpose, blandness, ineffectiveness and a loss of autonomy and control. It is a position which echoes some of the more libertarian aspects of the previous option. It can be found, for instance, amongst many of the newer environmental groups and campaigns who often see no advantage in becoming locked into more general political and organizational alliances. Their cause is best served, it is argued, by retaining the freedom to pursue their interests in ways which they define and control for themselves. What might be called 'non-socialist vanguardism' is not, in this context, seen as either contradictory or inevitably self-defeating.

A second version of this option starts from a recognition that, in a competitive environment, there is no reason why voluntary organizations should eschew external relations strategies modelled on those of successful commercial enterprises. Provided that quality of service remains one's central objective, co-operation with other agencies – voluntary, statutory or commercial – is not necessarily to be preferred over competition. Indeed, different strategies can be adopted by different sections of one's organization. Rather than being constrained by forms of inter-agency working drawn from institutional arrangements and political projects which no longer pertain, voluntary organizations should manage their external relations in exactly the same way as discrete commercial enterprises manage their affairs in complex and uncertain operating environments.

☐   **Strategies and processes**

There is a sense in which there are no distinguishing strategies and processes within the Entrepreneuralism option. Beyond an assumed imperative to defend and advance the interests of one's organization, there are no pre-defined strategies which are deemed either desirable or inadmissible. By definition, the choice of appropriate strategies in inter-agency relationships is a matter for an organization itself to determine, unconstrained by wider sectoral identities and allegiances. So, paradoxically, a commitment to autonomy and self-determination can give rise to widely divergent practices, ranging from highly principled disengagement to ostensibly amoral opportunism.

Groups with very distinctive moral and social purposes – membership and mutual aid organizations, for instance, whose methods of working reflect and prefigure wider social aspirations – often refuse to co-operate with any agencies which do not make equally stringent demands on themselves. At the same time, similar commitments can result in organizations being drawn into a wide range of collaborative schemes to further their own interests. Radical campaigns which engage in marketing highlight the tensions. Look, for instance, at the transition of many street-wise community arts groups in the 1960s – such as Inter-Action in Kentish Town – into cultural entrepreneurs in the late 1980s. Or the contradictory allegiances of some third world and environmental groups which try to hold together expanding commitments to political campaigning, charitable service-provision and commercial fund-raising and promotion.

The strategies adopted by an all-round entrepreneurial voluntary organiza-tion and those of a self-determining, community campaign can converge. Both derive their strategies and tactics from an assessment of what is to their best advan-tage at any given time in given circumstances. From this perspective, co-operation and competition are not necessarily incompatible; they are techniques whose use is to be judged by their efficacy – which can clearly include criteria drawn from what is and is not consonant with an organization's social values, purposes and definitions of good practice.

It is, nevertheless, worth noting several possible tendencies that characterize this option. One is that voluntary organizations will 'contractualize' the whole gamut of their external relations, not just, as in the New Pluralism option, key agreements for the provision of particular services. The motif of 'the contract culture' will inform working practices and arrangements at individual, intra and inter-organizational levels. Relationships of co-operation, mutuality, solidarity, helping, kindness, service, support, advocacy and contestation are likely to be recast into the all-embracing mould of the contract relationship. As always in such relationships, there is a danger that the formal equality of the transaction will mask the substantive inequalities of the underlying relationship.

Another tendency will be towards competition with other agencies. Butler and Wilson (1990), in their work on organizational strategies amongst larger charities, have charted how they have tried to 'achieve a "market niche" in which their organization is perceived as a consistently good performer in comparison to others in the same field of activity. In commercial parlance, the attempt is one of becoming brand leader in the provision of services' (Wilson, 1990). Given the political and ideological milieu within which they have to operate, it is inevitable for the whole panoply of competitive strategies to be unfurled by voluntary organizations. At a more local level, it has been argued that the process of 'contrac-ting' with local authorities to provide services – particularly as a result of competi-tive tendering – will induce comparable competitive entrepreneurialism amongst smaller organizations. The risks are seen, to some extent, as an irreconcilable opposition between an ethic of voluntarism and mutuality and one of competition and individualism (Addy, 1990). The processes of competition can also skew an organization's relationship to its whole operating environment; clients become other agencies rather than the beneficiaries of an organization's services.

Within the broad framework of competitive strategies, charging fees for services is perhaps the ideological rubicon for many voluntary organizations. As Rose-Ackerman (1990) has shown, once that step is taken and non-profit organizations come to rely on fee-paying individuals for a high proportion of their income, the resulting pattern of inter-agency relationships raises a whole barrow-load of contradictions. On what basis should non-profit and for-profit organizations co-exist within the same market or sector? One can argue that, by virtue of their access to subsidies and tax exemptions for charitable purposes, voluntary organizations have grossly unfair advantages in a market environment. Established notions of the distinctive roles and purposes of different sorts of organization are further confused when commercial agencies receive grants and contracts from public sources. How can commercialism be distinguished from charitable mission in the same organization? Recent research in America has even begun to show that, in some health and welfare sectors, not only do voluntary organizations pay higher wages but also they charge higher fees than commercial organizations competing to provide the same service (Holtmann *et al.*, 1990).

☐　**Discussion**

The fiercest debates rage around the option of Entrepreneurialism in the early 1990s. Some authors, such as Kramer in his article, have argued that there is a need to detach the pragmatic from the ideological in this debate. Others maintain that such a manoeuvre concedes too much ground to the privatizers and advocates of unbridled market forces.

Voluntary organizations opting for an entrepreneurial strategy face the familiar dichotomy within any open market system, namely that rational choices by individual consumers/clients and organizations do not necessarily result in an adequate pattern of provision by the system as a whole. In specific circumstances, it is not at all improper for a voluntary organization to opt for competitive strategies to both defend and extend its work; for all voluntary organizations to do so, as a general rule, creates contradictions, waste, duplication and/or areas of under-provision.

To some extent, voluntary organizations are developing entrepreneurial strategies on the basis of outmoded theories of how so-called free markets actually operate (see Wilson's article on co-operation and competition). Ever since Adam Smith first pointed out that competitive markets do not inevitably maximize everyone's interests, organizations have always sought ways of coming to some sort of 'arrangement' with others to achieve system and order in an uncertain environment.

Perhaps the central conundrum for voluntary organizations in this option is the ideological ambiguity of principles of autonomy and self-determination. On the one hand, they are often central to the purposes of many of the more radical and oppositional campaigning groups. On the other hand, they are frequently articulated as part of the rhetoric of organizations adopting a highly commercial approach to their work. The more a voluntary organization detaches itself, for whatever reasons, from its sectoral moorings and allegiances, the more it is likely, in the 1990s, to find itself having to grapple with this ambiguity. That process, in its turn, is likely to raise questions about the extent to which the distinction between co-operation and competition – between partnership and rivalry – is necessarily a defining distinction for voluntary organizations. The American *non-profit* and *for-profit* distinction may be, in a wholly disaggregated system, more meaningful.

■ Movement-building

☐ Assumptions

The assumptions underpinning our fourth option for managing inter-agency relationships can be drawn from the ideas of the American philosopher Richard Rorty (1989). On the face of it, Rorty's notion of the contingency of values and identity in individual and social life appears to rule out any possibility of collaboration. As far as voluntary organizations are concerned, Rorty would certainly contend that it is not possible to sustain common cause on the basis of an appeal to some essential moral or political components of voluntarism. Solidarity between organizations and individuals cannot be directly derived either from sectoral identity or from social location – class, gender, race, etc. However, the fact that solidarity is not automatically *given* in this way in no way obviates the fundamental imperative to *create* solidarity in the face of manifest suffering, injustice and oppression.

This analysis has far-reaching implications for how value-led organizations should approach inter-agency relationships. It means that the option of 'going it alone' is not justifiable but nor is the search for co-operation on the basis of general principles about, for example, voluntarism. What is called for is an approach to collaboration which sees solidarity, alliances and coalition-building not as tactical options but as central to the integrity of an organization's purposes and mode of operation. It is inconsistent and self-defeating for voluntary organizations not to work with other agencies to achieve their ends; it is equally self-defeating, however, not to acknowledge that the processes of co-operation will re-define those ends. In stark contrast to the option of entrepreneurialism, this approach requires voluntary organizations to acknowledge that their aims and purposes can be legitimately re-ordered by other, external agencies and constituencies. Organization independence and self-determination are inconsistent with a commitment to collaboration.

In such a contingency-based approach to inter-agency relationships, conventional sectoral boundaries and identities – state, voluntary, market – will be of little consequence. This fourth option, therefore, opens up possibilities for the creation of forms of collaboration which have, to date, had little place within the dominant traditions and structures of social and political organization in the UK.

☐ Strategies and processes

Strategies and processes for building alliances and coalitions that are not shaped by particular sectoral identities have been much more elaborated in the USA than in the UK. As we have already seen in our first two options, there are well-established approaches in the UK to managing relationships between voluntary and statutory bodies; there are also long-standing ways of working together and organizing joint campaigns. What has not been developed to the same extent or with the same subtlety are the theory and practice of creating and managing coalitions.

As 'organizations of organizations', coalitions of voluntary agencies raise complex management problems. They invariably require the co-ordination of explicitly political and non-political purposes. They are often temporary and, by conventional standards, remarkably unstable associations of people and groups. They can take a variety of forms, ranging from *ad hoc* networks concerned with single issues to quite diffuse, multi-purpose groupings. As Table 16.1 shows, all coalitions involve shifting assemblages of individuals and agencies (Dluhy, 1990).

Maintaining coalitions as inherently dynamic entities committed to change calls for quite distinctive ways of dealing with standard organizational questions of structure, communications, conflict, etc. They demand considerable openness in their management, given the in-built tendency to factionalism and hidden agendas that arises from their lack of organizational rigidity. Questions of style are central to coalitions, as is the need to develop tactics that are both politically efficacious and politically acceptable to all coalition members.

There are other, more far-reaching, features of the alliance and coalition processes. First, they are not constrained by any particular institutional forms or identities. They can, and do, operate across conventional sectoral boundaries. Second, given the growing size and complexity of many voluntary agencies,

Table 16.1 Typology of coalitions. (Source: Dluhy, 1990)

Group base of coalition	Focus of coalition	
	Single issue *or* Narrow focus	Multi-issue *or* Broad focus
Professional or agency[a]	Bread-and-butter	Pre-association
Community[b]	Consciousness raising	Pre-federation
Mixed[c]	Network	Pre-social movement

[a] Individual joins coalition to further the interests of the agency or organization of which he or she is a member. Personal or individual professional considerations are secondary.
[b] Individual joins coalition to further personal, individual, or professional considerations or altruistic goals. Agency or organizational interests are secondary.
[c] Motivations for membership and participation are mixed.

they can be hewn out of, and built around, particular sections and groupings within organizations. Third, alliances and coalitions are not simply instrumental mechanisms to enable groups of voluntary organizations to maximize their own individual advantages in concert. Creating, maintaining and participating in a coalition or alliance all give rise to new purposes and possibilities.

Arising from this, a fourth characteristic of coalitions is their potential for re-creating the relationships between different agencies, organizational forms and social purposes. Voluntary organizations cannot easily disentangle questions of their own survival and continuity from questions about the continuing validity of their core values and social and political purposes. Coalitions can provide a framework within which such complex matters as changing forms and purposes amongst voluntary organizations can be progressed.

☐ Discussion

The American experience of coalitions and alliances points to several new possibilities for forms of inter-agency co-operation in the UK. Perhaps the most exciting is the potential for re-creating and giving more organizational focus to the notion of a 'movement'. For the most part, the idea of a movement – Labour Movement, Women's Movement, Community Movement, Green Movement, Voluntary Movement – has become increasingly devoid of organizational form. (For instance, the restructuring of the Labour Party in the 1980s has very consciously moved it away from its original, complex structure as a coalition of organizations, groups and constituencies towards a much more limited structural form as an association of individual members.) Compared to the growing preoccupation with the management of discrete organizations, the idea of a movement has tended to become an ideological abstraction, with only limited expression in particular forms of collaboration. To claim commitment to a movement tends to be an assertion of aspiration or a view of society, rather than a statement about how one's organization defines itself in relation to others.

Voluntary organizations that approach inter-agency relationships on the basis of solidarity and coalition-building will, therefore, be obliged to rethink their identities and purposes. Entry into coalitions on this basis – and not just as a calculated means of securing advantage – will oblige them to be much more critical of their goals and purposes. The sacrosanct and all-defining 'core values' and 'mission statements' cannot but be open to scrutiny and redefinition, not solely by an organization acting autonomously, but in relation to the wider demands and processes of the coalition. In this way, coalitions could be powerful vehicles, not for advancing established interests but for creating new forms of common cause.

■ Conclusions

'The Enterprise Culture' is not the most important outcome of the social and political upheaval of the 1980s. Of much wider significance has been the breakdown of the post-war political and ideological consensus. Our survey of four very different approaches to the management of inter-agency relationships needs to be set squarely in the context of that collapse of consensus.

We will not, therefore, try to end with a hitherto undiscovered set of principles or criteria which enable voluntary organizations to pick 'the right strategy' from the four broad options we have discussed. Nor are we going to extract some common elements from those strategies, as if they were merely a set of roughly similar levers to be pulled for roughly similar reasons to achieve roughly similar ends. It is implicit in our analysis that different approaches to inter-agency relationships reflect quite fundamentally opposed social purposes and priorities.

What we can do is to identify some of the factors involved in opting for a particular approach to inter-agency relationships.

- Decisions about an organization's relationships with other agencies cannot be divorced from its sense of autonomy and the strength of its sectoral identity. In following a particular strategy, a voluntary organization is also expressing a wider set of beliefs about the nature and purposes of voluntary organizations in general.

- In deciding how to order its links with other agencies, a voluntary organization is inextricably faced with political choices and commitments. Once it has to define its roles and purposes, not in relation to users, clients and members but in relation to other agencies, it cannot avoid the sorts of political and ideological contestation we have been discussing.

- Voluntarism does not, of itself, guarantee unity of purpose between organizations.

- Not all options or approaches to the conduct of external relations are compatible with one another. The choice of one strategy is not necessarily consonant with another; it may well involve an organization in conflict, difference and contestation.

- All external relations strategies involve dilemmas and ambiguities. Living with social, political and organizational contradictions is arguably the major management problem posed by inter-agency relationships.

- All forms of inter-agency co-operation and competition involve risk. Operating on the terrain of values and principles, voluntary organizations are peculiarly vulnerable when it is not possible to justify their actions by appealing to commonly held norms and ideologies.

- Solidarity and common cause are not automatically given; they have to be created.

Pluralism, State-orientated Radicalism, Entrepreneurialism and Movement-building are all valid approaches to the conduct of inter-agency relationships. They represent different responses to the 'new times' within which voluntary organizations find themselves. None avoids ambiguities, tensions, political choices or risks.

What is not valid is for voluntary organizations to see those strategies as simply alternative techniques or tactics. Hopefully our analysis has demonstrated that each of the strategies not only reconstructs an organization's identity, it also shapes and determines its aims, aspirations and possibilities. They are not alternative ways of expressing an essential, underlying or unchanging spirit of 'voluntary-ism'. They are different ways – often quite radically different ways – in which voluntary organizations can engage with the wider environment. They launch voluntary organizations on very different social and political journeys ... it will be interesting to see where they all get to during the 1990s.

Notes

(1) See, for instance, Article 1 in this book. At a theoretical level, our analysis implies a different focus from that proposed by Rob Paton. Less emphasis would be placed on the relationship between organizational forms and sectoral identities; more account would be taken of an organization's strategic and political orientations towards other organizations and sectors in determining its sectoral location. On the other hand, both analyses highlight the blurring of sectoral boundaries and the tensions concerning the nature and purpose of many voluntary organizations.

(2) It is worth noting that this matrix relates to debates during the 1980s over welfare ideologies. Lee and Raban (1983) identified a pervasive analysis based on two variables: commitment to state intervention and commitment to equality. The modified version of this in Figure 16.3 was used by Taylor and Lansley (1990) to examine the implications of welfare ideologies for voluntary organizations.

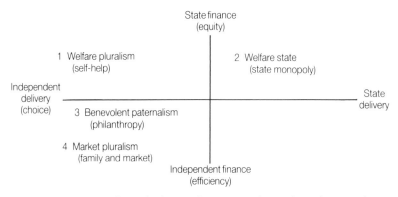

Figure 16.3 Welfare ideologies. (Source: Taylor and Lansley, 1990)

References

Addy, T. (1990) 'Take the money and run?', in *Strategies for the '90s: The Future of the Voluntary Sector*, pp. 3–9. Greater Manchester Council for Voluntary Service.

Brody, R. (1982) *Problem Solving: Concepts and Methods for Community Organizations*. New York: Human Sciences Press.

Butler R. J. and Wilson, D. C. (1990) *Managing Voluntary and Non-profit Organizations: Strategy and Structure*. London: Routledge.

Cockburn, C. *et al.* (1980) *In and Against the State*. London: Pluto Press.

Dluhy, S. (1990) *Building Coalitions in the Human Services*. London: Sage.

Gladstone, F. (1979) *Voluntary Action in a Changing World*. London: Bedford Square Press.

Gutch, R. and Young, K. (1988) *Partners or Rivals? The Changing Relationship between Local Government and the Voluntary Sector*. Luton: Local Government Training Board.

Hadley, R. and Hatch, S. (1981) *Social Welfare and the Failure of the State*. London: Allen and Unwin.

Hall, S. (1989) *The Voluntary Sector under Attack ...?* London: Islington Voluntary Action Council.

Holtmann, A. G., Todd, L. I. and Ullmann, S. (1990) Wage determination of registered nurses in proprietary and non-profit nursing homes, *Proceedings of the 1990 Conference of the Association of Voluntary Action Scholars*. London: Centre for Voluntary Organization, LSE.

Lee, P. and Raban, C. (1983) 'Welfare and ideology', in Loney, M., Boswell, D. and Clarke, J. (eds) *Social Policy and Social Welfare*, pp. 18–32. Milton Keynes: Open University Press.

McCarthy, M. (ed.) (1989) *The New Politics of Welfare: An Agenda for the 1990s?* London: Macmillan.

MacFarlane, R. (1990) *Contracting – In or Out? The Impact on Management and Organisation*, NCVO Guidance Notes on Contracting for Voluntary Organizations 3. London: National Council for Voluntary Organizations.

MacGregor, S. (1990) 'The voluntary sector and the state', in *Strategies for the '90s: The Future of the Voluntary Sector*, pp. 15–29. Greater Manchester Council for Voluntary Service.

NCVO (1989) *Joint Projects: Patterns of Management*. London: Community Care Project, National Council for Voluntary Organizations.

Rorty, R. (1989) *Contingency, Irony, Solidarity*. Cambridge University Press.

Rose-Ackerman, S. (1990) 'Competition between non-profits and for-profits: entry and growth', *Voluntas*, Vol. 1:1, pp. 13–25.

Salamon, L. (1989) 'The voluntary sector and the future of the welfare state', *Non-profit and Voluntary Sector Quarterly*, Vol. 18:1, pp. 11–24.

Scott, D. and Wilding, P. (eds) (1985) *What Price Voluntary Action?* Manchester Council for Voluntary Service.

Scott, D. and Wilding P. (eds) (1986) *Beyond Welfare Pluralism*, 2nd edn. Manchester Council for Voluntary Service.

Taylor, M. (1989) *New Times, New Challenges: Voluntary Organisations Facing 1990*. London: National Council for Voluntary Organizations.

Taylor, M. and Lansley, J. (1990) 'Ideological ambiguities of welfare', *Proceedings of the 1990 Conference of the Association of Voluntary Action Scholars*. London: Centre for Voluntary Organization, LSE.

Wilson, D. C. (1990) 'Co-operation and competition in the voluntary sector: the strategic challenges of the 1990s', *Proceedings of the 1990 Conference of the Association of Voluntary Action Scholars*. London: Centre for Voluntary Organization, LSE.

Index